Lecture Notes in Economics and Mathematical Systems 509

Springer
Berlin
Heidelberg
New York
Barcelona
Hong Kong
London
Milan
Paris
Tokyo

Dietmar Hornung

Investment, R&D, and Long-Run Growth

Springer

Author

Dr. Dietmar Hornung
DGZ Deka Bank
Deutsche Kommunalbank
Emerging Markets Research
Mainzer Landstrasse 16
60325 Frankfurt/Main, Germany

Cataloging-in-Publication data applied for

Die Deutsche Bibliothek - CIP-Einheitsaufnahme

Hornung, Dietmar:
Investment, R&D, and long run growth / Dietmar Hornung. - Berlin ; Heidelberg ; New York ; Barcelona ; Hong Kong ; London ; Milan ; Paris ; Singapore ; Tokyo : Springer, 2001
(Lecture notes in economics and mathematical systems ; 509)
ISBN 3-540-42528-4

ISSN 0075-8450
ISBN 3-540-42528-4 Springer-Verlag Berlin Heidelberg New York

Springer-Verlag Berlin Heidelberg New York
a member of BertelsmannSpringer Science+Business Media GmbH

http://www.springer.de

Printed in Germany

Typesetting: Camera ready by author
Cover design: *design & production*, Heidelberg

Printed on acid-free paper SPIN: 10849430 55/3142/du 5 4 3 2 1 0

The study at hand has been honored by the Faculty of Economics and Management at the Otto-von-Guericke University Magdeburg with the Fakultätspreis 2000.

Acknowledgements

This book represents my doctoral thesis which I wrote during my time as an assistant at the Faculty of Economics and Management at the Otto-von-Guericke University Magdeburg. First of all, I would like to thank my supervisor Professor Paqué for his continuous guidance. The discussions we shared have deepened my understanding of many of the issues explored in a tremendous way. Furthermore, I owe a great amount of gratitude to Professor Schwödiauer and Professor Bretschger who, as members of my doctoral committee, commented on numerous parts of this study in a very helpful manner. Moreover, I am grateful to my colleagues at the Faculty of Economics and Management. Particulary, I would like to thank Ludwig von Auer, Bettina Büttner, Bertrand Koebel, Philipp Reiß, and Frank Silber for challenging discussions as well as encouragement and support.

Frankfurt am Main, June 2001 Dietmar Hornung

Contents

List of Tables

List of Figures

Introduction

In the 1990s, growth theory has incorporated imperfect competition in its investigations. This innovation has proven to be seminal: deviating from growth models with perfect competition, the new framework featured forward-looking entrepreneurs. Firms maximize profits intertemporarily, i.e. their investment leads to instantaneous sunk costs and offers flows of future profits. Firms finance this investment by launching shares. The capital market is perfectly competitive, implying that the return on a share is equal to the return on a bond. As opposed to the capital market, the goods market is imperfectly competitive. As a result of investment, firms enjoy market power. That is, firms may acquire the capability to provide a product that is differentiated in, e.g., styling, technology, accessibility, or reputation. The launch of a differentiated product allows to capture a market niche, and successful firms may price above marginal cost. The resulting profit flows are channelled to the firms' shareholders. The introduction of monopolistic competition into growth theory is valuable: real world economies may be portrayed rather by such an imperfect competition framework than by a perfect competition approach.

Starting with Romer (1990), in growth theory, modeling of imperfect competition has been notoriously bound to a focus on the impact of research and development (R&D) on economic growth. In the existing literature, growth-affecting investment is restricted to R&D investment. R&D-based models propose a quite ready relationship between R&D expenditure and economic growth: the more research is done, the higher the economy's long-run growth rate. In the present study, we leave the narrow R&D focus that growth theory has taken. Choosing a broader view, we seek to rehabilitate physical capital investment back to growth theory. More specifically, the contribution of this study consists of the subsequent three points.

First, we present growth models that are based on investment rather than mere R&D. Taking a comprehensive view, we model economic growth as a process that is driven by the complementary processes of physical capital accumulation and innovation, i.e. R&D capital accumulation. Accordingly, deviating from recent growth models, we represent economic growth as being more than only R&D, stressing the importance of entrepreneurial activity in

		Physical Capital	Human Capital	R&D Capital
Part II	Ch. 3, 4			X
Part III	Ch. 5, 6, 7	X		
Part IV	Ch. 8, 9, 10			X
Part V	Ch. 11	X		X
	Ch. 12	X	X	

Table 1: Foci of the study's models.

general. In a first approach, we model a homogeneous physical capital stock, assuming that capital equipment embodies technical knowledge. Later on, we make the complementarity of physical capital and R&D capital explicit: in the respective approach, entrepreneurs may invest in physical capital and R&D capital separately.

Second, we consider the capability of physical capital investment to differentiate products. In the existing literature, investment other than R&D does not lead to product differentiation. Apparently, this contrasts with real world experience: a firm may appropriate market power by physical capital investment, too. Certainly, in real world, shares in capital markets do represent more than pure R&D investment. Apart from the consideration of physical capital's capability to differentiate products, we present a model in which schooling leads to skill differentiation. In this model, a growing economy is characterized by an increasing specialization of its labor force.

Third, we thoroughly investigate the external effects of both physical capital investment and R&D investment. In the case of physical capital investment, a negative static congestion externality is opposed to a positive intertemporal learning-by-doing effect. We derive the result that physical capital investment in real world is most probably below the social optimum. In the case of research, a positive static productivity externality contrasts with a negative intertemporal exhaustion spillover. Thus, we present R&D-based models that capture cases in which the laissez-faire growth rate is above the social optimum, i.e. models that permit growth to be excessive. In turn, we investigate the likelihood of excessive growth. We find that for realistic parameter values, the case of excessive growth appears to be fairly unlikely.

The present study comprises five parts. In part I, we survey related literature. In part II, we set forth two standard models. In parts III, IV, and V, we present our own research. Table 1 provides an overview of the models presented. The table shows what kind of capital the different models focus on.

The first part provides a selective outline of recent research. In the first chapter, we appraise the literature on R&D-based growth. We show that, considering the history of growth theory, the strong R&D bias that the field has taken since the 1990s certainly sticks out. Moreover, we comment on the recent debate on "growth with or without scale effects". In the second chapter, we analyze the empirical evidence, surveying qualitative historical studies and econometric investigations. We present studies that support the view that physical capital accumulation is essential to economic growth.

In the second part, we set forth two standard growth models in which the capability to differentiate products is restricted to R&D. In chapter 3, we investigate the basic model of Grossman/Helpman's book on *Innovation and Growth in the Global Economy* [Grossman/Helpman (1991a), ch. 3]. It features an expanding product variety. In chapter 4, we introduce a model that represents an improving product quality. The model is quite close to the one that Aghion/Howitt use as the basic model in their book on *Endogenous Growth Theory* [Aghion/Howitt (1998), ch. 3].

In the third part, we extend product-differentiating investment beyond R&D. The models of this part feature a homogeneous physical capital stock. Physical capital equipment embodies technical knowledge. Chapter 5 gives the Ramsey model with imperfect competition. This model is an exogenous growth model, i.e. growth peters out due to market saturation. This model is the basic model of the present study. The subsequent two chapters introduce models capturing endogenous growth. In chapter 6, we present a generalized AK model. Chapter 7 yields a model where learning-by-doing sets off the market saturation effect.

The fourth part revisits R&D-based models. We take a closer look at R&D externalities, allowing for a broad variety of different external effects, including an exhaustion effect. We find that the sign of the overall R&D externality is ambiguous, contradicting the result of Romer/Grossman/Helpman-type growth models. Chapter 8 introduces R&D's exhaustion effect in an expanding product variety framework. In chapter 9, we show that the exhaustion effect may also be set into an improving product quality framework. Chapter 10 models growth without scale effects. It relates to the recent literature on this topic.

The fifth part takes an integrated perspective: the models presented allow for two-stage input differentiation. While in this part, the idea of extending product-differentiating investment beyond R&D is carried on, the models differ from second part's models. Here, we allow for a heterogeneous capital stock, separating different kinds of investment. In chapter 11's model, individuals may invest in either R&D or physical capital. Chapter 12 introduces human capital investment. Here, schooling leads to a differentiation of labor. The model features an imperfectly competitive labor market.

Part I

An Outline of Related Research

Chapter 1

Literature on R&D-Based Growth

In this chapter, we give an outline of recent theoretical research and point to the strong R&D focus that the field has taken since the 1990s. In addition, we comment on the debate on "growth with or without scale effects". For the sake of clarity, we relate growth models to five generations: models of *exogenous growth*, endogenous growth models with perfect competition (*endogenous growth I*), endogenous growth models with imperfect competition (*endogenous growth II*), models of *semi-endogenous growth*, and endogenous growth models without scale effects (*endogenous growth III*) [cf. table 1.1].

The literature on endogenous growth with imperfect competition (cf. endogenous growth II) has introduced forward-looking entrepreneurs to the field. It consists of two strands. The first strand comprises models that represent a horizontal product differentiation, i.e. an expanding product variety [Romer (1990), Grossman/Helpman (1991a, ch. 3), Barro/Sala-i-Martin (1995, ch. 6)]. The second strand encompasses models that assign economic growth to a vertical product differentiation, i.e. an improving product quality [Segerstrom/Anant/Dinopoulos (1990), Grossman/Helpman (1991a, ch. 4, 1991b), Aghion/Howitt (1992), Barro/Sala-i-Martin (1995, ch. 7), Aghion/Howitt (1998, ch. 3)]. Throughout both strands, the models are based on R&D. That is, the capturing of imperfect competition is inevitably bound to a focus on the impact of R&D on economic growth. In R&D-based endogenous growth models, the pace of long-run growth is solely determined by the number of researchers, respectively by the level of research expenditure. Consequently, according to these models, subsidization of research leads unambiguously to a higher long-run growth rate.

	Seminal Paper	Endogen. Growth	Imperfect Comp.	No Scale Effect
Exogenous Growth	Solow *QJE 1956*			X
Endogenous Growth I	Romer *JPE 1986*	X		X
Endogenous Growth II	Romer *JPE 1990*	X	X	
Semi-endogen. Growth	Jones *JPE 1995*		X	X
Endogenous Growth III	Young *JPE 1998*	X	X	X

Table 1.1: Five generations of growth models.

Using post-war time series for major OECD economies, Jones (1995b) indicates that whereas the numbers of scientists and engineers engaged in R&D exhibit rapid exponential growth, aggregate total factor productivity growth rates are stationary. This finding is at odds with the essential prediction of R&D-based endogenous growth models, according to which the dependence of growth rates on the numbers of researchers is monotonically positive. Considering Jones' finding, semi-endogenous growth models that overcome this inconsistency have been developed [Jones (1995a), Kortum (1997), Segerstrom (1998)].[1] In these models, the long-run growth rate is affected neither by the level of research nor by the degree of R&D subsidization. Moreover, these models deviate from earlier endogenous growth models in their representation of a long-run growth rate that does not depend on the size of the economy, i.e. these models do not exhibit *scale effects*. But by the same token, in semi-endogenous growth models, the long-run growth rate depends linearly on the population growth rate. Hence, the models cannot explain economic growth without population growth.

This shortcoming of semi-endogenous growth models has been addressed by recent endogenous growth models (cf. endogenous growth III) [Aghion/Howitt (1998, ch. 3), Dinopoulos/Thompson (1998), Peretto (1998), Young (1998)]. These models combine endogenous growth with the absence of scale effects. The absence of scale effects in these models hinges on a knife-edge solution, though [cf. Jones (1999)]. Moreover, as their predecessors with scale effects, these models feature an R&D-dependent long-run growth rate, and, in turn, may be rejected by the empirical findings of Jones (1995b).

[1] The term *semi-endogenous growth* has been coined by Jones (1995a). He argues that in semi-endogenous growth models, "although growth (...) is generated endogenously through R&D, the long-run growth rate depends only on parameters that are usually taken to be exogenous, including the rate of population growth" [p. 759].

	Physical Capital	**Human Capital**	**R&D Capital**
Exogenous Growth	Solow *QJE 1956*	Uzawa *IER 1965*	Shell *AER 1966*
Endogenous Growth I	Rebelo *JPE 1991*	Lucas *JME 1988*	Romer *JPE 1986*
Endogenous Growth II			Romer *JPE 1990*
Semi-endogenous Growth			Jones *JPE 1995*
Endogenous Growth III			Young *JPE 1998*

Table 1.2: Foci of seminal papers.

The narrow focus on R&D that growth theory has taken since the 1990s is fairly striking if one considers the fact that before the introduction of imperfect competition into the field, different kinds of capital have been investigated as possible engines of growth. Until the dominance of R&D-based models, growth theory had a broader scope, considering physical capital, human capital, and R&D capital as promising candidates to shed light on the process of economic growth. In the era of exogenous growth models, physical capital [Solow (1956), Swan (1956), Cass (1965), Koopmans (1965)], human capital [Uzawa (1965)], and R&D capital [Shell (1966, 1967, 1973)] were analyzed. In the era of endogenous growth models with perfect competition (cf. endogenous growth I), models that focused on R&D capital [Romer (1986)], human capital [Lucas (1988)], and physical capital [Jones/Manuelli (1990), Rebelo (1991)] were presented. Thus, considering the history of growth theory, the strong R&D bias of recent research is certainly conspicuous [cf. table 1.2]

In the remainder of this chapter, we comment on the recent debate on "growth with or without scale effects". In this debate, models of the endogenous growth II-generation are criticized for their exhibition of scale effects [cf., e.g., Jones (1995a, 1995b, 1999)]. It is claimed that in real world, running counter to the models' prediction, larger countries do not grow faster than small countries. We argue that the representation of scale effects follows from suggestive theoretical reasoning. We also present studies that support the empirical validity of models that consider scale effects.

Theoretical reasoning suggests the showing-up of scale effects. A firm invests into capital, and this investment allows to provide a differentiated product that, in turn, yields profit. Hence, the profitability of investment depends on the relation of profit opportunities to sunk investment costs. It is apparent that with a larger accessible market, the profitability of investment increases. Since, at the aggregate level, more investment implies higher growth, scale effects are implied. In particular, studies that investigate the implications of economic integration on long-run growth emphasize the presence of scale effects [see Grossman/Helpman (1991a), Rivera-Batiz/Romer (1991)].

Romer (1990) points out that an appropriate test of the scale effect implication would be a controlled experiment in which the level of research activity was monitored before and after an economy was opened to trade. In line with Romer (1990), Sokoloff (1988) suggests a link between economic growth and the size of the accessible market. Analyzing historical data from counties in the United States in the early nineteenth century, he documents that counties that had access to navigable waterways experienced higher rates of patenting than counties that did not. Moreover, he finds that the counties adjacent to waterways enjoyed a further increase in the rates of patenting when additional counties were connected to the system of waterways.

Kremer (1993) argues that the long-run history of population growth and technical change confirms the existence of scale effects. Kremer's model is based on two assumptions. First, each individual's chance of inventing is independent of the population size. Second, following Lee (1988), the population size is limited by the available technology. Kremer presents empirical evidence that supports the existence of scale effects. In particular, he finds that through most of history, the growth rate of world population has been approximately proportional to the level of world population. Furthermore, among nations with no technical interaction, those with a larger initial population have grown faster.

Apart from historical studies that are based on time series evidence like Sokoloff (1988) and Kremer (1993), the empirical validity of growth models with scale effects may also be tested by cross-sectional regressions. Utilizing cross-sectional data, Backus/Kehoe/Kehoe (1992) find that there is no significant relation between scale and growth at the aggregate level. The scale variable that Backus/Kehoe/Kehoe employ is somewhat problematic, though: instead of using the size of the accessible market, as would be appropriate on theoretical grounds, Backus/Kehoe/Kehoe take the gross domestic product (GDP) as the regressor that captures scale. In real world however, firms that produce a differentiated product usually deliver this product beyond the confines of the domestic market, and, in turn, the profitability of investment depends rather on the size of the accessible market than on the size of the domestic economy. Consistent with this argument, empirical studies that find a significantly positive relation of economic growth to the openness to trade hint that scale effects are present [cf. Kormendi/Meguire (1985), Harrison (1995), Frankel/Romer (1996), Frankel/Romer/Cyrus (1996)].

To conclude: the presented studies suggest that, employing appropriate setups, growth models that exhibit scale effects may well be empirically confirmed. Thus, we cannot follow Jones (1995a, 1995b) who claims that the scale property poses a problem. Accordingly, the present study gives growth models in which the scale effects are not eliminated. In two places, we relate directly to the literature on growth without scale effects, though. In appendix A, we show that by the consideration of scale-dependent costs, the scale effects in the presented models may be eliminated. In chapter 10, we set forth a growth model in which a process of imitation complements the innovation process, and, in turn, leads to non-scale growth.

Chapter 2

Evidence that Suggests a Broader View

In the introduction, we have given the main contributions of this study: first, a presentation of growth models that are based on investment rather than mere R&D, second, a consideration of the capability of physical capital investment to differentiate products, and, third, a careful theoretical investigation of external effects of physical capital investment and R&D investment. In the current chapter, we present studies that complement these contributions with empirical evidence.

The chapter is organized as follows. In the first section, we survey empirical studies that examine physical capital's role in the growth process. In the second section, we present empirical evidence that sheds light on the relationship between physical capital investment and imperfect competition. In the third section, we appraise studies that measure the externalities of both physical capital investment and R&D.

2.1 Physical Capital's Role in the Growth Process

Studies on the contribution of input factors to growth may be associated with one of the subsequent four strands: first, qualitative historical studies, second, growth accounting studies that are in the tradition of Abramovitz (1956) and Solow (1957), third, econometric studies that employ informal growth equations, a strand that has been popularized by Barro (1991), and fourth, econometric studies that estimate theory-based growth equations, following Mankiw/Romer/Weil (1992) and Benhabib/Spiegel (1994).[1]

[1] For recent surveys of the empirical literature on economic growth, see Durlauf/Quah (1999) and Temple (1999).

In this section, we investigate to what extent empirical studies support our view according to which physical capital investment has essential explanatory power for the course of economic growth. In this context, we may wonder what empirical studies say about R&D's role in the growth process. It is certainly striking that, in sharp contrast to the impressive theoretical literature on R&D-based growth, econometric studies that examine the impact of R&D on aggregate economic growth are relatively rare.[2] Fagerberg (1987, 1988) finds a significant positive association between patent applications in foreign countries and national gross domestic product (GDP) growth. Contrarily, Jones (1995a, 1995b) raises doubts whether R&D has an effect on long-run growth. In particular, he documents that growth rates in OECD countries since World War II have not exhibited any persistent upwards trend in spite of a substantial rise in R&D efforts. Summarizing, we may say that the picture of R&D's impact on aggregate economic growth is unclear.

In the remainder of this section, we focus on empirical studies that examine physical capital's role in the growth process. First, we turn to the field of qualitative historical studies. Economic historians have regularly pointed to the importance of physical capital accumulation for economic growth. Rostow (1958, 1959) and Gerschenkron (1962) attribute rapid growth to rapid acquisition and installation of machinery and equipment. In addition, we may cite Landes (1969) who explores Western Europe's economic development since 1750. He finds that the role of machinery investment has been essential to economic growth, concluding that "the machine is at the heart of the new economic civilization" (p. 40). Pollard (1982) construes the same field, suggesting that the richest countries are the ones that were first in applying capital-intensive technologies. Mokyr (1990) characterizes technology embodied in equipment and machinery as "the lever of riches".

Second, opposed to these qualitative studies, investigations that are based on classical growth accounting typically measure that the accumulation of physical capital accounts for only a relatively small fraction of productivity growth. The most influential papers have been the ones by Abramovitz (1956), Solow (1957), and Denison (1962, 1967). These studies base their analysis on the assumption of a perfectly competitive economy, implying that capital is paid its marginal product. As has been argued, the assumption of perfect competition appears to be questionable.

Jorgenson/Gollop/Fraumeni (1987) have advanced growth accounting by estimating sectoral production functions. They conclude that "productivity is a much less important source of growth than the contributions of intermediate, capital, and labor inputs" (p. 210). The highly disaggregated exercises of Jorgenson (1988) yield the result of a substantial association between equipment investment and total factor productivity growth. Jorgenson documents

[2] The rarity of empirical studies that examine R&D-driven growth is reflected in Durlauf/Quah (1999)'s recent survey. Discussing the empirical growth literature, Durlauf/Quah report not a single study that investigates the role of R&D in the growth process.

	Estim. proced.	Dependent variable	Investment share's coefficient	
			Overall investm.	Equipm. investm.
Kormendi/ Meguire (1985)	OLS (cross section)	Growth rate of per-capita GDP	0.12 (0.04)	
Dowrick/ Nguyen (1989)	OLS (cross section)	Growth rate of per-capita GDP	0.11 (0.03)	
De Long/ Summers (1991)	OLS (cross section)	Growth rate of per-capita GDP		0.27 (0.07)
Levine/ Renelt (1992)	OLS (cross section)	Growth rate of per-capita GDP	0.17 (0.03)	
De Long/ Summers (1993)	OLS (cross section)	Growth rate of per-capita GDP		0.31 (0.05)
Sala-i-Martin (1997)	OLS (cross section)	Growth rate of per-capita GDP		0.22 (0.04)

Table 2.1: Investment and economic growth.

that in most industries technical change is capital-using: at given prices, isoquants with higher levels of total factor productivity are related to higher ratios of capital to labor.

Third, we address the strand of studies that estimate informal growth equations. *Ad hoc* cross-country regressions have been pioneered by Robinson (1971), Landau (1983), Kormendi/Meguire (1985), and Dowrick/Nguyen (1989). In the 1990s, an impressive body of respective literature has evolved. The research has been certainly favored by the construction of the Penn world tables (PWT). The standard data sets are PWT mark 4 (PWT 4) [Summers/Heston (1988)], and PWT mark 5 (PWT 5) [Summers/Heston (1991)]. To make national data comparable, the PWT use purchasing power parity benchmarks that have been derived by the United Nations International Comparison Project [cf. Kravis (1984)]. The Penn World Tables currently include data for 152 countries, covering the period from 1950 to 1992.

A seminal paper by Barro (1991) has promoted the field of informal cross-country regressions. In his analysis, Barro focuses strongly on the importance of human capital to economic growth. With respect to physical capital, Barro finds that the estimated coefficient that measures the correlation between the growth rate of per capita real GDP and the investment share is significantly positive [table IV, p. 429]. He interprets this finding by suggesting that human capital investment implies both physical capital investment and economic growth. Barro bases his ordinary least squares (OLS) regressions on PWT 4, comprising 98 countries from 1960 to 1985.

An influential econometric analysis that focuses particularly on the role of physical capital accumulation for economic growth has been undertaken by De Long/Summers (1991). The study is based on PWT 4. De Long/Summers find that countries that invest heavily in equipment relative to other countries at the same stage of economic development exhibit rapid growth. According to their analysis, in the period between 1960 and 1985, each extra percent of GDP invested in equipment is associated with an increase in GDP growth of almost one third of a percentage point per year [cf. table 2.1[3]]. De Long/Summers conclude that there is a much stronger relation between growth and equipment investment than between growth and any of the other components of investment.

In their study, De Long/Summers (1991) address the problem of causality: does investment cause growth, or does growth cause investment? They find a strong negative association between equipment prices and growth. This is a result that more recently has been backed by Jones (1994). De Long/Summers argue that the finding of a strong negative relation between equipment prices and growth suggests that equipment investment drives growth, and not the other way round. It is claimed that, if high investment shares were a result rather than a cause of growth, it would be certainly to be expected that the price of equipment would be bid up.

In a follow-up to their article from 1991, De Long/Summers (1993) investigate how strongly developing countries benefit from equipment investment. For these countries, they find a close link between equipment investment and economic growth, too: fast growth is found where equipment investment is high, and slow growth where equipment investment is low. Whereas De Long/Summers (1991) is based on PWT 4, in De Long/Summers (1993), the range of information sources is extended, including data provided by Aitken (1991) and Lee (1992).

Levine/Renelt (1992) engage in a sensitivity analysis of cross-country growth regressions. They conclude that "the cross-country statistical relationship between long-run average growth rates and almost every particular macroeconomic indicator is fragile" [p. 960]. Nevertheless, they find that the correlation between growth rate and investment share is the least fragile among the many candidate explanations for growth that have been suggested. Levine/Renelt use data from PWT 4, World Bank, and International Monetary Fund.

[3]Throughout this chapter, in the case that a surveyed study documents alternative regressions that differ by the sample they are based on, we report the regression that is based on the largest sample.

Sala-i-Martin (1997) disagrees with the "nothing is robust" of Levine/Renelt (1992). He documents that a substantial number of variables can be found to be strongly related to growth. In one point however, Sala-i-Martin confirms the view of Levine/Renelt: he backs their finding according to which physical capital investment is explanatory to economic growth [see table 2.1]. In Sala-i-Martin's analysis, the variable "equipment investment" proves to be the most robust one [p. 181]. Sala-i-Martin (1997) employs data provided by the World Bank.

Fourth, there is a strand of studies that utilize growth equations that are explicitly derived from aggregate production functions. Seminal is the paper by Mankiw/Romer/Weil (1992) that caused a neoclassical revival in growth theory. Mankiw/Romer/Weil examine determinants of differences in the levels of per-worker real GDP. Regarding the role of physical capital, Mankiw/Romer/Weil measure that the coefficient on investment share is significantly positive for the complete set of 98 countries. The result holds for both the standard Solow model [cf. table I, p. 414], and the Solow model with human capital augmentation [cf. table II, p. 420]. Mankiw/Romer/Weil use PWT 4 and UNESCO data.

Whereas Mankiw/Romer/Weil (1992) base their study on flows of investment and school enrollment rates, Benhabib/Spiegel (1994) construe estimates of physical and human capital stocks. Moreover, Benhabib/Spiegel investigate, apart from differences in per-capita output levels, differences in per-capita output growth rates, too. They find that physical capital is a significantly positive explanatory variable to real output. Benhabib/Spiegel acquire data from PWT 5, Barro/Lee (1993), and Kyriacou (1991).

Islam (1995) advances Mankiw/Romer/Weil (1992) by utilizing panel data. Employing the same regression equations as Mankiw/Romer/Weil, he confirms their essential findings. In particular, he finds a strong convergence between economies at different stages of development. With respect to the importance of physical capital, he measures that the coefficient on saving is significantly positive [cf. table I, p. 1141, and table II, p. 1142]. Islam bases his analysis on data from PWT 4 and Barro/Lee (1993).

Hamilton/Monteagudo (1998) relate their paper to Mankiw/Romer/Weil (1992), too. Using data from PWT 4 and World Bank, they examine determinants of changes in the growth rates of per capita output. They find that "physical capital seems to be quite important for economic growth, though the reasons for this importance may not be fully captured by the augmented Solow growth model" [p. 495].

To sum up: the results of qualitative historical studies and econometric studies – either with informal or theory-based growth equations – suggest that physical capital investment plays indeed a decisive role in the process of economic growth.

2.2 Physical Capital and Imperfect Competition

Empirical evidence for physical capital's capability to differentiate products is reported by Jovanovic (1993). He finds that product differentiation depends positively on physical capital accumulation. In this section, we pursue a more indirect approach to indicate that physical capital investment and product differentiation are closely related. We argue that without capturing physical capital's capability to differentiate products, technology parameter estimates that result from regression analyses are inconsistent with the income shares of capital as they are documented in national income accounts.

In neoclassical models with perfect competition, a factor's income share is equal to its output elasticity. This prediction can hardly be supported by evidence: whereas, according to national income accounts, the benchmark value for the capital share is roughly 0.3 [cf. Maddison (1987)], empirical studies find capital's output elasticity to be in a range from 0.3 to 0.9 [see table 2.2]. The empirical finding that the capital shares that are documented in national income accounts are systematically below the capital shares that are implied by estimations of aggregate production technology suggests that growth models that employ a perfect competition framework come short.

When perfect competition growth models fail to explain the data, does the income share puzzle make a case for R&D-based growth models? We are sceptical. Whereas R&D-based growth models loosen the link between a factor's income share and a factor's output elasticity, the data from national income accounts pose a fundamental problem for R&D-based models, too. These models imply that a major share of national income goes to researchers. This is certainly at odds with the evidence from national income accounts.

In contrast to neoclassical as well as R&D-based growth models, our investment-based approach fits the empirical evidence from both technology estimations and national income accounts quite well. As will be set forth, in our theoretical investigations, we employ a Cobb/Douglas-type production function at the aggregate level. Nevertheless, deviating from neoclassical growth models, we break up the counterfactual link between capital share and capital's output elasticity. This is achieved by allowing for imperfect competition.

In the remainder of this section, we survey studies that estimate physical capital's output elasticity. In parts III and V of the present study, we will see that the values that our investment-based models predict are consistent with the estimates reported.

For the standard Solow model, Mankiw/Romer/Weil (1992) estimate an output elasticity of physical capital as high as 0.60 (standard error of 0.02)

	Estim. proced.	Dependent variable	Physical capital's output elasticity	
			Stand. Solow model	Augm. Solow model
Mankiw/ Romer/ Weil (1992)	OLS (cross section)	log level of per-capita GDP	0.60 (0.02)	0.31 (0.04)
Benhabib/ Spiegel (1994)	OLS (cross section)	log level of per-capita GDP		0.85 (0.06)
		Δ log levels of per-capita GDP		0.46 (0.09)
Islam (1995)	OLS (cross s.)	log level of per-capita GDP	0.83 (0.11)	0.69 (0.07)
	OLS (panel)	log level of per-capita GDP	0.83 (0.09)	0.80 (0.05)
	LSDV (panel)	log level of per-capita GDP	0.44 (0.05)	0.52 (0.06)
Hamilton/ Monteagudo (1998)	OLS (cross section)	Δ growth rates of per-capita GDP	0.42 (0.08)	0.47 (0.08)

Table 2.2: Estimates of physical capital's output elasticity.

[cf. table 2.2]. Mankiw/Romer/Weil attribute the high elasticity to the correlation between investment in physical and human capital. In a further step, they augment the Solow model by human capital, and obtain a lower output elasticity of physical capital [cf. table 2.2]. However, this human capital augmentation has been found not to be robust to alternative specifications of the econometric model [see Pritchett (1996) and Hamilton/Monteagudo (1998)].

Benhabib/Spiegel (1994) find that physical capital has an impact on growth that is larger than would be predicted on the basis of physical capital's income share [cf. table 2.2]. Using maximum likelihood estimators, Benhabib/Spiegel also run a CES instead of a Cobb/Douglas specification. They report that with the CES specification, the estimated elasticity of substitution is not significantly different from unity. The capital share that is implied by the CES model is 0.5 [p. 151].

Islam (1995) applies different estimation techniques to Panel data. In a pooled regression, he finds an output elasticity of physical capital at 0.83 (standard error of 0.09). In a least squares estimation with dummy variables (LSDV), he finds an output elasticity of 0.44 (standard error of 0.05). The human capital augmentation changes the elasticities only slightly [see table 2.2].

The OLS regression analysis of Hamilton/Monteagudo (1998) yields estimates for the output elasticity of physical capital of 0.42 (standard error 0.08) and 0.47 (standard error 0.08) [see table 2.2]. The latter estimate results from a setup that includes human capital.

Apart from papers that obtain estimates for the physical capital's output elasticity by running regressions of an aggregate production function, there are studies that derive the elasticity by investigating the convergence properties of alternatively specified aggregate production functions. Employing this approach, Barro/Sala-i-Martin (1992) and King/Rebelo (1993) find that the neoclassical growth model can only be reconciled with the observed persistence in differences in per-capita output across countries if one assumes a relatively high value for the output elasticity of physical capital. With the assumption of perfect competition, such a high value implies a capital share that is significantly larger than the capital shares that are documented in national income accounts.

Barro/Sala-i-Martin (1992) examine the process of convergence among U.S. states over various periods from 1840 to 1988. Regardless of the time period, the speed of convergence is found to be at roughly two percent per year. To simulate this speed of convergence with an aggregate neoclassical production function, the model requires an output elasticity of physical capital in the neighborhood of 0.8 [Barro/Sala-i-Martin (1992), p. 227].

We conclude that the assumption of perfect competition leads to an inconsistency, both in studies on aggregate technology and in studies on convergence processes: the capital shares that follow from the estimations are significantly above the capital shares that are documented by national in-

	Kind of capital	**Social rate of return to investment**
De Long/Summers (1991)	Equipment	≥ 0.30
Lichtenberg/Siegel (1991)	R&D	0.35
De Long/Summers (1993)	Equipment	0.25 to 0.35
Griliches (1994)	R&D	0.30 to 0.36
Jones/Williams (1998)	R&D	0.35

Table 2.3: Investment and externalities.

come accounts. As we will see, this puzzle can be solved by allowing for imperfectly competitive markets, and, in particular, by considering physical capital's capability to differentiate products.

2.3 Investment Externalities vs. R&D Externalities

In the preceding two sections, we have surveyed studies that investigate the role of physical capital investment in the growth process and its relation to the presence of imperfect competition. In the current section, we turn to the normative aspect of investment. In particular, we outline studies that examine the externalities of physical capital investment and R&D. The importance of the respective evidence is apparent: if positive externalities are present, laissez-faire investment is below the social optimum, and the recommendation for governments is to encourage investment.

First, we outline studies that investigate externalities to physical capital investment. De Long/Summers (1991) suggest that the social return to equipment investment is at least 30 percent per year. They propose that "much of this return is not captured by private investors" (p. 485). With respect to developing economies, De Long/Summers (1993) estimate that the social return to equipment investment is in a range between 25 to 35 percent per year.

As reported in the previous section, Hamilton/Monteagudo (1998) find evidence according to which physical capital investment has a bigger impact on economic growth than suggested by its factor share. Consistent with De Long/Summers (1991, 1993), Hamilton/Monteagudo argue that a reasonable explanation for this finding is that there are significant externalities associated with investment in machinery.

Second, we appraise studies that examine externalities to research. Mohnen (1990) and Griliches (1992) give surveys of the respective literature. Griliches (1992) concludes that "there has been a significant number of reasonably well done studies pointing in the same direction: R&D spillovers are present, their magnitude may be quite large, and social rates of return remain significantly above private rates" [p. S43]. In table 2.3, we complement the surveys of Mohnen (1990) and Griliches (1992) by reporting the social rates of return that are found by the more recent studies of Lichtenberg/Siegel (1991), Griliches (1994), and Jones/Williams (1998). The social rates of return to research that these studies find are in the neighborhood of 35 percent per year. Based on these results, the social returns to research certainly exceed the private returns, and, in turn, R&D spillovers are present.

Hence, the literature on investment externalities yields a consistent picture: although it remains difficult to tag numbers to the external effects of different kinds of investment, it is apparent that, in general, significant spillovers are present. Whereas the presence of externalities to R&D has become common wisdom, the presence of spillovers to physical capital investment is at least in recent growth models rarely considered. Thus, the evidence of remarkable spillovers to equipment investment challenges existing growth models. Hamilton/Monteagudo (1998) propose that models that allow for a divergence between private and social returns to physical capital – apart from approaches that consider either vintage effects or legal structure effects – "may be the most promising way to make sense of existing results" [p. 508]. The evidence suggests that, for an appropriate modeling of investment externalities, growth models should pursue an approach that includes the externalities to physical capital investment rather than stick to frameworks that consider solely R&D externalities.

Part II

Product Differentiation due to R&D

Chapter 3

Expanding Product Variety

In their seminal study on *Innovation and Growth in the Global Economy*, Grossman/Helpman (1991a) present a framework in which the pace of economic growth is determined by the intentional investment of forward-looking, profit-seeking entrepreneurs that act on imperfectly competitive markets. Together with Romer (1990), Grossman/Helpman's contribution has certainly been most influential in originating the strand of endogenous growth with monopolistic competition.

Grossman/Helpman see their investigations in the tradition of Joseph Schumpeter. In *Capitalism, Socialism and Democracy*, Schumpeter (1942) expresses his view of the growth process as follows: "It is quite wrong (...) to say, as so many economists do, that capitalist enterprise was one, and technological progress a second, distinct factor in the observed development of output; they were essentially one and the same thing or, as we may also put it, the former was the propelling force of the latter" [p. 110].

Moreover, Grossman/Helpman relate their investigations to Schmookler (1966)'s *Invention and Economic Growth*. In this study, Schmookler analyzes the inventing activity in four U.S. industries between 1800 and 1957. He concludes that the stimulus for inventions is rather "the recognition of a costly problem to be solved or a potentially profitable opportunity to be seized" than "scientific discoveries and major inventions" [p. 199].

Grossman/Helpman's investigations have had enormous impact within and beyond the confines of the scientific community. Within the discipline, they have been seminal to theory, triggering a vast strand of literature. The framework proved to be helpful to investigate the growth implications of knowledge diffusion, trade, factor movement, patent rights, and intellectual property rights [cf., e.g., Helpman (1993), Walz (1995), Bretschger (1997, 1999)]. Furthermore, beyond the scientific community, Grossman/Helpman's investigations have also been influential to policy. Particularly the prediction according to which an increase in the number of researchers leads to an increase of the long-run growth rate has caught much attention.

In the present chapter, we reproduce Grossman/Helpman's basic model, refering to it as the standard expanding product variety model, i.e. *EPV model*.[1] The represented economy consists of three sectors: an intermediate goods sector, a final output sector, and an R&D sector [cf. figure 3.1].

Looking at the model's structure, it is striking that final output is a mere consumption good. Whereas in traditional growth theory, final output is exposed to the consumption-saving decision of the representative utility-maximizing individual [cf. Cass (1965), Koopmans (1965)], in the EPV model, it is the economy's allocation of labor that mimics the individual's consumption-saving decision. An economy the representative individual of which has a relatively high propensity to save employs a relatively high share of its labor force in research laboratories. Contrarily, an economy the representative individual of which is prone to consume employs a relatively high share of its labor force in the production of intermediate goods, and, hence, expands the production of the consumption good.

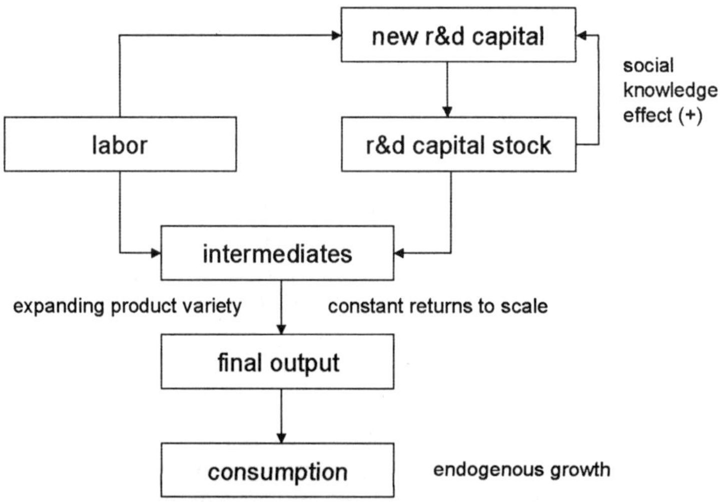

Figure 3.1: A schematic representation of the model.

[1] Cf. Grossman/Helpman (1991a, ch. 3). The EPV model shares many similarities with the models presented in Romer (1990), and Barro/Sala-i-Martin (1995, ch. 6).

The remainder of the chapter is organized as follows. In section one, we present the economy's technology. Section two investigates the laissez-faire outcome. Section three yields the social planner's solution. Section four derives policy implications. Section five gives an appraisal of the model.

3.1 Technology

3.1.1 Final Output

The economy is populated by a continuous mass of identical individuals. There is no population growth. For simplicity's sake, we assume that every individual works, i.e. both labor force and population are of size L. Final output Y_t being a mere consumption good implies $Y_t = c_t L$, where c_t is the level of consumption per capita. The technology of final output is given by the following constant elasticity of substitution (CES) production function

$$Y_t = \left[\int_0^{A_t} x_{at}^{\alpha} da\right]^{\frac{1}{\alpha}} \tag{3.1}$$

where $0 < \alpha < 1$.[2] The inputs into the production of final output are the differentiated intermediate goods a, where $a \in [0, A_t]$. We take the intermediate goods space to be continuous, assuming an infinite set of varieties. The quantity of intermediate a that is used in the production of final output at point t is denoted by x_{at}.

The elasticity of substitution between any two intermediates is given by $\epsilon = 1/[1-\alpha]$.[3] For $\alpha \to 0$, the elasticity of substitution approaches unity, and the intermediates become complements. The intermediates suppliers enjoy maximum market power. For $\alpha \to 1$, the elasticity of substitution tends to infinity, the intermediates become perfect substitutes, and the intermediates market becomes perfectly competitive.

The intermediate goods sector's technology is given by the subsequent one-to-one production functions $x_{at} = l_{at}$, where $a \in [0, A_t]$. To open up an intermediates production unit, it takes a blueprint, i.e. a unit of R&D capital. The output of the production unit a depends on the size of the labor force l_{at} that it employs: one unit of labor is transformed into one unit of the respective intermediate.

We define u_t as the share of the economy's labor force that is employed in the production of intermediates, where $0 \leq u_t \leq 1$. Thus, in the remainder, we will refer to u_t as the production share, and to $u_t L$ as the production

[2]Taking up the Dixit/Stiglitz (1977) specification of imperfect competition, we follow Ethier (1982) who interpreted the differentiated products as intermediate goods.

[3]This follows directly from the definition of the elasticity of substitution, i.e. $\epsilon \equiv d\log[x_{a't}/x_{a''t}] / \{d\log[\{\partial Y_t/\partial x_{a''t}\} / \{\partial Y_t/\partial x_{a't}\}]\}$, with $a', a'' \in [0, A_t]$, and $a' \neq a''$ [cf. Varian (1992), p. 14].

labor force, i.e. $u_t L = \int_0^{A_t} l_{at} da$. Assuming that all intermediates firms have the same market share, i.e. $x_{at} = x_t$, we obtain $x_t = [u_t L] / A_t = l_t$, i.e. each firm employs a labor force of the same size l_t.[4] Moreover, we may rewrite final output production function (3.1) as follows

$$Y_t = A_t^{\frac{1-\alpha}{\alpha}} u_t L \tag{3.2}$$

where $[1-\alpha]/\alpha > 0$.[5]

Notice that equation (3.1) yields three interpretations of A_t. First, A_t represents the amount of intermediates production units that have been opened up before time t. Second, since A_t denotes the amount of production units that produce differentiated intermediates, it denotes the amount of differentiated intermediates itself. Third, since the amount of differentiated intermediates equals just the economy's amount of blueprints, A_t represents furthermore the size of the accumulated R&D capital stock.

3.1.2 R&D

The R&D sector's technology is given by

$$\dot{A}_t = \frac{1}{\omega} S_t [1-u_t] L \tag{3.3}$$

$\dot{A}_t$ may be interpreted as the amount of new blueprints, i.e. the increase in R&D capital stock, A_t.[6] S_t represents the level of social knowledge, i.e. the social knowledge capital stock. The input requirement parameter ω is assumed to be positive, i.e. $\omega > 0$. The higher ω is, the lower is the labor productivity in research. The share of the economy's labor force that does R&D is denoted by $[1-u_t]$. Hence, we will refer to $[1-u_t]$ as the R&D share, and to $[1-u_t]L$ as the R&D labor force.

The intertemporal R&D spillover features two characteristics. First, production function (3.3) implies a labor productivity in research given by S_t/ω. Thus, the costs of developing a blueprint decrease linearly in the accumulated social knowledge capital stock. Second, Grossman/Helpman assume that the economy's level of social knowledge depends linearly on the R&D capital stock that has been accumulated by private firms, i.e. $S_t = A_t$.[7] Hence, we

[4] In subsection 3.2.1, we show that the identical size of the A_t market shares is implied by intermediates firms' profit-maximization.

[5] Notice that $0 < \alpha < 1$ implies $[1-\alpha]/\alpha > 0$.

[6] A dot over a variable denotes total differentiation with respect to time.

[7] By an appropriate choice of units of measuring social knowledge capital, the factor of proportionality may be set to one. With respect to the intertemporal R&D spillover, Grossman/Helpman (1991a) suggest two kinds of generalizations. First, they investigate a model with a nonlinear relationship between private R&D investment and social knowledge capital. They formulate a function $S_t = f(A_t)$, with $f'(A_t) > 0$. The resulting model encompasses the present EPV model as a special case when $f(A_t) = A_t$. It is shown that a linear accumulation of social knowledge capital is not a necessary condition for

obtain a fourth interpretation of A_t: it works as an index for the amount of social knowledge that has been accumulated before time t. Accordingly, we may modify technology (3.3) to

$$\dot{A}_t = \frac{1}{\omega} A_t [1 - u_t] L \tag{3.4}$$

For the subsequent analysis, it is helpful to derive the sectoral labor demand functions. First, since $Y_t = c_t L$, production function (3.2) leads to the following labor demand function for the intermediates sector

$$u_t L = A_t^{-\left[\frac{1-\alpha}{\alpha}\right]} c_t L \tag{3.5}$$

The higher the *level* of consumption, the higher the intermediates sector's demand for labor. Second, production function (3.4) implies for the steady state a labor demand function for the R&D sector as follows

$$[1 - u_t] L = \frac{\alpha\omega}{[1-\alpha]} \gamma \tag{3.6}$$

where γ is the steady-state growth rate of consumption.[8] The higher the *growth rate* of consumption, the higher the R&D sector's demand for labor. Since negative employment in an activity is meaningless, the equilibrium consumption level must satisfy $c_t \leq A_t^{\frac{1-\alpha}{\alpha}}$, and the equilibrium consumption growth rate has to meet $\gamma \leq [1-\alpha] L/\alpha\omega$.

3.2 Laissez-faire Outcome

3.2.1 Intermediate Market

Since both the producers of final output and the researchers face constant returns to scale and perfect competition, both earn zero profits. In contrast, the suppliers of differentiated intermediates enjoy market power. The flow profit rates at time t are given by

$$\pi_{at} = p_{x_a t}(x_{at}) x_{at} - w_t x_{at} \tag{3.7}$$

where $p_{x_a t}$ denotes the price of the intermediate a, and $a \in [0, A_t]$. The intermediates firms maximize their flow profits by charging

$$p_{x_a t} = \frac{w_t}{\alpha} = p_{xt} \tag{3.8}$$

balanced growth [Grossman/Helpman (1991a), pp. 75-78]. Second, Grossman/Helpman extend the EPV model by allowing for lags in the dissemination of knowledge. They find that the long-run growth rate of an economy with dissemination lags is lower than the long-run growth rate of an economy in which knowledge diffuses instantaneously. The findings of the EPV model are not affected by the introduction of dissemination lags, though [Grossman/Helpman (1991a), pp. 78-81].

[8] In subsection 3.2.3, we find that the economy jumps immediately to the steady state.

The greater the firm's market power, the higher the markup $1/\alpha$ on the marginal costs, i.e. on the wage rate. Since all A_t intermediates firms charge a common price, p_{xt}, we obtain a symmetric solution where $x_{at} = x_t$, and $l_{at} = l_t$, for all A_t varieties. Thus, in the remainder, we may indeed use production function (3.2).

In order to determine the evolution of relative prices, we derive the cost function of the final output sector. The cost function C_Y which is dual to production function (3.1) is given by[9]

$$C_Y(\{p_{x_a t}\}_{a=0}^{A_t}, Y_t) = \left[\int_0^{A_t} p_{x_a t}^{-\left[\frac{\alpha}{1-\alpha}\right]} da\right]^{-\left[\frac{1-\alpha}{\alpha}\right]} Y_t \tag{3.9}$$

By symmetry [cf. equation (3.8)], and production function (3.2), total cost may be stated as

$$C_Y(p_{xt}, L) = p_{xt} u_t L \tag{3.10}$$

Since perfect competition prevails on the market for final output, revenue equals cost. Hence, the price of final output, p_{Yt}, is equal to aggregate cost (3.10) over aggregate output (3.2), i.e. $p_{Yt} = A_t^{-[1-\alpha]/\alpha} p_{xt}$. Solving for p_{xt}, and setting $p_{Yt} = 1$ for all t, yields the intermediates price[10]

$$p_{xt} = A_t^{\frac{1-\alpha}{\alpha}} \tag{3.11}$$

The wage rate follows from price equation (3.8)

$$w_t = \alpha A_t^{\frac{1-\alpha}{\alpha}} \tag{3.12}$$

The intermediates price and the wage rate increase with an expanding product variety, since additional intermediates raise the marginal productivity of each intermediate.

---

[9] To derive cost function (3.9), we employ a Lagrangian given by $L = \int_0^{A_t} p_{x_a t} x_{at} da + \mu\left\{Y_t - \left[\int_0^{A_t} x_{at}^{\alpha} da\right]^{1/\alpha}\right\}$. Apart from a restatement of production function (3.1), the first order conditions imply $x_{at} = \mu^{1/[1-\alpha]} p_{x_a t}^{-1/[1-\alpha]} Y_t$, where $a \in [0, A_t]$. Inserting the latter equations into production function (3.1), and solving for μ, we obtain $\mu = \left[\int_0^{A_t} p_{x_a t}^{-\alpha/[1-\alpha]} da\right]^{-[1-\alpha]/\alpha}$. Substituting for μ in our equations, we obtain the demand functions $x_{at} = p_{x_a t}^{-1/[1-\alpha]} \left[\int_0^{A_t} p_{x_{a'} t}^{-\alpha/[1-\alpha]} da'\right]^{-1/\alpha} Y_t$, where $a \in [0, A_t]$ and $a' \in [0, A_t] \setminus a$. Using $C_Y = \int_0^{A_t} p_{x_a t} x_{at} da$ yields cost function (3.9).

[10] The choice of numéraire is arbitrary. Taking p_{Yt} as numéraire yields, as long as R&D is done, a steady rise of intermediates price and wage rate, i.e. an inflationary effect. If we took p_{xt} as numéraire, we would obtain a steady fall in p_{Yt}, i.e. a deflation in the price of final output. With either choice, an expanding variety in the intermediates lowers the relative price between final output and intermediates. Notice that Grossman/Helpman (1991a) choose a different numéraire: they set prices in a way that nominal spending remains constant, i.e. $p_{Yt} Y_t = 1$ for all t. Of course, the choice of numéraire does not affect the findings on real magnitudes.

Inserting price equation (3.8) into profit equation (3.7), and using $x_t = [u_t L] / A_t$ yields

$$\pi_t = [1 - \alpha] p_{xt} A_t^{-1} u_t L \tag{3.13}$$

The profit of the representative firm increases with its market power, the intermediates' price, and its physical output. The latter is given by $A_t^{-1} u_t L$. An increase in the number of varieties has two opposite effects on profit. First, a positive productivity effect: it follows from the induced rise in the intermediates' price. Second, a negative market-saturation effect: the intermediate's share of a market the size of which is given by the production labor force $u_t L$ is negatively related to the number of varieties. To determine the sign of the overall effect, we insert price equation (3.11) into profit equation (3.13). We obtain a modified profit equation which depends only on the R&D capital stock and the production labor force

$$\pi_t = [1 - \alpha] A_t^{-\left[1 - \frac{1-\alpha}{\alpha}\right]} u_t L \tag{3.14}$$

Profit equation (3.14) shows that for $\alpha > 0.5$ – i.e. a relatively high elasticity of substitution of intermediates – the negative market-saturation effect dominates the positive productivity effect. Hence, for $\alpha > 0.5$, the overall effect of the launch of an additional variety on profits is negative. Using labor demand function (3.5) allows to rewrite profit equation (3.14) as

$$\pi_t = [1 - \alpha] A_t^{-1} c_t L \tag{3.15}$$

Profit equation (3.15) shows that the profit of the representative intermediates production unit depends proportionally on its nominal output which is given by $A_t^{-1} c_t L$.

3.2.2 Asset Market

Individuals are willing to finance the development of a blueprint as long as the value of a blueprint, v_t, does not fall below the cost of developing a blueprint, p_{At}. If the value of a blueprint falls below its cost, R&D stops, i.e. $\dot{A}_t = 0$. The value of a blueprint cannot exceed its cost, because this would imply an unbounded demand for blueprints. Such a situation cannot arise in a competitive equilibrium. The condition of a free entry into the production of intermediates follows as

$$v_t \leq p_{At} \tag{3.16}$$

with equality whenever R&D is undertaken, i.e. whenever $\dot{A}_t > 0$. R&D capital's production function (3.4) yields[11]

$$p_{At} = \omega A_t^{-1} w_t \tag{3.17}$$

[11] Setting $\partial \dot{A}_t / \partial \{[1 - u_t] L\} = w_t / p_{At}$, and solving for p_{At} yields equation (3.17).

The cost of developing a blueprint increases with a lower research productivity, a lower social technical knowledge, and a higher wage rate. An increase in the number of varieties has two opposite effects on a blueprint's costs. First, a productivity effect: since a broader variety increases the wage rate, the blueprint's costs rise, too. Second, a social technical knowledge effect: since a broader variety raises the social technical knowledge, the costs of developing a blueprint fall. To determine the sign of the overall effect, we insert wage rate (3.12) into price equation (3.17). We obtain the subsequent modified price equation

$$p_{At} = \alpha\omega A_t^{-\left[1-\frac{1-\alpha}{\alpha}\right]} \tag{3.18}$$

Price equation (3.18) shows that for $\alpha > 0.5$ – i.e. a relatively high elasticity of substitution of intermediates –, the social technical knowledge effect dominates the productivity effect. Thus, for $\alpha > 0.5$, the costs of developing a blueprint decrease with the launch of an additional variety. Using price equation (3.18) allows to rewrite free entry condition (3.16) as follows

$$v_t \leq \alpha\omega A_t^{-\left[1-\frac{1-\alpha}{\alpha}\right]} \tag{3.19}$$

with equality whenever $\dot{A}_t > 0$.

The value of a blueprint equals the discounted stream of future profits that accrues to this blueprint subsequent to time t. Our setup implies perfect foresight. Thus, we rule out speculative bubbles. This yields

$$v_t = \int_t^\infty e^{-R_{ts}}\pi_s ds$$

where $R_{ts} \equiv \int_t^s r_u du$ is the cumulative discount factor from time t to time s.

Differentiating with respect to time, and using Leibniz's rule, we obtain no-arbitrage condition

$$\pi_t + \dot{v}_t = r_t v_t$$

It reflects the individual's indifference between purchasing a blueprint, and buying a bond: the total return that accrues to the owner of the representative blueprint in the interval between t and $t + dt$ – the flow profit that the blueprint yields, $\pi_t dt$, plus the absolute change in the value of the blueprint, $\dot{v}_t dt$ – equals the interest on the value of the blueprint, $r_t v_t dt$. Dividing by the value of the blueprint gives

$$\frac{\pi_t}{v_t} + \frac{\dot{v}_t}{v_t} = r_t \tag{3.20}$$

This allows a slightly different interpretation of no-arbitrage: the rate of return on a blueprint, i.e. the rate of return on a share, in the interval $[t, t + dt]$ – the dividend, $\pi_t dt/v_t$, plus the relative change in the value of the share, $\dot{v}_t dt/v_t$ – is equal to the rate of return on a bond, i.e. the interest rate multiplied by the length of the interval, $r_t dt$.

3.2.3 Steady-State Growth

The representative utility-maximizing individual is assumed to be infinitely lived.[12] Her overall utility at time t is given by

$$U_t = \int_t^{\infty} e^{-\rho[s-t]} u(c_s) ds \tag{3.21}$$

i.e. the overall utility is a weighted sum of all future flows of utility $u(c_s)$ from time t to infinity. The weights hinge upon the individual's time preference, i.e. her subjective discount rate, ρ, where $\rho > 0$. The higher the rate of time preference, ρ, the less patient the individual is to consume. The instantaneous utility is given by the constant intertemporal elasticity of substitution (CIES) utility function

$$u(c_s) = \begin{cases} \frac{c_s^{1-\theta}-1}{1-\theta} & \text{for } \theta > 0, \quad \theta \neq 1 \\ \log c_s & \text{for } \theta = 1 \end{cases} \tag{3.22}$$

The function $u(c_s)$ relates the instantaneous flow of utility per capita to the level of consumption per capita. The intertemporal elasticity of substitution, σ, is the negative inverse of the elasticity of marginal utility, $-\theta$, i.e. $\sigma \equiv 1/\theta = -u'(c_s)/u''(c_s)c_s$. With a lower intertemporal elasticity of substitution, the individual is less willing to accept deviations from a uniform pattern of consumption over time.

The representative individual faces the subsequent flow budget constraint[13]

$$c_t + \dot{q}_t = w_t + r_t q_t \tag{3.23}$$

where q_t are the assets held by the individual, w_t is the wage rate, and r_t is the rate of return on investment, i.e. the interest rate. Individuals can borrow or lend freely at the interest rate. Since perfect competition prevails on the markets for labor and assets, the individual takes the wage rate and the interest rate as given. Due to her inelastic supply of one unit of labor per unit of time, the individual has labor income w_t at her disposal. The ownership of assets yields income $r_t q_t$. Total income can either be spent on consumption c_t, or saved and used for the purchase of $\dot{q}_t$ assets. Since all blueprints are held by individuals, assets per capita equals R&D capital stock per capita. To rule out that the individual uses chain letters to increase her utility, we assume in the remainder that the credit market imposes a constraint on the

[12] The infinitely lived individual may be interpreted as a family the generations of which are linked to each other through bequests [cf. Barro (1974)].

[13] Flow budget constraint (3.23) may be derived as follows. The assets that the representative individual holds at point t are given by $q_t = \int_t^{\infty} e^{-R_{ts}} [c_s - w_s] ds$, i.e. real wealth at point t is equal to the discounted stream of future consumption that exceeds labor income. Total differentiation with respect to time yields flow budget constraint (3.23).

amount of borrowing

$$\lim_{t\to\infty} e^{-R_{0t}} q_t \geq 0 \tag{3.24}$$

where $R_{0t} \equiv \int_0^t r_u du$ is the cumulative discount factor from time 0 to time t. The no-Ponzi-game condition (3.24) means that an individual's level of debt cannot grow asymptotically faster than at rate r_t.[14]

The representative individual maximizes overall utility (3.21) with respect to flow budget constraint (3.23). The problem can be solved by formulating an appropriate current-value Hamiltonian

$$H = u(c_t) + \lambda_t[w_t + r_t q_t - c_t]$$

The first-order conditions for an optimum consumption path are

$$\frac{\partial H}{\partial c_t} = 0 \tag{3.25}$$

$$\dot{q}_t = \frac{\partial H}{\partial \lambda_t} \tag{3.26}$$

and

$$\dot{\lambda}_t = \rho\lambda_t - \frac{\partial H}{\partial q_t} \tag{3.27}$$

The transversality condition is

$$\lim_{t\to\infty} [e^{-\rho t}\lambda_t q_t] = 0 \tag{3.28}$$

Condition (3.25) states that instantaneous consumption should maximize the current-value Hamiltonian at every point in time. Thus, it equates assets' shadow price, λ_t, with consumption's marginal utility. The condition yields a first equation of motion for the shadow price

$$\frac{\dot{\lambda}_t}{\lambda_t} = \frac{u''(c_t)\dot{c}_t}{u'(c_t)} = -\frac{1}{\sigma}\frac{\dot{c}_t}{c_t} \tag{3.29}$$

As the level of consumption increases, assets' shadow price and, hence, consumption's marginal utility decrease. The decrease of the marginal utility goes up with a lower intertemporal elasticity of substitution.

Condition (3.27) requires that the utility gain from a marginal unit of an asset, $\partial H/\partial q_t$, matches the utility gain that would follow from postponing

[14] Flow budget constraint (3.23) and condition (3.24) yield an intertemporal budget constraint: the present value of consumption is equal to total wealth, which is the sum of initially held assets q_0, and the present value of labor income [cf. Blanchard/Fischer (1989), p. 50].

the accumulation for a moment. This gain is the difference between the cost for the forgone consumption, $\rho\lambda_t$, and the instantaneous rate of change in the shadow price, $\dot{\lambda}_t$. Condition (3.27) yields a second equation of motion for the shadow price

$$\frac{\dot{\lambda}_t}{\lambda_t} = -[r_t - \rho] \tag{3.30}$$

The larger the difference between the rate of return on investment and the rate of time preference, the faster the decline of the shadow price.

If we combine equations (3.29) and (3.30), we obtain the Keynes/Ramsey rule

$$\frac{\dot{c}_t}{c_t} = \sigma[r_t - \rho] \tag{3.31}$$

The level of consumption grows at an instantaneous rate equal to the difference between the rate of return on investment and the rate of time preference, premultiplied by the intertemporal elasticity of substitution. Condition (3.26) restates constraint (3.23): to attain an optimal spending program, the individual's income flow has to equate her expenditure flow at every point in time. Together with equation (3.30), transversality condition (3.28) implies that, in the long run, the rate of asset accumulation has to be below the rate r_t. If the individual were to accumulate assets forever at a rate equal to or above r_t, she could increase her utility by consuming some of these assets in finite time.

Inserting the no-arbitrage condition (3.20) into equation (3.31) yields a modified Keynes/Ramsey rule

$$\frac{\dot{c}_t}{c_t} = \sigma\left[\frac{\pi_t}{v_t} + \frac{\dot{v}_t}{v_t} - \rho\right] \tag{3.32}$$

The level of consumption grows as long as the return on a share – dividend plus relative change in the share's value – exceeds the rate of time preference.

For the analysis of the equilibrium dynamics, the evolution of two variables is crucial: the value of a blueprint, and the profit that accrues to the owner of a blueprint. Notice that in the steady state, the allocation of the non-growing labor force between production and R&D is fixed. First, we analyze the evolution of the profit. Differentiating profit equation (3.14) with respect to time yields the subsequent steady-state equation of motion

$$\frac{\dot{\pi}}{\pi} = -\left[\frac{\alpha}{1-\alpha} - 1\right]\gamma \tag{3.33}$$

where γ denotes the laissez-faire steady-state growth rate. Second, we investigate the evolution of the value of a blueprint, i.e. the value of a share. The steady-state evolution of a share's value is given by [cf. condition (3.19) with equality]

$$\frac{\dot{v}}{v} = -\left[\frac{\alpha}{1-\alpha} - 1\right]\gamma \tag{3.34}$$

Equations of motion (3.33) and (3.34) imply for the steady state a constant dividend, since the profit that accrues to a representative blueprint falls with the same rate as the value of the blueprint does. The steady-state dividend follows from profit equation (3.14) and condition (3.19) with equality as

$$\frac{\pi}{v} = \frac{1-\alpha}{\alpha\omega} uL \tag{3.35}$$

where u represents the laissez-faire steady-state production share. The dividend valorizes with a higher productivity in developing blueprints, a larger market power, and a larger production labor force. Since dividend (3.35) is independent of the size of the R&D capital stock, the model exhibits endogenous growth. Using labor demand function (3.6), the steady-state dividend may be stated as[15]

$$\frac{\pi}{v} = \frac{1-\alpha}{\alpha\omega} L - \gamma \tag{3.36}$$

The interpretation is straight-forward: the higher the steady-state growth rate, the more workers do R&D, and the smaller the production labor force. Therefore, a higher steady-state growth rate leads to a lower steady-state dividend.

Inserting dividend (3.36) and equation of motion (3.34) into the modified Keynes/Ramsey rule (3.32) yields the laissez-faire steady-state growth rate[16]

$$\gamma = \frac{\sigma\left[\frac{1-\alpha}{\alpha\omega} L - \rho\right]}{1 + \sigma\frac{\alpha}{1-\alpha}} \tag{3.37}$$

where for a positive growth rate, i.e. $\gamma > 0$, $[1-\alpha] L / [\alpha\omega] > \rho$ has to be met. Moreover, the condition for a bounded attainable utility, $\rho > [\sigma - 1]\gamma/\sigma$, must be satisfied. It ensures that the transversality condition holds. The economy jumps immediately to the steady state. Considering equation (3.37), we find that the decentralized growth rate increases with a higher research productivity, a lower elasticity of substitution of intermediates, and a larger

[15] Recall that we exclude negative employment in the production sector, i.e. $\gamma \leq [1-\alpha] L/\alpha\omega$ [cf. equation (3.6)]. Hence, dividend (3.36) is nonnegative.

[16] For $\sigma = 1$, consumption growth rate (3.37) is equivalent to the laissez-faire steady-state innovation rate that Grossman/Helpman derive [1991a, p. 61]. Notice that there, the analysis is restricted to a logarithmic instantaneous utility function, i.e. $\sigma = 1$. The relation between consumption growth rate γ and innovation rate γ_A is given by $\gamma = [1-\alpha]\gamma_A/\alpha$ [cf. production function (3.2)].

labor force. Furthermore, a lower rate of time preference, and a higher intertemporal elasticity of substitution set incentives to do more R&D and, in turn, accelerate growth.[17]

3.3 Social Planner's Solution

After having analyzed the laissez-faire outcome, we investigate the social planner's solution. This solution will be the reference for our welfare analysis. The preferences of the representative individual are given by equations (3.21) and (3.22). Using production functions (3.2) and (3.4), the intertemporal maximization problem can be stated in terms of the subsequent current-value Hamiltonian

$$H = u(c_t) + \lambda_t \frac{1}{\omega} A_t^{1-\left[\frac{1-\alpha}{\alpha}\right]} \left[A_t^{\frac{1-\alpha}{\alpha}} L - c_t L\right]$$

The first-order conditions can be obtained in the usual manner by setting the derivative of the current-value Hamiltonian with respect to c_t equal to zero, setting $\dot{A}_t$ equal to $\partial H_t / \partial \lambda_t$, and equating $\dot{\lambda}_t$ to $\rho\lambda_t - \partial H_t/\partial A_t$. Furthermore, we obtain a transversality condition given by $\lim_{t\to\infty}[e^{-\rho t}\lambda_t A_t] = 0$. A first equation of motion for the shadow price of R&D capital follows as

$$\frac{\dot{\lambda}_t}{\lambda_t} = \frac{u''(c_t)\dot{c}_t}{u'(c_t)} - \left\{1 - \left[\frac{1-\alpha}{\alpha}\right]\right\} \frac{\dot{A}_t}{A_t}$$

For the steady state follows

$$\frac{\dot{\lambda}}{\lambda} = -\left[\frac{1}{\sigma} - 1 + \frac{\alpha}{1-\alpha}\right] \gamma_S \tag{3.38}$$

where γ_S is the social optimum growth rate. A further equation of motion for the shadow price may be stated as

$$\frac{\dot{\lambda}_t}{\lambda_t} = -\left\{\frac{1}{\omega} L \left[1 - \left[1 - \frac{1-\alpha}{\alpha}\right] c_t A_t^{-\left[\frac{1-\alpha}{\alpha}\right]}\right] - \rho\right\}$$

Using labor demand functions (3.5) and (3.6), the respective steady-state equation of motion is given by[18]

$$\frac{\dot{\lambda}}{\lambda} = -\left\{\left[\frac{1-\alpha}{\alpha\omega} L + \left\{\frac{\alpha}{1-\alpha} - 1\right\} \gamma_S\right] - \rho\right\} \tag{3.39}$$

[17] The laissez-faire steady-state R&D share, $[1-u]$, may be derived using growth rate (3.37) and labor demand function (3.6) as $[1-u] = \sigma\left\{1 - \alpha\omega\rho / \left[\{1-\alpha\} L\right]\right\} / \left\{1 + \alpha\sigma / \left[1-\alpha\right]\right\}$. Thus, the model's parameters affect the laissez-faire steady-state R&D share and the laissez-faire steady-state growth rate (3.37) in a uniform manner.

[18] Social planner's allocation of labor is not biased as can be seen from the fact that the social technical knowledge effect is considered in both equations (3.38) and (3.39). This result is opposed to the laissez-faire outcome. Firms do not consider the external effect of their R&D efforts. Hence, the laissez-faire allocation of labor is biased towards production, i.e. towards today's consumption.

Equations (3.38) and (3.39) give the social optimum steady-state growth rate[19]

$$\gamma_S = \sigma \left[\frac{1-\alpha}{\alpha\omega} L - \rho \right] \tag{3.40}$$

The social optimum growth rate is raised by a higher research productivity, a lower elasticity of substitution of intermediates, and a larger labor force. Furthermore, a lower rate of time preference, and a higher intertemporal elasticity of substitution increase the rate.[20]

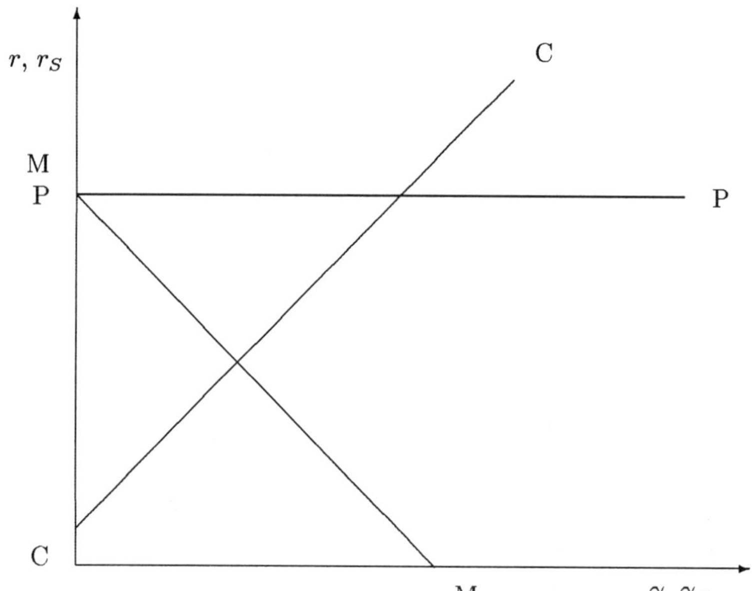

Figure 3.2: Equilibrium conditions.

[19]For $\sigma = 1$, consumption growth rate (3.40) is equivalent to the social optimum steady-state innovation rate that Grossman/Helpman derive [1991a, p. 71].

[20]The social optimum steady-state R&D share, $[1 - u_S]$, may be derived using growth rate (3.40) and labor demand function (3.6) as $[1 - u_S] = \sigma \{1 - [\alpha\omega\rho / \{1-\alpha\} L]\}$. Analogous to the laissez-faire case, the model's parameters affect the social optimum steady-state R&D share and the social optimum steady-state growth rate (3.40) in a uniform manner.

How does laissez-faire growth (3.37) compare to social optimum growth (3.40)? Both solutions involve a steady-state equilibrium condition (CC) that follows from Keynes/Ramsey rule (3.31). We obtain

$$r = r_S = \rho + \frac{1}{\sigma}\gamma \tag{CC}$$

where r_S denotes the steady-state social return on investment. The CC line is upward-sloping in γ-r-space [cf. figure 3.2]. Individuals ask for a higher return on investment, the lower their willingness to postpone consumption, i.e. the higher their rate of time preference, and the higher their actual postponement, i.e. the higher the economy's growth rate.

For laissez-faire, the second equilibrium condition (MM) follows from no-arbitrage condition (3.20) along with equations (3.34) and (3.36) as

$$r = \frac{1-\alpha}{\alpha\omega}L - \frac{\alpha}{1-\alpha}\gamma \tag{MM}$$

The MM line is downward-sloping in γ-r-space. The rate of return is negatively related to the growth rate, since a higher growth rate leads to a faster depreciation of the representative share. To rule out a negative return on R&D investment, we require that the steady-state growth rate is below an upper boundary, i.e. $\gamma \leq \{[1-\alpha]/\alpha\}^2 L/\omega$.

Social planner's equilibrium condition (PP) is implied by social optimum growth rate (3.40) as

$$r_S = \frac{1-\alpha}{\alpha\omega}L \tag{PP}$$

The PP graph is a horizontal line in γ-r-space. Deviating from the private return on R&D investment, the social return on R&D investment does not depend on growth.

Equations (CC), (MM), and (PP) imply that the laissez-faire growth rate is unambiguously below the social optimum [cf. figure 3.2].[21] We may describe this gap either in terms of the ratio $\gamma_S/\gamma > 1$, or in terms of the difference $[\gamma_S - \gamma] > 0$. The ratio γ_S/γ increases with a higher elasticity of substitution of intermediates, and a higher intertemporal elasticity of substitution [cf. growth rates (3.37) and (3.40)]. The difference $[\gamma_S - \gamma]$ increases for all parameter values that raise decentralized growth. Thus, although a higher elasticity of substitution between intermediates increases the ratio γ_S/γ, it decreases the difference $[\gamma_S - \gamma]$.[22] It is readily checked that the gap between the two growth rates is reflected in differing R&D shares: the laissez-faire R&D share is unambiguously below the social optimum.

[21] Notice that if the economy were stationary, the positive intertemporal R&D spillover would disappear, and laissez-faire's zero growth would be socially optimal.

[22] The reasoning is straightforward. The difference $[\gamma_S - \gamma]$ may be written as $\{[\gamma_S/\gamma] - 1\}\gamma$. It can be shown that the impact of a lower substitutability between intermediates on γ dominates its impact on the ratio γ_S/γ. Thus, a lower substitutability between intermediates leads to a higher difference $[\gamma_S - \gamma]$.

3.4 Policy Implications

The model suggests that the laissez-faire growth rate is below the social optimum. This finding poses the question whether there are policy measures that have the ability to close this gap. We introduce a government which faces the following flow budget constraint

$$t_\pi \pi_t A_t + t_I w_t[1-u_t]L + TL = 0 \tag{3.41}$$

where t_π is a tax on profits, t_I is a tax on R&D investment, and T is a lump-sum tax. Taxes obey the condition $-1 < t_\pi, t_I < 1$. To obtain a balanced budget, as soon as one tax is positive, at least one tax has to turn negative. A negative tax is a subsidy.

The after-tax profit rate is given by [cf. equation (3.14)]

$$\pi_t = [1-t_\pi][1-\alpha]A_t^{-\left[1-\frac{1-\alpha}{\alpha}\right]} u_t L \tag{3.42}$$

The introduction of a R&D tax changes the value of a blueprint [cf. condition (3.19) with equality] to

$$v_t = [1+t_I]\alpha\omega A_t^{-\left[1-\frac{1-\alpha}{\alpha}\right]} \tag{3.43}$$

Inserting profit equation (3.42), blueprint's value (3.43), and equation of motion (3.34) into the modified Keynes/Ramsey rule (3.32), we obtain the after-tax steady-state growth rate.

What are appropriate policy measures to raise this decentralized growth rate to the social optimum growth rate (3.40)? The decentralized growth rate may be increased by strengthening the incentive to save. More saving leads to a reallocation of labor from the intermediates sector to the R&D sector. Hence, the R&D share increases. Strengthening the incentive to save is accomplished by subsidizing either profit or investment.

To keep expressions handy, in the remainder of this chapter, we assume that the intertemporal elasticity of substitution is equal to unity, i.e. we postulate a logarithmic instantaneous utility function. Thus, the optimum combinations of subsidies $[t_\pi, t_I]^*$, i.e. combinations that make the after-tax growth rate and the social optimum growth rate coincide, are given by the subsequent equation

$$t_\pi = 1 - [1+t_I]\left[1 + \frac{1}{\omega\rho}L - \frac{\alpha}{1-\alpha}\right]$$

Hence, for optima, there is a trade-off between subsidizing profit and investment. For $t_I^* = 0$, the optimum profit subsidy, $t_\pi^* < 0$, follows as

$$t_\pi^* = -\left[\frac{1}{\omega\rho}L - \frac{\alpha}{1-\alpha}\right]$$

For $t_\pi^* = 0$, the optimum investment subsidy, $t_I^* < 0$, may be derived as[23]

$$t_I^* = -\left[1 - \frac{\rho}{\frac{1}{\omega}L + \left[1 - \frac{\alpha}{1-\alpha}\right]\rho}\right]$$

The optimum subsidies ought to be financed by imposing a lump-sum tax, since this tax does not deteriorate the accumulation of R&D capital.

3.5 Discussion

In the EPV model, growth is driven by forward-looking, profit-seeking entrepreneurs. Firms invest in today's R&D laboratories so they will hold a differentiated product in their tomorrow's product portfolio. Thus, firms finance today's research by tomorrow's profits. Since in the EPV model, R&D is assumed to have an unambiguously positive intertemporal spillover, laissez-faire research is unambiguously below the social optimum. The policy implications are straighforward: since firms disregard the positive external effect of their research, governments should encourage R&D by appropriate subsidies.

Our critique of the EPV model encompasses four points. First, the model's restriction to R&D as the single kind of growth-affecting investment contradicts empirical evidence [cf. chapter 2]. Second, the model does not represent the capability of physical capital to differentiate products, and, in turn, to create monopoly power. These two points have been set forth in the study's introduction. Third, the EPV model assumes that final output is a mere consumption good. This implies a severely asymmetrically modelled economy in which imperfect competition in the production of the consumption good contrasts with perfect competition in the production of the capital good [cf. figure 3.1]. We address this point in chapter 5 below. Fourth, the EPV model takes labor as the only input into R&D [again, cf. figure 3.1]. This representation contradicts evidence that suggests that research is rather capital intensive than labor intensive. We investigate this point in chapter 8.

[23] Cf. Grossman/Helpman (1991a), p. 73.

Chapter 4

Improving Product Quality

New products may be either horizontally or vertically differentiated from earlier vintage products, and, in turn, their launch may imply either an expanding product variety or an improving product quality. In the previous chapter, we investigated a growth model that focuses on an expanding product variety (EPV model). In the present chapter, we analyze a model that explains long-run growth by an improving product quality. We will refer to this model as the standard improving product quality model, i.e. *IPQ model.*

In the IPQ model, economic growth is generated by a random sequence of quality improving innovations that result from research activities. Innovators drive incumbent producers out of the market by launching products that turn earlier vintage products obsolete. In its setup, the IPQ model is inspired by the quality ladder models of Segerstrom/Anant/Dinopoulos (1990), Grossman/Helpman (1991a, ch. 4, 1991b), Aghion/Howitt (1992), and Barro/Sala-i-Martin (1995, ch. 7). Nevertheless, it is certainly closest to the multisector model that Philippe Aghion and Peter Howitt use as the basic model in their investigations on *Endogenous Growth Theory* (1998) [cf. Aghion/Howitt (1998, ch. 3)].

The structure of the IPQ model resembles the structure of the EPV model [cf. figures 3.1 and 4.1]. Again, the economy consists of three sectors: an intermediate goods sector, a final output sector, and an R&D sector. As in the EPV model, labor has two competing uses: producing the consumption good and performing research. The representative individual's consumption-saving decision is reflected in the economy's allocation of labor.

The plan of this chapter is as follows. In section one, we present the economy's technology. Section two investigates the laissez-faire outcome.

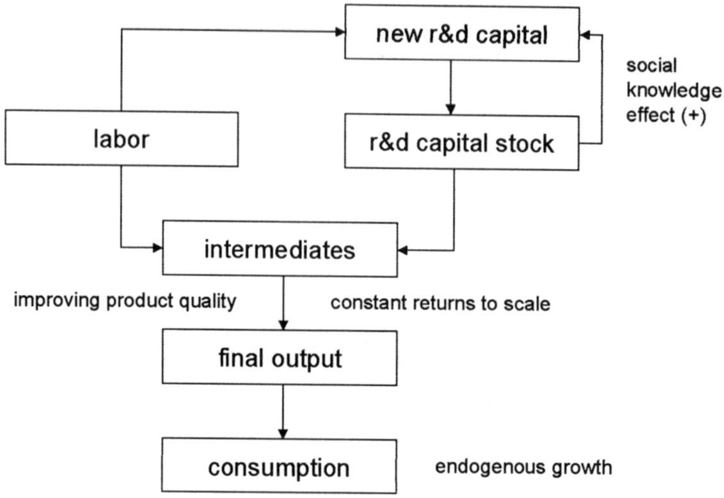

Figure 4.1: A schematic representation of the model.

Section three yields the social planner's solution. Section four derives policy implications. Section five provides a discussion of the model.

4.1 Technology

4.1.1 Final Output

The technology of final output is given by the subsequent CES production function[1]

$$Y_t = \left[\int_0^1 A_{it} x_{it}^{\alpha} di \right]^{\frac{1}{\alpha}} \tag{4.1}$$

where $0 < \alpha < 1$. The inputs into the production of final output are the differentiated intermediate goods i, where $i \in [0, 1]$. The intermediates space is continuous, which implies an infinite set of varieties. x_{it} denotes the quantity of intermediate i that is used in the production of final output at time t. The parameter α determines the substitutability between intermediates. A_{it} represents technical knowledge capital that is used in the production of intermediate i: a higher A_{it} increases the intermediate's product quality, i.e. the productivity of the specific intermediate in producing final output.

[1] Aghion/Howitt employ a final output production function given by $Y_t = \int_0^1 A_{it} x_{it}^{\alpha} di$ [cf. Aghion/Howitt (1998), p. 87]. Thus, the CES technology they use implies diseconomies of scale of size α. In order to stress the analogy of the improving product quality framework and the expanding product quality framework, we deviate from Aghion/Howitt by imposing the EPV model's assumption of constant returns to scale on the IPQ model.

The intermediate goods sector's technology is given by production functions $x_{it} = l_{it}/A_{it}$, where $i \in [0,1]$. l_{it} denotes the labor force that is used in the production of intermediate i. The technology implies that the production of intermediates that incorporate a more recent technology, i.e. a higher A_{it}, are more resource-intensively produced.[2] The index i serves to count the intermediates firms, the differentiated intermediates themselves, and the niches of the intermediates market. Notice that at each point in time, the same amount of intermediates firms operate, the same amount of differentiated intermediates are available, and the same amount of market niches are targeted by researchers.

4.1.2 R&D

Innovation is the result of successful R&D. Within each product niche i, an R&D race takes place. When an innovation is made, the innovator captures the respective niche of the intermediates market by launching a new product. The innovative supplier drives the incumbent supplier out of the market, and the new product replaces the earlier vintage product completely. That is, we assume drastic innovations.[3]

We define a *Schumpeterian clock* as a clock that progresses with every innovation that occurs. Employing such a clock, we index a technology parameter, A, by the number of innovations, n, rather than by real time, t. For niche i, each innovation advances the innovation counter, n_i, by one, and increases the technology parameter, A_i, by the constant factor e^δ, where $\delta > 0$. Thus, we obtain

$$A_{i,n_i+1} = e^\delta A_{in_i} \tag{4.2}$$

Taking the log of the factor e^δ yields the size of the innovation, δ.

To innovate, the prospective intermediates supplier i has to employ researchers. The R&D labor force that targets niche i is denoted by l_{it}^A. R&D is considered to be an activity the success of which is uncertain. We assume that the sequence of innovations in market niche i is a random process that follows a Poisson distribution with parameter ψl_{it}^A, where $\psi > 0$. Hence, in market niche i, innovations arrive randomly at a Poisson arrival rate of ψl_{it}^A. Notice that ψ reflects the productivity of research laboratories in producing blueprints, whereas it says nothing on the quality of these blueprints relative to their predecessors.

---

[2]The formulation of a resource-intensifying production of intermediates is owed to Aghion/Howitt's extension of their basic multisector model [cf. Aghion/Howitt (1998), pp. 94-95]. We draw this assumption because, in our framework, it allows to employ one identical aggregate production function for both the EPV model and the IPQ model [cf. production functions (3.2) and (4.5)]. Notice that the IPQ model's findings do not hinge on the assumption of a resource-intensifying intermediates production.

[3]Aghion/Howitt show that the assumption of drastic innovations may be readily relaxed. The findings of the IPQ model remain valid [cf. Aghion/Howitt (1992), pp. 339-341, Aghion/Howitt (1998), pp. 74-76].

With respect to the innovation prospects of a specific R&D laboratory, our formulation implies two things. First, the laboratory's probability of inventing is proportional to its resource input, i.e. its labor force. Second, the laboratories share a common productivity, i.e. all researchers are equal. That follows from the fact that any laboratory may dismantle the current state-of-art-product, and, thus, has complete access to the up-to-date technical knowledge. This means that researchers do not learn from their own research, may it be successful or not. In our economy, research is a memoryless process.

Thus, the evolution of the technology parameter, A_i, in a unit-time interval depends on two parameters. First, on the innovation size, i.e. on δ. Second, on the number of innovations $[n_{i,t+1} - n_{it}]$ that occur in a unit-time interval between t and $[t+1]$. The expected value of the number of innovations between t and $[t+1]$ is given by the Poisson arrival rate, i.e. $E(n_{i,t+1} - n_{it}) = \psi l_{it}^A$. Equation (4.2) implies that the expected value of the difference between $\log A_{i,t+1}$ and $\log A_{it}$ is given by the expected amount of innovations that occur in the unit-time interval, premultiplied by the innovation size. Hence, we may express A_i's evolution in real time, i.e.

$$E\left(\log A_{i,t+1} - \log A_{it}\right) = \delta\psi l_{it}^A$$

which may be approximated by

$$E\left(\frac{\dot{A}_{it}}{A_{it}}\right) = \delta\psi l_{it}^A \tag{4.3}$$

where $\dot{A}_{it}/A_{it}$ represents the growth rate of intermediate i's product quality.

In the remainder of this subsection, we impose that market and research niches are of same size, i.e. $x_{it} = x_t$, $l_{it} = l_t = u_t L$, and $l_{it}^A = l_t^A = [1 - u_t] L$, where $0 \leq u_t \leq 1$.[4] Thus, the normalization of the amount of differentiated intermediates to unity implies that, by symmetry, $u_t L$ denotes, first, the economy's total production labor force, $\int_0^1 l_{it} di$, and, second, the labor force that is employed in the representative intermediates firm, l_t. Accordingly, $[1 - u_t] L$ represents, first, the economy's total R&D labor force, $\int_0^1 l_{it}^A di$, and, second, the R&D labor force that targets the representative niche of the intermediates market, l_t^A.

We turn now to the externalities of research. Empirical studies show that R&D has often an even bigger effect on productivity in other sectors than in the sector doing R&D itself.[5] We consider this finding of strong intersectoral R&D spillovers in our model. When a firm innovates, the other

[4] In subsection 4.2.1, we show that the identity of the A_t market shares is implied by intermediates firms' profit-maximization. In subsection 4.2.2, we show that the identity of the sizes of the A_t research niches follows from the absence of arbitrage opportunities in the capital market.

[5] See Scherer (1982), Terleckyj (1982), Griliches/Lichtenberg (1984), and Goto/Suzuki (1989).

intermediates suppliers benefit from the innovation just as the innovating firm does itself. Since only incumbent suppliers of intermediates benefit from these intersectoral R&D spillovers, the incentive to do research is given. Thus, the level of technical knowledge increases in a symmetric manner, implying that there is a common level of technical knowledge across the economy, i.e. $A_{it} = A_t$, where $i \in [0,1]$.[6]

The infinite number of market niches i implies an infinite number of research projects i, where $i \in [0,1]$. Thus, the law of large numbers prevents the uncertainty of the sectoral innovation processes from showing up at the aggregate level. Accordingly, at the macroeconomic level, the technology parameter A_t grows steadily, and the economy's innovation process is deterministic.[7]

By symmetry, we may sum up the supply side of the economy as follows. The production function of the economy's R&D sector is given by [cf. equation (4.3)]

$$\frac{\dot{A}_t}{A_t} = \delta\psi\,[1 - u_t]\,L \tag{4.4}$$

The intermediate goods sector's technology may be written as $x_t = [u_t L]/A_t$. Furthermore, symmetry allows to rewrite final output production function (4.1) as follows

$$Y_t = A_t^{\frac{1-\alpha}{\alpha}} u_t L \tag{4.5}$$

where $[1-\alpha]/\alpha > 0$.

Considering the economy's technology, we derive the sectoral labor demand functions. First, production function (4.5) yields the following labor demand function for the intermediates sector

$$u_t L = A_t^{-\left[\frac{1-\alpha}{\alpha}\right]} c_t L \tag{4.6}$$

[6] Whereas in our model, the intermediates suppliers benefit symmetrically from the most recently launched innovation, in Aghion/Howitt (1992, 1998), the intersectoral dissemination of knowledge is discriminatory. In both models, Aghion/Howitt assume that only the economy's next innovator has access to the R&D technical knowledge that is incorporated in the most recently launched state-of-the-art product. The two models differ in their assumptions on the sectoral sequence of innovations. In Aghion/Howitt (1992), the innovating sector is necessarily the one with the lowest productivity parameter. Hence, the sectoral sequence of innovations is deterministic [Aghion/Howitt (1992), p. 346]. In Aghion/Howitt (1998), the innovating sector is arbitrarily chosen. Thus, the sectoral sequence of innovations is stochastic [Aghion/Howitt (1998), pp. 87-89]. The improving product quality models of Segerstrom et al., Grossman/Helpman, and Barro/Sala-i-Martin do not consider an intersectoral dissemination of knowledge [Segerstrom/Anant/Dinopoulos (1990), Grossman/Helpman (1991a, ch. 4), Barro/Sala-i-Martin (1995, ch. 7)].

[7] The variance of the Poisson distributed random variable $\dot{A}_{it}/A_{it}$ is given by $var\left(\dot{A}_{it}/A_{it}\right) = \delta\psi l_{it}^A = \delta\psi\,[1-u_t]\,L$ [cf. equation (4.3)]. Hence, for an infinite number of research projects i, we obtain $var\left(\dot{A}_t/A_t\right) = 0$.

The higher the *level* of consumption, the higher the intermediates sector's demand for labor. Second, production function (4.4) implies a labor demand function for the R&D sector as follows

$$[1-u_t]L = \frac{\alpha}{[1-\alpha]\,\delta\psi}\gamma \tag{4.7}$$

where γ is the steady-state growth rate of consumption.[8] The higher the *growth rate* of consumption, the higher the R&D sector's demand for labor. Since employment in every sector must be nonnegative, the equilibrium consumption level must satisfy $c_t \leq A_t^{\frac{1-\alpha}{\alpha}}$, and the equilibrium consumption growth rate has to fulfill $\gamma \leq [1-\alpha]\,\delta\psi L/\alpha$.

4.2 Laissez-faire Outcome

4.2.1 Intermediate Market

The firm that succeeds in innovating may monopolize the respective niche of the intermediates market until it is replaced by the next innovator. The flow profit rates of the suppliers of differentiated intermediates at time t are given by

$$\pi_{it} = p_{x_it}(x_{it})x_{it} - w_t A_{it} x_{it} \tag{4.8}$$

where p_{x_it} denotes the price of the intermediate i, and $i \in [0,1]$. With $A_{it} = A_t$, the profit-maximizing price is given by $p_{x_it} = w_t A_t/\alpha$, implying a common intermediates price, i.e. $p_{x_it} = p_{xt}$, a common intermediates output, i.e. $x_{it} = x_t$, and a common production labor force, i.e. $l_{it} = l_t$, where $i \in [0,1]$. This is our first result on symmetry.

The cost function that is dual to production function (4.1) is given by[9]

$$C_Y(\{p_{x_it}\}_{i=0}^1, Y_t) = \left[\int_0^1 A_{it}^{\frac{1}{1-\alpha}} p_{x_it}^{-\left[\frac{\alpha}{1-\alpha}\right]} di\right]^{-\left[\frac{1-\alpha}{\alpha}\right]} Y_t \tag{4.9}$$

Using the symmetry result, setting $A_{it} = A_t$ for all $i \in [0,1]$, and employing production function (4.5), total cost can be stated as $C_Y(p_{xt}, L) =$

[8] In subsection 4.2.3, we find that the economy jumps immediately to the steady state.

[9] To derive cost function (4.9), we use a Lagrangian given by $L = \int_0^1 p_{x_it}x_{it}di + \mu\left\{Y_t - \left[\int_0^1 A_{it}x_{it}^{\alpha}di\right]^{1/\alpha}\right\}$. Apart from a restatement of production function (4.1), the first order conditions imply $x_{it} = \mu^{1/[1-\alpha]}p_{x_it}^{-1/[1-\alpha]}A_{it}^{1/[1-\alpha]}Y_t$, where $i \in [0,1]$. Inserting these equations into production function (4.1), and solving for μ, we obtain $\mu = \left[\int_0^1 A_{it}^{1/[1-\alpha]}p_{x_it}^{-\alpha/[1-\alpha]}di\right]^{-[1-\alpha]/\alpha}$. Substituting for μ in our equations, we obtain the demand functions $x_{it} = A_{it}^{1/[1-\alpha]}p_{x_it}^{-1/[1-\alpha]}\left[\int_0^1 A_{i't}^{1/[1-\alpha]}p_{x_{i'}t}^{-\alpha/[1-\alpha]}di'\right]^{-1/\alpha}Y_t$, where $i \in [0,1]$ and $i' \in [0,1] \setminus i$. Hence, using $C_Y = \int_0^1 p_{x_it}x_{it}di$, we obtain cost function (4.9).

$p_{xt}A_t^{-1}u_tL$. Since in the final good sector, revenue equals cost, the price of final output, p_{Yt}, is equal to aggregate cost over aggregate output. Thus, setting $p_{Yt} = 1$ for all t, yields the intermediates price

$$p_{xt} = A_t^{\frac{1}{\alpha}} \tag{4.10}$$

The wage rate may be derived as

$$w_t = \alpha A_t^{\frac{1-\alpha}{\alpha}} \tag{4.11}$$

As the intermediates price, the wage rate increases with an improving product quality. Notice that the wage rate increases at a lower rate, reflecting the rising labor intensity in the production of intermediates.

Using $x_t = [u_tL]/A_t$, we may rewrite profit rate (4.8) as

$$\pi_t = [1-\alpha]p_{xt}A_t^{-1}u_tL \tag{4.12}$$

The profit of the representative firm increases with its market power, the intermediates price, and its physical output which is given by $A_t^{-1}u_tL$. We insert price equation (4.10) into profit equation (4.12). A modified profit equation which depends only on R&D capital stock and production labor force results as

$$\pi_t = [1-\alpha]A_t^{\frac{1-\alpha}{\alpha}}u_tL \tag{4.13}$$

We obtain an unambiguous result: quality improvements increase profits.[10] Considering labor demand function (4.6) allows to rewrite profit equation (4.13) as

$$\pi_t = [1-\alpha]c_tL \tag{4.14}$$

Profit equation (4.14) shows that the profit of an intermediates production unit depends proportionally on its nominal output which is given by c_tL.

4.2.2 Asset Market

Blueprint i enables its owner to launch an innovative intermediate i, and, thus, to capture market niche i, where $i \in [0,1]$. The value of blueprint i is given by the discounted expected flow of future profits that accrues to the firm that owns the respective blueprint. The profit flow starts at time t and stops when the innovation becomes obsolete. Product obsolescence occurs at flow probability ψl_{is}^A, where $s \geq t$. Thus,

$$v_{it} = \int_t^{\infty} e^{-R_{ts}-\psi l_{is}^A[s-t]}\pi_{is}ds \tag{4.15}$$

[10] This finding is opposed to the respective result in the EPV model. There, the accumulation of R&D capital has an ambiguous effect on the profit rate [cf. equation (3.14)].

where $R_{ts} \equiv \int_t^s r_u du$ denotes the cumulative discount factor from time t to time s. The flow probability ψl_{it}^A is the arrival rate for a complete capital loss that the firm incurs when it is replaced by a new innovator. In this case, the value of the incumbent's blueprint jumps from v_{it} to zero. The flow probability, ψl_{it}^A, presupposes that the incumbent does not engage in R&D herself, so that ψl_{it}^A is indeed the flow probability for the occurrence that the incumbent firm loses the market niche.[11]

Equation (4.15) implies a second result on symmetry, stating that the R&D labor forces that target the different market niches are of same size. The reasoning is straightforward. If the R&D labor force that addresses market niche i were relatively small, i.e. $l_{it}^A < [1-u_t]L$, the flow probability that market niche i's most recent innovator incurs a complete capital loss would be relatively low, i.e. $\psi l_{it}^A < \psi[1-u_t]L$. Accordingly, by equation (4.15), the value of an innovation in the respective niche, v_{it}, would be relatively high. Recall that the research process is memoryless. Hence, we find a strong incentive for researchers to join the relatively small R&D labor force that addresses market niche i. We may conclude that in equilibrium, there is a common value for the differentiated blueprints, i.e. $v_{it} = v_t$, and, furthermore, the R&D labor forces are of same size, i.e. $l_{it}^A = l_t^A$, where $i \in [0,1]$. The latter implies that the market niches share a common innovation arrival rate, i.e. $\psi l_{it}^A = \psi[1-u_t]L$. This is our second result on symmetry. Notice that, applying our two symmetry findings, we may indeed use production functions (4.4) and (4.5). Moreover, the value of the representative blueprint follows as

$$v_t = \int_t^\infty e^{-R_{ts}-\psi[1-u_s]L[s-t]}\pi_{is}ds \tag{4.16}$$

Individuals are willing to invest in the development of the representative blueprint as long as the value of the blueprint is not below its price. The price of the blueprint is equal to the cost that an investor expects to incur if she seeks to develop the blueprint. If the value of the blueprint happens to be below the price, the economy performs no research, i.e. $\dot{A}_t = 0$. With free entry, the value of the blueprint cannot exceed its price. Thus, $v_t \leq p_{At}$, where p_{At} is the price of the representative blueprint. R&D capital's production function (4.4) implies price equation $p_{At} = \psi^{-1}w_t$. The expected cost of developing the blueprint increases with a lower probability that research is successful. It is independent from the innovation size. Applying wage rate

[11] This assumption reflects the replacement effect, or *Arrow effect*. The reasoning goes as follows. Assume that an intermediates supplier has captured a market niche. The expected cost of developing a new blueprint is both for the incumbent and the non-incumbent the same. But the net value of a new blueprint for the two agents differ: while the net value for the incumbent is zero, the net value for the non-incumbent is v_{it}. Thus, the net value that the incumbent attaches to the blueprint is strictly lower. It would not be reasonable for the incumbent supplier to perform research in the market niche she occupies. Hence, we may indeed use ψl_{it}^A as the flow probability of replacement.

(4.11), we obtain the following free-entry condition

$$v_t \leq \frac{\alpha}{\psi} A_t^{\frac{1-\alpha}{\alpha}} \tag{4.17}$$

with equality whenever $\dot{A}_t > 0$. Since an improvement of the product quality increases the wage rate, the price of the representative blueprint increases unambiguously.[12]

Differentiating equation (4.16) with respect to time, and using Leibniz's rule, we obtain no-arbitrage condition

$$\pi_t + \dot{v}_t - \psi\left[1 - u_t\right] L v_t = r_t v_t$$

It reflects the individual's indifference between the development of a blueprint, and the purchase of a bond: the expected total return that accrues to the owners of a blueprint in the interval between t and $t + dt$ equals the interest on the expected cost of developing a blueprint. Dividing by the value of a blueprint yields

$$\frac{\pi_t}{v_t} + \frac{\dot{v}_t}{v_t} - \psi\left[1 - u_t\right] L = r_t \tag{4.18}$$

This allows a slightly different interpretation of no-arbitrage: the expected rate of return on a blueprint, i.e. the expected rate of return on a share, in the interval $[t,\ t + dt]$, is equal to the rate of return on an investment in a bond, i.e. the interest rate multiplied by the length of the interval.

4.2.3 Steady-State Growth

Preferences [equations (3.21) and (3.22)], budget constraint (3.23), and utility maximization [conditions (3.25) to (3.28)] remain unchanged. The Keynes/Ramsey rule holds, i.e. $\dot{c}_t / c_t = \sigma\left[r_t - \rho\right]$, where $\rho, \sigma > 0$. Inserting no-arbitrage condition (4.18) yields the subsequent equation of motion of the consumption level

$$\frac{\dot{c}_t}{c_t} = \sigma\left[\frac{\pi_t}{v_t} + \frac{\dot{v}_t}{v_t} - \psi[1 - u_t]L - \rho\right] \tag{4.19}$$

Differentiating profit equation (4.14) with respect to time yields the subsequent steady-state evolution of profit

$$\frac{\dot{\pi}}{\pi} = \gamma \tag{4.20}$$

[12] As with the evolution of the profit rate, this finding is opposed to the respective result in the EPV model. There, the accumulation of R&D capital has an ambiguous effect on the price of the representative blueprint [cf. condition (3.19)].

In the steady state, the evolution of a share's value is given by [cf. condition (4.17)]

$$\frac{\dot{v}}{v} = \gamma \tag{4.21}$$

Equations of motion (4.20) and (4.21) imply for the steady state a constant dividend. Taking profit equation (4.13), condition (4.17), and labor demand function (4.7), the steady-state dividend follows as[13]

$$\frac{\pi}{v} = \frac{1-\alpha}{\alpha}\psi L - \frac{\gamma}{\delta} \tag{4.22}$$

The dividend increases with a higher market power of the representative intermediates firm, a higher productivity of research, and a larger total labor force. Furthermore, the dividend increases with a lower steady-state growth rate, adjusted by the innovation size. The latter result may be explained as follows. First, the higher the steady-state growth rate is for a given innovation size, the more workers do R&D. Second, the lower the innovation size is for a given steady-state growth rate, the more worker are employed in research laboratories. Thus, for both an increase in γ and a decrease in δ, the R&D labor force goes up, whereas the production labor force decreases. A smaller production labor force implies lower sales per intermediates firm. Hence, we obtain a lower steady-state profit rate, and, accordingly, a lower steady-state dividend.

Inserting dividend (4.22) and a blueprint value's steady-state equation of motion (4.21) into Keynes/Ramsey rule (4.19), we obtain the laissez-faire steady-state growth rate

$$\gamma = \frac{\sigma\left[\frac{1-\alpha}{\alpha}\psi L - \rho\right]}{1+\sigma\left[\frac{1}{[1-\alpha]\delta} - 1\right]} \tag{4.23}$$

where for a positive growth rate, i.e. $\gamma > 0$, first, $[1-\alpha]\psi L/\alpha > \rho$ must hold, and, second, $1/\sigma > 1 - 1/[1-\alpha]\delta$ must be fulfilled. The transversality condition implies $\rho > [\sigma - 1]\gamma/\sigma$. The economy is instantaneously in the steady state. Growth increases with a higher market power of the representative intermediates firm, a higher innovation size, a higher productivity of research, and a larger labor force. Furthermore, a lower rate of time preference, and a higher intertemporal elasticity of substitution speed up growth.[14]

---

[13] Recall that we exclude negative employment in the production sector, i.e. $\gamma \leq [1-\alpha]\delta\psi L/\alpha$ [cf. equation (4.7)]. Thus, dividend (4.22) is nonnegative.

[14] The laissez-faire steady-state R&D share follows as $[1-u] = \sigma\{\delta - \alpha\rho/[1-\alpha]\delta\psi L\}/\{1+\sigma[1/\{1-\alpha\}\delta - 1]\}$ [cf. labor demand function (4.7) and growth rate (4.23)]. Restricting their analysis to a linear instantaneous utility function, i.e. $\sigma \to \infty$, Aghion/Howitt derive the laissez-faire steady-state innovation rate by employing no-arbitrage condition $w_t = \psi v_t$ [cf. Aghion/Howitt (1998), pp. 90-92].

4.3 Social Planner's Solution

Using utility function (3.22) and production functions (4.4) and (4.5), the intertemporal maximization problem can be stated in terms of the subsequent current-value Hamiltonian

$$H = u(c_t) + \lambda_t \delta\psi A_t^{1-\left[\frac{1-\alpha}{\alpha}\right]} \left[A_t^{\frac{1-\alpha}{\alpha}} L - c_t L\right]$$

The first-order conditions for an optimum consumption path can be derived in the usual manner. We obtain a first steady-state equation of motion for the shadow price of R&D capital as follows

$$\frac{\dot{\lambda}}{\lambda} = -\left[\frac{1}{\sigma} - 1 + \frac{\alpha}{1-\alpha}\right]\gamma_S \tag{4.24}$$

where γ_S is the social optimum growth rate. A further steady-state equation of motion may be stated as

$$\frac{\dot{\lambda}}{\lambda} = -\left\{\left[\frac{1-\alpha}{\alpha}\delta\psi L + \left\{\frac{\alpha}{1-\alpha} - 1\right\}\gamma_S\right] - \rho\right\} \tag{4.25}$$

Equations (4.24) and (4.25) give the social optimum steady-state growth rate

$$\gamma_S = \sigma\left[\frac{1-\alpha}{\alpha}\delta\psi L - \rho\right] \tag{4.26}$$

where for a positive growth rate, i.e. $\gamma_S > 0$, $[1-\alpha]\,\delta\psi L/\alpha > \rho$ has to be fulfilled. The social optimum growth rate increases with a lower elasticity of substitution of intermediates, a higher innovation size, a higher productivity of research laboratories, and a larger labor force. Furthermore, a lower rate of time preference, and a higher intertemporal elasticity of substitution raise the rate.

How does laissez-faire growth (4.23) compare to social optimum growth (4.26)? Both solutions involve the following steady-state equilibrium condition (CC)

$$r = r_S = \rho + \frac{1}{\sigma}\gamma \tag{CC}$$

where r_S denotes the steady-state social return on investment. The CC line is upward-sloping in γ-r-space [cf. figure 4.2].

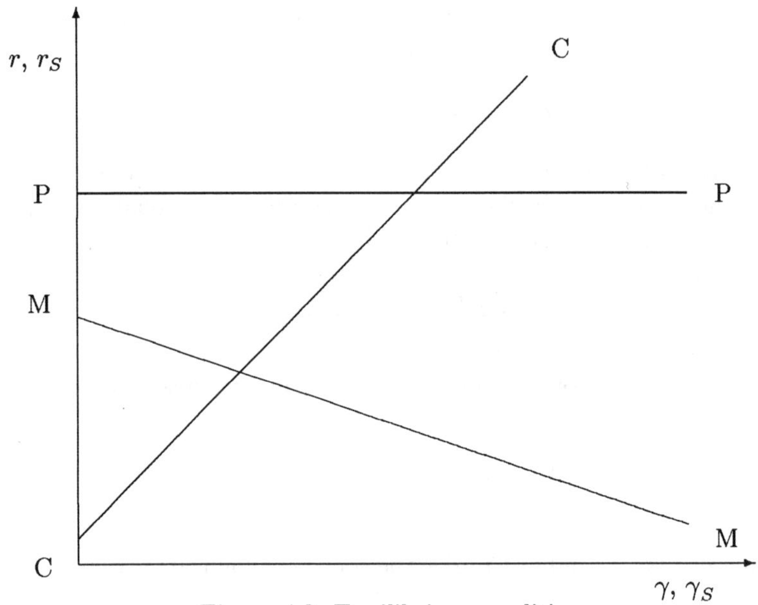

Figure 4.2: Equilibrium conditions.

The laissez-faire steady-state condition (MM) follows from no-arbitrage condition (4.18) along with equations (4.21) and (4.22) as

$$r = \frac{1-\alpha}{\alpha}\psi L - \left[\frac{1}{[1-\alpha]\,\delta} - 1\right]\gamma \qquad (MM)$$

The MM line is downward-sloping in γ-r-space. To rule out a negative return on R&D investment, we impose the subsequent conditions: $\gamma \leq [1-\alpha]^2\,\delta\psi L/\left\{[1-\{1-\alpha\}\,\delta]\,\alpha\right\}$ and $\delta \leq 1/\,[1-\alpha]$.

Social planner's equilibrium condition (PP) is implied by social optimum growth rate (4.26). We obtain

$$r_S = \frac{1-\alpha}{\alpha}\delta\psi L \qquad (PP)$$

The PP graph is a horizontal line in γ-r-space. Deviating from the private return, the social return does not depend on growth.

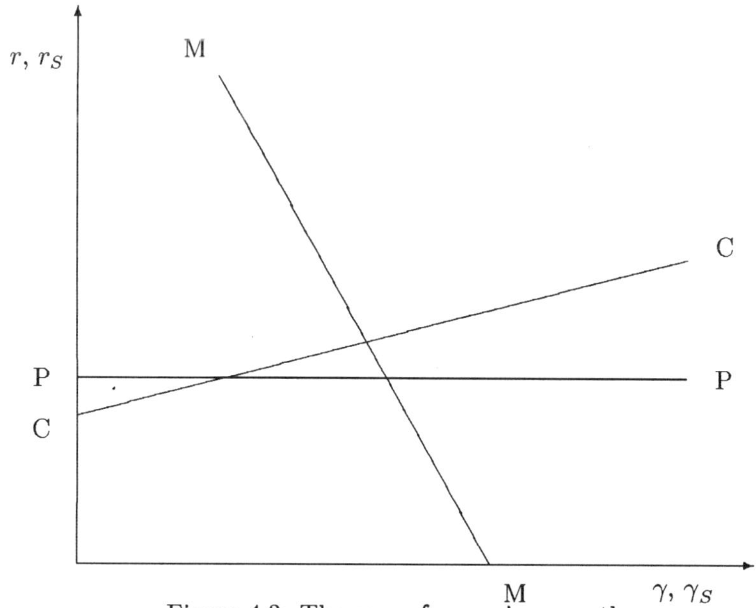

Figure 4.3: The case of excessive growth.

Equations (CC), (MM), and (PP) yield the subsequent results. First, an innovation size above unity implies unambiguously that laissez-faire growth is below the social optimum [cf. figure 4.2]. Second, for an innovation size below unity, laissez-faire growth may exceed social optimum growth, i.e. excessive laissez-faire growth may occur [cf. figure 4.3]. Excessive growth becomes more probable, the lower the innovation size is. Moreover, the probability of excessive growth increases for all parameter values that decrease the decentralized growth rate, except the elasticity of substitution of intermediates. The impact of the elasticity of substitution of intermediates on excessive's growth probability is ambiguous. However, imposing a logarithmic instantaneous utility function, i.e. $\sigma = 1$, its impact turns unambiguous: then, a higher elasticity of substitution of intermediates makes excessive growth more probable.[15]

4.4 Policy Implications

We introduce a government which faces flow budget constraint (3.41). For simplicity's sake, in the remainder of this chapter, we impose a logarithmic

[15] Cf. Aghion/Howitt (1992), pp. 348-349. In Aghion/Howitt (1998), for the multisector model, the social desirability of laissez-faire is not investigated.

instantaneous utility function. The optimum combinations of taxes $[t_\pi, t_I]^*$ are given by equation

$$t_\pi = 1 - [1 + t_I] \left\{ \delta \left[1 + \frac{\psi L}{\rho} \right] - \frac{\alpha}{1-\alpha} \right\}$$

where $\delta > \delta_L = [\alpha\rho] / \{[1-\alpha][\psi L + \rho]\}$. Summing up our findings on the parameter space of δ, we obtain

$$\frac{\alpha}{[1-\alpha]} \frac{\rho}{[\rho + \psi L]} < \delta \leq \frac{1}{1-\alpha}$$

For $t_I^* = 0$, the optimum profit tax is given by

$$t_\pi^* = \frac{1}{1-\alpha} - \delta \left[1 + \frac{\psi L}{\rho} \right]$$

The sign of the tax is ambiguous. Nevertheless, it is apparent that for a relatively small size of the innovation step, i.e. $\delta \longrightarrow \delta_L$, we obtain a positive optimum tax rate. Moreover, a relatively high elasticity of substitution of intermediates, i.e. $\alpha \longrightarrow 1$, turns the optimum tax rate positive. For $t_\pi^* = 0$, the optimum tax on R&D investment follows as

$$t_I^* = \left[\frac{1}{\delta \left[1 + \frac{\psi L}{\rho} \right] - \frac{\alpha}{1-\alpha}} \right] - 1$$

Again, for $\delta \longrightarrow \delta_L$, and $\alpha \longrightarrow 1$, the optimum tax is positive.

4.5 Discussion

In the present chapter, we put forth a model that describes economic growth as a process of creative destruction: research projects yield innovations, and these innovations turn existing products obsolete. Thus, creative research leads to the destruction of earlier vintage R&D capital. The propelling force behind this process is an entrepreneurship à la Schumpeter: profit-maximizing individuals compare the costs of research with the profit opportunities that innovations yield.

We have shown that the processes of expanding product variety and improving product quality may be modeled in a way that emphasizes the properties that they have in common. Moreover, we find that in the IPQ model, as in the EPV model, economic growth increases for a lower elasticity of substitution of products, a higher productivity of research laboratories, a larger resource base, a higher intertemporal elasticity of substitution, and a lower rate of time preference. It is apparent that our critique of the EPV model applies to the IPQ model, too.

Notice that despite the great analogy, the IPQ model deviates from the EPV model when it comes to normative issues: whereas in the EPV model, laissez-faire growth is due to the positive intertemporal R&D spillover unambiguously below the social optimum, in the IPQ model, we obtain an ambiguous result: if the innovation size is relatively small, laissez-faire growth may be excessive. Apart from its capturing of the uncertainty of the innovation process, the representation of excessive growth is the main novelty of the IPQ model.

Part III

Product Differentiation due to Investment

Chapter 5

The Ramsey Model with Imperfect Competition

Empirical studies show that, first, business formation and economic growth are related. Davis/Haltiwanger (1990) document that macroeconomic fluctuations are associated with business start-ups and failures. Chatterjee/Cooper (1993) find detrended real gross national product (GNP) and net business formation to be positively correlated. Second, there is empirical evidence that physical capital accumulation and product differentiation are linked. Jovanovic (1993) reports that product differentiation depends positively on physical capital accumulation. Third, there is evidence that product differentiation and economic growth are associated. Funke/Ruhwedel (1999) employ OECD panel data to show that a greater degree of product variety helps to explain per capita GDP levels. Fourth, empirical studies find that physical capital accumulation and economic growth are related. In section 2.1, we have surveyed the respective literature. Most prominent is certainly the study by De Long/Summers (1991).

In the present chapter, we apply a simple Ramsey-type model to represent the empirically supported relation between business formation, capital accumulation, product differentiation, and economic growth. Thus, we turn away from the R&D focus that the models of part II – the EPV model and the IPQ model – take.

Our starting point is the standard neoclassical growth model, usually referred to as the Ramsey model [cf., e.g., Barro/Sala-i-Martin (1995), ch. 2]. This textbook model encompasses three building blocks. First, the intertemporal allocation of income: Ramsey (1928) derived the utility-maximizing rate of saving. Second, the aggregation of the economy's capital stock: Solow (1956) solved the problem by postulating a one good economy. Third, the growth path' stability: Solow (1956) invoked stability by the use of a neoclassical aggregate production function. Putting the three blocks together,

Cass (1965) and Koopmans (1965) formulated what has become the textbook Ramsey model.

We generalize that model by modifying the second of its three building blocks. Hence, considering Romer's (1987) paper on increasing returns due to specialization, we replace the neoclassical aggregate production function by a CES final output production function with imperfectly substitutable intermediates as inputs.

With this basic model, we address three of the four points of critique that we have raised in our discussion of the EPV model [cf. chapter 3]. First, the Ramsey model with imperfect competition leaves the stark research focus of R&D-driven growth models. Second, physical capital's product differentiating capability is represented. Third, in our model, final output is more than a mere consumption good: final output may be either consumed or transformed into capital stock. The Ramsey model with imperfect competition does not tackle the fourth point of critique, though. The reason is obvious: the fourth point relates to EPV model's representation of labor being the only input into R&D, and our basic model does not feature an explicitly modelled R&D sector. In this model, we assume that capital equipment embodies technical knowledge.

The present model relates to Kiyotaki (1988), Hornstein (1993), and Judd (1999). In those models, physical capital accumulation with imperfect competition is featured, too. Our model deviates in its representation of the process of business formation and product differentiation, though. In those models, the amount of firms and the degree of product differentiation are assumed to be constant.

Whereas the textbook Ramsey model finds laissez-faire growth to be unambiguously socially optimal, in our model, due to the introduction of imperfect competition, we obtain a deviating result. Our model shows that laissez-faire growth is not socially optimal: the decentralized growth rate is unambiguously below the social optimum growth rate. We find that the difference between the two growth rates increases with the degree of imperfectness of competition. For the boundary case of perfect competition, our model confirms the normative finding of the textbook Ramsey model, though.

The structure of the present model is given by figure 5.1. There is one primary input, which is labor, and one reproducible input, which is capital. Output can either be consumed or transformed into capital. Thus, apart from the introduction of intermediate goods, the model indeed replicates the structure of the textbook Ramsey model. Accordingly, in its structure, the model follows traditional growth theory. By the same token, the structure of the model deviates from the standard models of endogenous growth with imperfect competition [cf. EPV model, figure 3.1, IPQ model, figure 4.1].

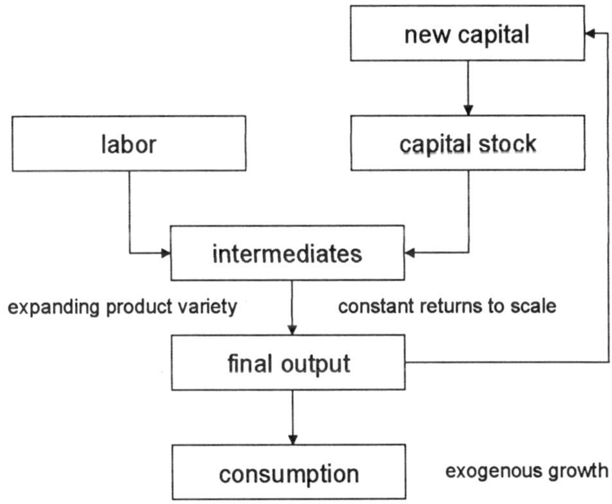

Figure 5.1: A schematic representation of the model.

The present chapter is organized as follows. In section one, we present the technology of our Ramsey-type model. Section two investigates the model's laissez-faire outcome. Section three yields the social planner's solution. Section four derives policy implications. Section five gives a recapitulation.

5.1 Technology

Final output Y_t is produced according to the following CES production function

$$Y_t = \left[\int_0^{K_t} x_{kt}^{\alpha} dk \right]^{\frac{1}{\alpha}} \tag{5.1}$$

where $0 < \alpha < 1$. The inputs into the production of final output are the differentiated intermediate goods k, where $k \in [0, K_t]$. The quantity of intermediate k that is used in final output production is denoted by x_{kt}. The parameter α determines the elasticity of substitution of intermediates ϵ, i.e. $\epsilon = 1/[1-\alpha]$.

A one-to-one transformation of final output into capital implies $\dot{K}_t = I_t$, where I_t is investment, i.e. the part of final output which is not consumed. We rule out negative investment, i.e. $I_t \geq 0$. Thus, the market-clearing condition for final output is given by

$$Y_t = c_t L + I_t = c_t L + \dot{K}_t \tag{5.2}$$

Notice that equation (5.1) yields three interpretations of K_t. First, K_t denotes the amount of intermediates production units that have been opened up before time t. Second, since each of the K_t production units produces a unique differentiated intermediate, it is also a measure for the amount of varieties that have been launched before time t. Third, since the sum of production units is just the economy's capital stock, K_t represents furthermore the size of the accumulated capital stock.

The intermediate goods sector's technology is given by the subsequent one-to-one production functions $x_{kt} = l_{kt}$, where $k \in [0, K_t]$. To open up an intermediates production unit, it takes a unit of capital. The output of the production unit k is determined by the size of the labor force l_{kt} that it employs: one unit of labor is transformed into one unit of the respective intermediate.

Imposing full employment and symmetric market shares on the K_t intermediates suppliers, i.e. $x_{kt} = x_t$, we obtain the condition $L = \int_0^{K_t} l_{kt} dk = K_t x_t$. That is, the output per intermediates production unit is negatively related to the amount of varieties. Furthermore, by symmetry, we may formulate final output production function (5.1) as[1]

$$Y_t = K_t^{\frac{1-\alpha}{\alpha}} L \tag{5.3}$$

where $[1-\alpha]/\alpha > 0$.[2] To rule out exploding as well as endogenous growth, we assume $[1-\alpha]/\alpha < 1$, i.e. $\alpha > 0.5$. With $\alpha < 0.5$, growth would explode. If $\alpha = 0.5$ were to hold, the model would turn into a model of endogenous growth.[3] Here, we abstract from the possibility of endogenous growth without the amendment of an explicit engine of growth, and assume that $\alpha > 0.5$.

5.2 Laissez-faire Outcome

5.2.1 Intermediate Market

The profit rates of the intermediates suppliers at time t are given by

$$\pi_{kt} = p_{x_k t}(x_{kt})x_{kt} - w_t x_{kt} \tag{5.4}$$

where $p_{x_k t}$ denotes the price of the intermediate k, where $k \in [0, K_t]$. The suppliers maximize their flow profits by charging $p_{x_k t} = w_t/\alpha$. Thus, we obtain a symmetric solution, where $p_{x_k t} = p_{xt}$, $x_{kt} = x_t$, and $l_{kt} = l_t$ for all

[1] In subsection 5.2.1, we show that the identity of the K_t market shares is implied by intermediates firms' profit-maximization.

[2] Notice that $0 < \alpha < 1$ implies $[1-\alpha]/\alpha > 0$.

[3] A model with $[1-\alpha]/\alpha = 1$ may be portrayed as an AK model with imperfect competition. Unfortunately, such an AK model is quite restrictive on the required elasticity of substitution between intermediates, which has to meet exactly 0.5. In the following chapter, we will investigate a more general AK model.

K_t varieties. Accordingly, in the remainder, we may indeed use production function (5.3).

The cost function C_Y that is dual to production function (5.1) may be stated as[4]

$$C_Y(\{p_{x_k t}\}_{k=0}^{K_t}, Y_t) = \left[\int_0^{K_t} p_{x_k t}^{\frac{-\alpha}{1-\alpha}} dk\right]^{-\left[\frac{1-\alpha}{\alpha}\right]} Y_t$$

By symmetry, total cost follows as $C_Y(p_{xt}, L) = p_{xt}L$. Since perfect competition prevails on the market for final output, revenue equals cost. Accordingly, the price of final output, p_{Yt}, is equal to aggregate cost over aggregate output. Setting $p_{Yt} = 1$ for all t, and solving for p_{xt} yields the intermediates price

$$p_{xt} = K_t^{\frac{1-\alpha}{\alpha}} \tag{5.5}$$

The wage rate follows as $w_t = \alpha K_t^{[1-\alpha]/\alpha}$. Intermediates price and wage rate increase with an expanding product variety, since additional intermediates raise the marginal productivity of existing intermediates. The stimulant medium is the intermediates price which rises. This inflationary effect magnifies with a lower substitutability between intermediates. Since, for a given number of varieties, the intermediates price is pegged to the numéraire by equation (5.5), a rise of the representative intermediates supplier's market power does not affect the intermediates price, but lowers the wage rate.

Using $w_t = \alpha p_{xt}$, profit equation (5.4) may be stated as

$$\pi_t = [1-\alpha] p_{xt} K_t^{-1} L \tag{5.6}$$

The profit of the representative firm increases with its market power and with the intermediates price. An increase in the amount of varieties has two opposite effects on the profit. First, a positive productivity effect: it follows from the induced rise in the intermediates price. Second, a negative market-saturation effect: the intermediate's share of a market the size of which is given by the non-growing population L is negatively related to the amount of intermediates. To determine the sign of the overall effect, we insert price equation (5.5) into profit equation (5.6). We obtain a modified profit equation which depends only on capital stock and labor force, i.e.

$$\pi_t = [1-\alpha] K_t^{-\left[1-\frac{1-\alpha}{\alpha}\right]} L \tag{5.7}$$

Profit equation (5.7) shows that for $\alpha > 0.5$, the negative market saturation effect dominates the positive productivity effect. Hence, the overall effect of the launch of an additional intermediate on profits is negative.

[4] The cost function is the solution to the problem $\min\left\{\int_0^{K_t} p_{x_k t} x_{kt} dk + \mu\left[Y_t - \left[\int_0^{K_t} x_{kt}^{\alpha} dk\right]^{1/\alpha}\right]\right\}$.

In the Ramsey model with imperfect competition, $[1-\alpha]$ denotes capital's income share, whereas α depicts labor's income share. Hence, the present model follows the neoclassical growth model in the finding that the respective shares of national income are independent of the sizes of both labor force and capital stock [cf. equations (5.3) and (5.7)].

The present model deviates from the neoclassical growth model in a crucial point, though. Recall that empirical studies that base their analysis on the assumption of perfect competition typically face a puzzle: the income share of physical capital that is implied by the respective regressions tends to exceed the share that follows from national income accounts [cf. section 2.2]. We find that, opposed to the neoclassical growth model, the present model is in line with the evidence. Recall that national income accounts document a capital share $[1-\alpha]$ of roughly 0.3 [cf. Maddison (1987), table 7, p. 659]. Based on this estimate, our model predicts that capital's output elasticity is given by $[1-\alpha]/\alpha \approx 0.4$ [cf. production function (5.3)]. This prediction fits exactly the output elasticity that the recent studies by Islam (1995) and Hamilton/Monteagudo (1998) measure [cf. table 2.2].[5] Thus, by representing imperfectly competitive markets, the present model reconciles the Ramsey model with the empirical evidence.

5.2.2 Asset Market

The value of the representative unit of capital equals the discounted flow of future profits that accrues to this unit. This yields

$$v_t = \int_t^{\infty} e^{-R_{ts}} \pi_s ds \tag{5.8}$$

where $R_{ts} \equiv \int_t^s r_u du$ is the cumulative discount factor from time t to time s.

Differentiating equation (5.8) with respect to time, and using Leibniz's rule, we obtain the no-arbitrage condition $\pi_t + \dot{v}_t = r_t v_t$. It reflects the individuals' indifference between an investment in a firm on the one hand, and buying a bond on the other: the total return that accrues to the owners of a unit of capital in the interval between t and $t+dt$ – the flow profit that a unit of capital yields, $\pi_t dt$, plus the absolute change in the value of this unit, $\dot{v}_t dt$ – equals the interest on the value of a unit of capital, $r_t v_t dt$. Dividing by the value of a unit of capital yields

$$\frac{\pi_t}{v_t} + \frac{\dot{v}_t}{v_t} = r_t \tag{5.9}$$

[5] Notice that production function (5.3) restricts labor's output elasticity to unity. In this specific point, the present basic model is certainly at odds with the empirical evidence. However, by considering scale-dependent costs, this restriction may be easily relaxed. This is shown in appendix A. There, we derive an aggregate production function that is given by $Y_t = K_t^{[1-\alpha]/\alpha} L^{1-\phi}$, where the parameter $\phi > 0$ reflects the magnitude of the scale-dependent costs.

This allows a slightly different interpretation of no-arbitrage: the total return on a share in the interval $[t, t+dt]$ – the dividend, $\pi_t dt/v_t$, plus the relative change in the value of this share, $\dot{v}_t dt/v_t$ – is equal to the rate of return on an investment in a bond, i.e. the interest rate multiplied by the length of the interval, $r_t dt$.

5.2.3 Equilibrium Dynamics

Inserting no-arbitrage condition (5.9) into the Keynes/Ramsey rule, $\dot{c}_t/c_t = \sigma\left[r_t - \rho\right]$, where $\rho, \sigma > 0$, yields

$$\frac{\dot{c}_t}{c_t} = \sigma\left[\frac{\pi_t}{v_t} + \frac{\dot{v}_t}{v_t} - \rho\right] \tag{5.10}$$

The level of consumption grows as long as the return on a share – dividend plus relative change in the share's value – exceeds the rate of time preference. Since the rate of time preference is constant, the question whether our model exhibits fading growth boils down to the question whether the return on a share declines.

For the investigation of the equilibrium dynamics, the evolution of two variables is crucial: the value of a unit of capital, and the profit rate that accrues to a unit of capital. First, we analyze the evolution of the capital value. For $\dot{K}_t > 0$, the capital value is equal to unity, i.e. $v_t = 1$. Hence, the capital value is constant. For $\dot{K}_t = 0$, the economy is stationary, and the profit rate does not change. Since the capital value is the discounted flow of future profits [equation (5.8)], we obtain in this case, too, a constant capital value.

Second, we investigate the evolution of the profit rate. Differentiating profit equation (5.7) with respect to capital stock yields a falling profit rate. A falling profit rate and a constant capital value imply a decrease in the return on a share, i.e. a decrease in the return on investment. Thus, our model exhibits fading growth. The decrease in the return on investment makes the growth process grinding to a halt.[6] Notice that the decline in the return on investment in this model of imperfect competition resembles the falling return in a capital intensifying neoclassical economy: as capital gets relatively abundant, its marginal productivity decreases.

[6] A look on production function (5.3) confirms this finding. With $[1-\alpha]/\alpha < 1$, the production of final output exhibits decreasing returns to capital stock. Decreasing returns to the reproducible factor is a necessary condition for a petering-out of growth.

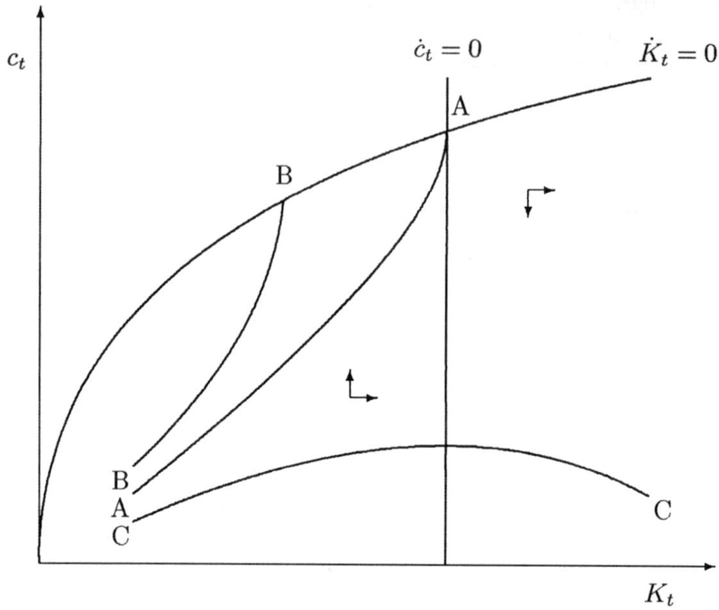

Figure 5.2: Equilibrium dynamics.

Taking Keynes/Ramsey rule (5.10), using profit equation (5.7), $v_t = 1$, and $\dot{v}_t = 0$, we obtain the following equation of motion for the level of consumption

$$\frac{\dot{c}_t}{c_t} = \sigma \left[[1-\alpha] K_t^{-[1-\frac{1-\alpha}{\alpha}]} L - \rho \right] \tag{5.11}$$

The level of consumption grows as longs as $[1-\alpha]K_t^{-\{1-[1-\alpha]/\alpha\}}L$ exceeds the rate of time preference, ρ. The condition is fulfilled for an appropriately low elasticity of substitution of intermediates, weak diseconomies of scale, a large labor force, a small capital stock, and a low rate of time preference.

Solving market-clearing condition (5.2) for the change in the capital stock, and using production function (5.3) we may derive the subsequent equation of motion for the capital stock

$$\dot{K}_t = \begin{cases} K_t^{\frac{1-\alpha}{\alpha}} L - c_t L & \text{for } v_t = 1 \\ 0 & \text{for } v_t < 1 \end{cases} \tag{5.12}$$

Equations (5.11) and (5.12) together with the respective transversality condition form a two-dimensional system of differential equations in K-c space. The $\dot{c}_t/c_t = 0$-locus is a vertical line, given by $\bar{K} =$

$\{[1-\alpha]\,L/\rho\}^{1/\{1-[1-\alpha]/\alpha\}}$. The $\dot{K}=0$-locus, defined by $c_t = K_t^{\frac{1-\alpha}{\alpha}}$, is an upward-sloping concave curve. It starts in the origin and tends to infinity for $K_t \to \infty$. With $K_0 < \bar{K}$, the existence of a unique saddle path AA and a unique steady-state equilibrium $[\bar{K}, \bar{c}]$ follows [cf. figure 5.2].

There are paths that start above the saddle path AA. In figure 5.2, these trajectories are represented by path BB. Along these trajectories, consumption and capital stock are both rising. When the paths hit the $\dot{K}=0$-locus, consumption and capital stock remain constant, both at suboptimal levels. Hence, these paths contradict the equation of motion for the level of consumption [cf. equation (5.11)]. Furthermore, there are paths that start below the saddle path AA. These trajectories are represented by path CC. Along such trajectories, both consumption and capital stock are initially rising. When the paths come across the $\dot{c}_t/c_t = 0$-locus, the level of consumption starts decreasing, while the capital stock approaches infinity. These paths contradict the transversality condition since, for $t \to \infty$, the capital stock, discounted at rate r_t, does not approach zero. The saddle path AA emerges as the unique path that satisfies equations of motion (5.11) and (5.12) as well as the transversality condition. It is straightforward to check the stability of this system.[7]

The saddle path AA is often referred to as the policy function. It relates the optimal value of the control variable, c_t, to the given state variable, K_t. In the remainder of this section, we investigate the curvature of the policy function. For this purpose, we define χ_t as the ratio of consumption over capital stock, i.e. $\chi_t = c_t L/K_t$. Considering figure 5.2, it is apparent that the curvature of the policy function depends on the sign of $\dot{\chi}_t$. Utilizing equations (5.11) and (5.12), we obtain the subsequent equation of motion:

$$\frac{\dot{\chi}_t}{\chi_t} = \{\sigma[1-\alpha]-1\}\,K_t^{-\left[1-\frac{1-\alpha}{\alpha}\right]}L - \sigma\rho + \chi_t \tag{5.13}$$

For the steady state, equation (5.13) implies $\bar{\chi} = \rho/[1-\alpha]$. Regarding the curvature of the policy function, we may distinguish three cases. First, $\sigma < 1/[1-\alpha]$ implies $\dot{\chi}_t < 0$, and, hence, we obtain a concave saddle path. The reasoning goes as follows. When σ is relatively low, the representative individual has a strong preference for smoothing her consumption over time. Accordingly, in the beginning, when the capital stock is low, she devotes a large part of her resources to consumption, i.e. χ_t is high. During transition, as capital is accumulated, the ratio of consumption over capital stock decreases, i.e. $\dot{\chi}_t < 0$. Since in the beginning, the investment rate is low, the economy approaches its steady state slowly. Second, $\sigma = 1/[1-\alpha]$ leads to $\dot{\chi}_t = 0$, and, accordingly, a linear trajectory follows. In this case, the policy function exhibits a simple closed-form solution, i.e. $c_t = \sigma\rho K_t/L$. Third, $\sigma > 1/[1-\alpha]$ implies $\dot{\chi}_t > 0$, and, hence, we obtain a convex saddle path. When σ is relatively high, the representative individual does not mind

[7] Cf. appendix B.

large swings in consumption over time. Hence, she chooses to consume little when the capital stock is low, that is, when the return on investment is high. During transition, the ratio of consumption over capital stock increases, i.e. $\dot{\chi}_t > 0$. As the initial investment rate is high, the economy approaches its steady state rapidly. This case is the one that is depicted in figure 5.2.[8]

5.3 Social Planner's Solution

After having analyzed the laissez-faire outcome, we investigate the social planner's solution. This solution will be the reference for our welfare analysis. The social planner's problem is to maximize overall utility (3.21) subject to technology constraint (5.12). The first-order conditions imply the following social optimum consumption path[9]

$$\frac{\dot{c}_t}{c_t} = \sigma \left[\frac{dY_t}{dK_t} - \rho \right] \tag{5.14}$$

where dY_t/dK_t is investment's social marginal productivity, i.e. the social return on investment. Equations of motion (5.12) and (5.14) together with the respective transversality condition depict a two-dimensional system of differential equations in K-c space.

To evaluate the social desirability of laissez-faire, we compare the private return on capital to the social return on capital. The social return is given by

$$\frac{dY_t}{dK_t} = \frac{1}{\alpha} r_t \tag{5.15}$$

i.e. the social return is equal to the private return premultiplied by the ratio $1/\alpha$. Thus, apart from the boundary case of perfect competition, where $\alpha \rightarrow 1$, the social return exceeds unambiguously the private return. Hence, for $0 < \alpha < 1$, the laissez-faire transitional growth to the steady state and the laissez-faire level of both physical capital stock and consumption in the steady state are both unambiguously below the social optimum.

The reason for laissez-faire's suboptimality is that the price of final output contains the monopoly rent that the intermediates suppliers levy. Since final output is transformed into capital, in laissez-faire, investment is inefficiently expensive, and, in turn, too little investment is undertaken. We will

[8] Thus, in this model, we obtain an analogous relation between the curvature of the policy function and the elasticity of intertemporal substitution as in the Ramsey model with perfect competition. That is, the ratio of consumption over capital stock is falling, constant, or rising on whether the elasticity of intertemporal substitution is smaller, equal to, or larger than the inverse of the capital share [cf. Barro/Sala-i-Martin (1995), pp. 89-90].

[9] Since instantaneous utility (3.22) and technology (5.3) are jointly concave in $[K, c]$, so is the Hamiltonian. This implies that the necessary conditions are also sufficient conditions.

refer to this effect as the *monopoly distortion effect.* Although the monopoly distortion effect is not a true externality, it is observationally equivalent to a positive externality. Hence, we will refer to this effect casually as a positive externality [cf. Romer (1987), p. 61].[10]

5.4 Policy Implications

The model suggests that both the laissez-faire transitional growth rate and the laissez-faire steady-state consumption level are below the social optimum. This finding poses the question whether there are policy measures that may close this gap. We introduce a government which faces the following flow budget constraint

$$t_\pi \pi_t K_t + t_I I_t + TL = 0$$

t_π is a profit tax, and t_I is an investment tax, where $-1 < t_\pi, t_I < 1$. T_t denotes a lump-sum tax. The size of the lump-sum tax adjusts endogenously in order to balance the governmental budget at every point in time.

Thus, we may derive the after-tax rate of return

$$r_t = \frac{1-t_\pi}{1+t_I}[1-\alpha]K_t^{-\left[1-\frac{1-\alpha}{\alpha}\right]}L \tag{5.16}$$

What are appropriate policy measures to raise the private return on investment (5.16) to the social return (5.15)? Closing the gap can be accomplished by granting either a subsidy on profit, $t_\pi < 0$, or a subsidy on investment, $t_I < 0$. The optimum combinations of subsidies $[t_\pi, t_I]^*$ that make the private return equal to the social return obey the condition

$$t_\pi = 1 - [1+t_I]\frac{1}{\alpha} \tag{5.17}$$

To stay with an optimum combination of subsidies, the higher the subsidization of investment, the lower the profit subsidization has to be, and vice

[10] How does the result of a suboptimal laissez-faire outcome compare to the evaluation of laissez-faire in a reinterpreted Grossman/Helpman-model? A reinterpretation involves the replacement of Grossman/Helpman's technical knowledge capital stock by a physical capital stock. A reinterpreted Grossman/Helpman-model implies a severe asymmetry in the economy's structure: imperfect competition in the production of the consumption good contrasts with perfect competition in the production of the capital good. The asymmetry implies the social efficiency of laissez-faire. This result contradicts our finding. The contrariety can be readily explained: in our model, the monopoly distortion effect makes investment inefficiently expensive, and, in turn, drives a wedge between the private and the social return on investment. The social inefficiency of laissez-faire follows. Since a reinterpreted Grossman/Helpman-model imposes perfect competition on the production of the capital good, there is no such effect, and the private return on investment is equal to the social return. Thus, in a reinterpreted Grossman/Helpman-model, the laissez-faire outcome is socially efficient. It is straightforward to check this argument analytically [cf. Grossman/Helpman (1991a), pp. 82-83].

versa. Furthermore, the less perfectly competitive the intermediates market is, the higher – ceteris paribus – the optimum subsidies. For $t_I = 0$, equation (5.17) implies the optimum profit subsidy $t_\pi^* = -[1-\alpha]/\alpha$. For $t_\pi = 0$, we obtain the optimum investment subsidy $t_I^* = -[1-\alpha]$.

How should these subsidies be financed? A lump-sum tax is a preferable choice to balance the budget: it has neither effects on capital accumulation, nor effects on income distribution.

5.5 Discussion

This chapter sets forth an exogenous growth model with forward-looking entrepreneurs who maximize profits on imperfectly competitive markets. The model represents a suggestive relation between business formation, capital accumulation, product differentiation, and economic growth: as long as there is economic growth, new businesses are established, capital is accumulated, and product diversity increases. Hence, the model is in line with the empirical literature cited at the beginning of this chapter.

Moreover, with the present model, we may explain evidence that is a puzzle to studies that are based on the neoclassical growth model. Recall that estimations of the Solow model reveal usually a contradiction: the income share of physical capital that is implied by these estimations tends to exceed the share that follows from national income accounts [cf. section 2.2]. We show that by representing imperfectly competitive markets, the Ramsey model may be reconciled with the empirical evidence.

The essential result of the Ramsey model with imperfect competition is stark: in the presence of imperfect competition, the laissez-faire steady-state level of physical capital stock is below the social optimum, i.e. the laissez-faire entrepreneurial activity is inefficiently low.

The policy implications are straightforward: since entrepreneurs disregard the positive external effect of their investment, governments ought to promote entrepreneurial activity, i.e. set incentives for an increase in business formation, and, thus, a rise in capital accumulation. The model recommends supply-side policies that strengthen the incentive to invest. Our model delivers a rationale to promote entrepreneurial activity through the institutional system. In particular, our model suggests that policies that hamper entrepreneurial activity have high social costs by pushing the decentralized capital accumulation below the social optimum.

Notice that the present model shares the textbook Ramsey model's petering-out of growth. Long-run growth could be attained by employing an exogenously determined rate of technological change. In the remainder of part III, we pursue a different approach, and turn our basic model into a model of endogenous growth. We propose two suggestive engines of growth: in chapter 6, we introduce a static network externality, and, in chapter 7, we represent an intertemporal learning-by-doing effect.

Chapter 6

A Generalized AK Model

In his seminal paper on *Long-Run Policy Analysis and Long-Run Growth*, Rebelo (1991) sets forth an unparalleled parsimonious endogenous growth model. The reason for the popularity of Rebelo's AK model is obvious: despite of its simplicity, it may explain the empirical phenomenon of sustained cross-country growth disparity. Recently, Crafts (2000) and De Long (2000) document that the gap between the richest and the poorest countries has widened dramatically during the past century.

The AK model represents long-run economic growth as being driven by the accumulation of a core of capital goods. It necessitates the assumption that this core of capital goods is produced without the use of non-reproducible factors. In particular, the AK model represents an economy where the labor force does not contribute to the production of final output. This assumption has been criticized, most prominently by Jones/Manuelli (1990).

In the present chapter, we show that by allowing for imperfect competition, we may introduce non-reproducible factors, i.e. labor, into the AK framework. Thus, our generalized AK model encompasses two features: first, the model allows for imperfect competition, and, second, it represents a non-reproducible factor, i.e. it captures labor as an input of production.

In spite of these innovations, our generalized AK model resembles Rebelo's AK model in many aspects. As in Rebelo (1991), there is a single reproducible input, i.e. capital. Deviating from Rebelo, though, in our model, the production of final output may exhibit constant returns to scale, economies of scale, or diseconomies of scale [cf. figure 6.1].

Apart from the representation of a single reproducible input, our model follows Rebelo (1991) also in the broad definition of this input. The justification of a broadly-defined capital stock is well-known. Empirical studies document that new physical capital investment is necessary to take advantage of new technical discoveries [cf. Jorgenson/Gollop/Fraumeni (1987) and Wolff (1996)]. Considering this evidence, it is suggestive to model technical knowledge as being embodied in physical capital.

We are indebted to Rebelo (1991) in one further point: in our model as in Rebelo's AK model, at the aggregate level, the economy exhibits non-decreasing returns to the reproducible factor, and, hence, endogenous growth. Accordingly, in our model, too, the determinants of the long-run growth rate include both economic fundamentals, i.e. parameters of tastes and technology, and government policy variables.

A fundamental prediction of both our generalized AK model and Rebelo's AK model is that a higher rate of income tax implies a lower long-run growth rate. Rebelo (1991) suggests that the share of government consumption is an appropriate proxy for the rate of income tax. Barro (1991, 1996, 1997) and Barro/Lee (1994) find indeed a negative relation between growth rates and the share of government consumption in GDP. In addition, Hall/Jones (1997) document that high government consumption lowers the level of income.

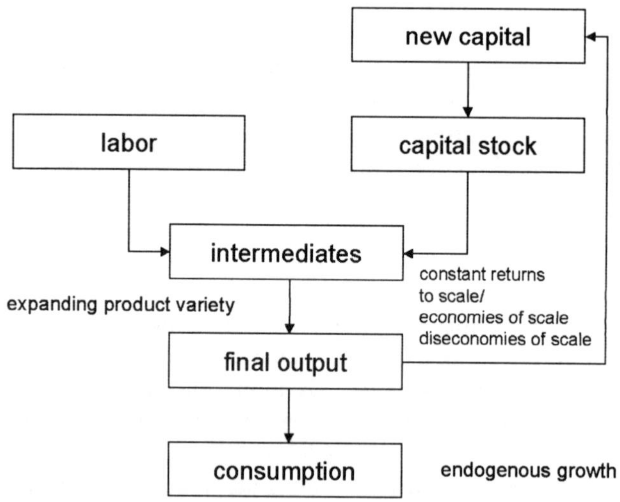

Figure 6.1: A schematic representation of the model.

The present chapter is organized as follows. In section one, we present the economy's technology. Section two investigates the laissez-faire outcome. Section three yields the social planner's solution. Section four derives policy implications, after which section five summarizes the findings.

6.1 Technology

The intermediate goods are produced by an infinite set of firms k, the amount of which is represented by K_t, i.e. $k \in [0, K_t]$. The technology that firm k faces is given by the one-to-one production function $x_{kt} = l_{kt}$. That is, firm k produces x_{kt} units of intermediate k, while it employs labor force l_{kt}. Hence, K_t may be interpreted as the amount of intermediates firms, the amount of differentiated intermediates, and the economy's capital stock. The elasticity of substitution of intermediates may be derived as $\epsilon = 1/[1-\alpha]$, where $0 < \alpha < 1$.

Final output Y_t is produced according to the following CES production function

$$Y_t = \left[\int_0^{K_t} x_{kt}^{\alpha} dk \right]^{\frac{\nu}{\alpha}} \tag{6.1}$$

where $\nu > 0$. The parameter ν reflects sign and size of economies of scale: for $0 < \nu < 1$, we obtain diseconomies of scale, for $\nu = 1$, the economy exhibits constant returns to scale, and $\nu > 1$ implies positive economies of scale. The overall economies of scale encompass two effects: a positive network effect, and a negative congestion effect. Hence, the sign and the size of the overall economies of scale hinges on the relative magnitude of these two effects.

The positive network effect is suggestive. It captures external benefits that spill from one firm to the other. The propelling force behind these positive spillovers may be, e.g., a common labor market that every firm can draw from, or a pool of social knowledge that all firms have readily access to.

The negative congestion effect may be motivated in two ways. First, the transportation of intermediates to final output production sites takes an appropriate infrastructure. If aggregate final output increases, the infrastructure becomes congested. Thus, congestion of infrastructure suggests diseconomies of scale. Second, the assembly of intermediates to final output takes organizational skills, and there may be a limit to the economy's supply of talented workers. An increase in aggregate final output raises the demand for talented labor force, and this resource becomes a bottleneck. Hence, the scarcity of talents may lead to diseconomies of scale, too.

Our examples suggest that neither positive economies of scale due to spillovers, nor diseconomies of scale as a result of congestion are affected by firm size. This is consistent with the empirical work by Caballero/Lyons (1990). Investigating internal vs. external economies of scale in European industry, they find very little evidence for internal economies of scale, but document strong evidence for external economies. Caballero/Lyons (1992a) find the same result for the U.S. industry. Accordingly, in our model, a single firm cannot exploit economies of scale by expanding, respectively by splitting up.

In the present model, we endogenize the overall economies of scale. It is argued that a higher elasticity of substitution of products increases the network effect, whereas it does not affect the congestion effect. That is, the more alike the economy's products are, the stronger are the firm-to-firm spillovers. Clearly, a firm benefits relatively more from a common labor market or a pool of social knowledge when it is surrounded by firms that produce similar products. Hence, an association that a higher elasticity of substitution increases the overall economies of scale is reasonable. We assume that this relation is given by $\nu = \alpha/[1-\alpha]$.[1]

Thus, with respect to the sign of the overall economies of scale, we may distinguish three cases. First, for $\alpha > 0.5$, we obtain positive economies of scale, i.e. the network effect dominates the congestion effect. Second, $\alpha = 0.5$ implies constant returns to scale, i.e. the two effects just neutralize. Third, $\alpha < 0.5$ yields diseconomies of scale, i.e. the congestion effect dominates the network effect effect.

Imposing symmetry, and with $\nu = \alpha/[1-\alpha]$, we may write production function (6.1) as follows[2]

$$Y_t = K_t L^{\nu} \tag{6.2}$$

6.2 Laissez-faire Outcome

6.2.1 Intermediate Market

By symmetry, total cost may be derived as $C_Y(p_{xt}, L) = p_{xt}L$. With perfect competition in the final output market, the price p_{Yt} is equal to aggregate cost over aggregate output. Normalizing on final output, i.e. setting $p_{Yt} = 1$ for all t, yields the intermediates price

$$p_{xt} = L^{\nu-1} K_t \tag{6.3}$$

For $\nu > 1$, i.e. a positive economies of scale, the intermediates price increases with a larger labor force. Moreover, the price increases with an expanding product variety, since additional intermediates raise the marginal productivity of existing intermediates.

[1] The assumption according to which $\nu = \alpha/[1-\alpha]$ may be perceived as stark, but drawing this assumption is required in order to make the economy exhibiting balanced growth. If $\nu < \alpha/[1-\alpha]$ were to hold, growth would peter out. Notice that, considering $\nu = \alpha/[1-\alpha]$, $0 < \alpha < 1$ implies $\nu > 0$.

[2] In subsection 6.2.1, we show that the identity of the K_t market shares is implied by intermediates firms' profit-maximization. Notice that production function (6.2) restricts labor's output elasticity to ν. This restriction may be relaxed by the modeling of scale-dependent costs. For the Ramsey model with imperfect competition, this is shown in appendix A. For the present model, the procedure is analogous. With the representation of scale-dependent costs, we obtain an aggregate production function that is given by $Y_t = K_t L^{\nu[1-\phi]}$, where the parameter $\phi > 0$ reflects the magnitude of the scale-dependent costs.

The intermediates suppliers profit rates at time t are given by

$$\pi_{kt} = p_{x_k t}(x_{kt})x_{kt} - w_t x_{kt} \tag{6.4}$$

where $p_{x_k t}$ denotes the price of the intermediate k, where $k \in [0, K_t]$. The suppliers maximize their flow profit rates by setting $p_{x_k t} = w_t/\alpha$.[3] Hence, we obtain indeed a symmetric solution with $p_{x_k t} = p_{xt}$, and $x_{kt} = x_t$. Thus, in the remainder, we may use production function (6.2) and intermediates price (6.3).

Applying intermediates price (6.3), we may modify profit equation (6.4) to

$$\pi_t = [1 - \alpha]p_{xt}LK_t^{-1} \tag{6.5}$$

The profit rate of the representative firm increases with its market power and with the intermediates price. An increase in the amount of varieties has two opposite effects on the profit rate. First, a positive productivity effect: it follows from the induced rise in the intermediates price. Second, a negative market-saturation effect: the representative intermediate's market share is negatively related to the amount of intermediates. To derive the overall effect, we insert price equation (6.3) into profit equation (6.5). We obtain the subsequent equation

$$\pi = [1 - \alpha]L^{\frac{\alpha}{1-\alpha}} \tag{6.6}$$

Profit rate (6.6) shows that the negative market-saturation effect neutralizes the positive productivity effect. Hence, the launch of an additional intermediate does not affect the profit rate, and equation (6.6) gives the steady-state profit rate.

6.2.2 Asset Market

Since the price of a unit of capital is at every point in time equal to unity, the steady-state rate of return on capital is just the steady-state profit rate, i.e. $r = \pi$. Thus, the rate of return on capital is independent from the economy-wide relative capital abundance, K/L. Deviating from the neoclassical model, our approach may explain why the return on capital in developed countries (with relatively high K/L-ratios) is not necessarily lower than the return on capital in developing countries (with relatively low K/L-ratios). The rationale is as follows. On the one hand, developed countries experience, due to their relatively high capital abundance, a relatively high market-saturation. This tends to lower capital stock's productivity. On the other hand, with a higher capital abundance, capital stock's productivity benefits from stronger network externalities. In our model, these two effects just neutralize, and, thus, capital stock's productivity is not affected by a country's relative capital abundance.

[3] Thus, the wage rate follows as $w_t = \alpha L^{\nu-1}K_t$ [cf. price equation (6.3)].

6.2.3 Steady-State Growth

The representative individual maximizes overall utility (3.21) with respect to flow budget constraint (3.23). The Keynes/Ramsey rule is given by $\gamma = \sigma[\pi - \rho]$, where γ denotes the steady-state growth rate. Moreover, ρ and σ are nonnegative. The laissez-faire steady-state endogenous growth rate follows as[4]

$$\gamma = \sigma\left\{[1-\alpha]L^{\frac{\alpha}{1-\alpha}} - \rho\right\} \tag{6.7}$$

where for a positive growth rate, i.e. $\gamma > 0$, $[1-\alpha]L^{\alpha/[1-\alpha]} > \rho$ has to be fulfilled. To ensure a bounded attainable utility, we require $\rho > [\sigma - 1]\,\gamma/\sigma$. The economy jumps instantaneously to the steady state. The decentralized growth rate increases for a larger labor force, a lower rate of time preference, and a higher intertemporal elasticity of substitution. The elasticity of substitution between intermediates has two opposite effects on growth. First, a direct effect: a lower elasticity of substitution, i.e. a higher market power of the representative intermediates firm, increases the profit rate, thereby accelerating growth. Second, an indirect effect: a lower elasticity of substitution implies lower positive economies of scale, respectively higher diseconomies of scale, and, thus, slows down growth. It is easily shown that for the likely case of $\alpha < L$, the direct effect dominates, i.e. a lower elasticity of substitution of intermediates increases the laissez-faire growth rate.[5]

6.3 Social Planner's Solution

The social planner's problem is to max U_t subject to the technology constraint $\dot{K}_t = L^{\alpha/[1-\alpha]}K_t - c_t L$. Solving the problem yields the following social optimum steady-state growth rate[6]

$$\gamma_S = \sigma\left[L^{\frac{\alpha}{1-\alpha}} - \rho\right] \tag{6.8}$$

The social optimum growth rate increases for a larger labor force, a lower rate of time preference, and a higher intertemporal elasticity of substitution. As opposed to the laissez-faire outcome, the elasticity of substitution of intermediates has a mere indirect effect on growth: since a lower elasticity of substitution between intermediates decreases positive economies of scale, respectively increases diseconomies of scale, it decreases the social optimum growth rate. Accordingly, a lower elasticity of substitution between intermediates unambiguously decreases the social optimum growth rate.[7]

---

[4] A look on production function (6.2) confirms the finding that growth is endogenous. The production of final output exhibits constant returns to capital. Constant returns to the reproducible factor is a necessary condition for balanced growth.

[5] The saving rate may be derived as $s = \dot{K}/Y = \sigma\left[[1-\alpha]L^{\alpha/[1-\alpha]} - \rho\right]/L^{\nu}$.

[6] Due to the concavity of the Hamiltonian, the necessary conditions are also sufficient conditions.

[7] The social optimum saving rate is given by $s_S = \sigma\left[L^{\alpha/[1-\alpha]} - \rho\right]/L^{\nu} > s$.

Recalling the results of last chapter's Ramsey model with imperfect competition, it may astonish that, in the generalized AK model, the elasticity of substitution of intermediates has no direct effect on the social optimum steady-state growth rate. The explanation is readily found, though. In the present model, if we had not linked the economies of scale and the elasticity of substitution by $\nu = \alpha/[1-\alpha]$, with a lower elasticity of substitution, a growth-increasing direct effect would be seen, too: for a lower α, social optimum growth would increase just as in the Ramsey model with imperfect competition. In the generalized AK model with $\nu = \alpha/[1-\alpha]$, for a lower α, the growth-increasing elasticity-of-substitution effect and the growth-decreasing economies of scale effect neutralize. Thus, we do not observe a direct effect of the elasticity of substitution of intermediates on the social optimum growth rate (6.8).

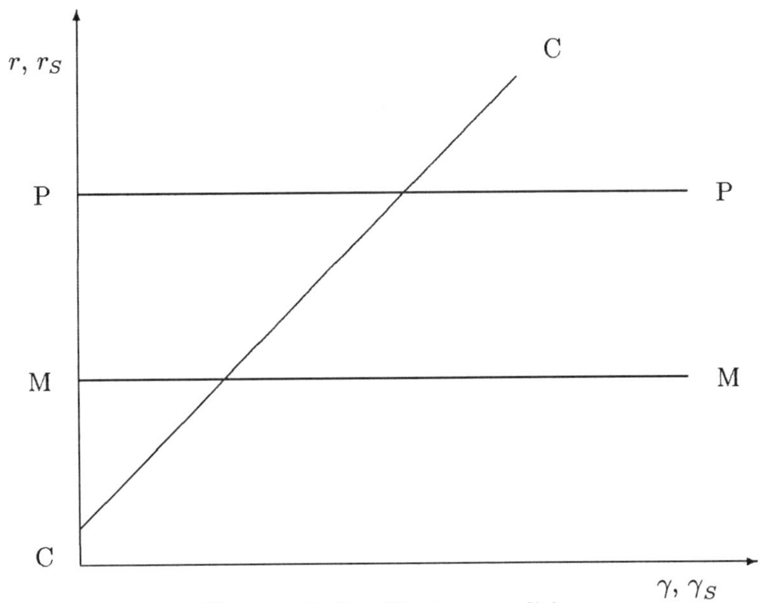

Figure 6.2: Equilibrium conditions.

How does laissez-faire growth (6.7) compare to social optimum growth (6.8)? Both solutions involve a steady-state equilibrium condition (CC) that follows from the Keynes/Ramsey rule. We obtain

$$r = r_S = \rho + \frac{1}{\sigma}\gamma \tag{CC}$$

where r_S denotes the social optimum steady-state return on capital. The CC line is upward-sloping in γ-r-space [cf. figure 6.2]. For laissez-faire, the equilibrium condition (MM) follows from profit rate (6.6) as

$$r = [1-\alpha]L^{\frac{\alpha}{1-\alpha}} \tag{MM}$$

Social planner's equilibrium condition (PP) is implied by social optimum growth rate (6.8) as

$$r_S = L^{\frac{\alpha}{1-\alpha}} \tag{PP}$$

Thus, both the MM line and the PP line are horizontal in γ-r-space.

Equations (CC), (MM), and (PP) imply that the laissez-faire growth rate is unambiguously below the social optimum [cf. figure 6.2]. The difference $[\gamma_S - \gamma] > 0$ increases with a higher elasticity of substitution between intermediates. Moreover, a larger labor force, a higher intertemporal elasticity of substitution, and stronger economies of scale, respectively weaker diseconomies of scale, increase the difference.

Notice that generalized AK model's finding according to which a higher substitutability between intermediates increases the difference between the social optimum growth rate and the laissez-faire growth rate deviates from the respective result of last chapter's Ramsey model with imperfect competition. The reason is obvious: the generalized AK model captures a network externality that is positively related to the substitutability between intermediates, and this network externality dominates the monopoly distortion effect that we are familiar with from the Ramsey model with imperfect competition. Hence, whereas both models find that with imperfect competition, laissez-faire investment is below the social optimum, they differ in their prediction regarding the relation of the difference $[\gamma_S - \gamma]$ to the elasticity of substitution between intermediates.

6.4 Policy Implications

What are appropriate policy measures to raise decentralized growth to the social optimum? The after-tax steady-state rate of return is given by

$$r_T = \frac{1-t_\pi}{1+t_I}[1-\alpha]L^{\frac{\alpha}{1-\alpha}} \tag{TT}$$

where t_π is a profit tax, t_I is an investment tax, and taxes obey $-1 < t_\pi, t_I < 1$.

The decentralized growth rate can be increased by strengthening the incentive to invest. This is accomplished by subsidizing either indirectly the return on investment, or directly the investment itself. In figure 6.2, both policy measures have the same effect: they shift the MM line upwards. The optimum combinations of subsidies $[t_\pi, t_I]^*$ that make the MM line and the PP line coincide are given by the equation

$$t_\pi = 1 - [1 + t_I] \frac{1}{1 - \alpha}$$

The optimum subsidies increase – ceteris paribus – with a higher elasticity of substitution of intermediates. For optima, there evolves a trade-off between subsidizing profit and investment. For $t_I = 0$, the optimum profit subsidy, $t_\pi^* < 0$, is given by $t_\pi^* = -\{\alpha / [1 - \alpha]\}$. For $t_\pi = 0$, the optimum investment subsidy, $t_I^* < 0$, is given by $t_I^* = -\alpha$.

6.5 Discussion

The generalized AK model is an endogenous growth model that represents an expanding product variety. The distinguishing characteristics from Rebelo's AK model are, first, the introduction of imperfect competition, and, second, the capturing of labor as an input factor.

We find that in an economy with imperfectly competitive markets, the social return on investment exceeds unambiguously the private return on investment. Consequently, the laissez-faire steady-state growth rate is unambiguously below the social optimum. The policy implications of this generalized AK model are as follows: since firms are not able to appropriate the full rent of their investment, government should promote entrepreneurial activity, i.e. set incentives for an increase in capital accumulation. Since for a higher elasticity of substitution of differentiated products, the economy's non-appropriability problem increases, the derived optimum subsidies increase, too.

The present model deviates from perfect competition growth models by relaxing the link between a factor's output elasticity and its income share. Here, capital's output elasticity exceeds unambiguously capital's income share. This property is backed by a number of empirical studies [cf. section 2.2].

Chapter 7

Learning-by-Doing and the Decline in the Relative Price of Capital

In the present chapter, we develop an endogenous growth model that is able to predict the following empirical evidence. First, countries with more sophisticated financial intermediaries experience higher growth rates. Seminal are the empirical studies by King/Levine (1993a, 1993b, 1993c). More recently, Levine/Zervos (1998) find a positive relationship between banking development, stock market liquidity, physical capital accumulation, and economic growth.[1] Second, there is empirical evidence that in growing economies, the relative price of capital decreases. Gordon (1990) provides data for the United States. He documents that during the postwar period, the relative price of equipment capital has fallen at an annual rate of more than three percent.

Deviating from the Ramsey model with imperfect competition and the generalized AK model, in the present model, we formulate an explicit capital good sector. This formulation enables us, first, to introduce a parameter that represents cross-country differences in the development of financial intermediaries, and, second, to implement learning-by-doing as an engine of growth.

Employing a learning-by-doing approach, the present model builds on Arrow (1962), Sheshinski (1967a), and Romer (1986). The model's structure is given by figure 7.1. The present model deviates from traditional learning-by-doing models in its featuring of imperfect competition and, in turn, in its comprehensive representation of investment externalities. With respect to our modeling of broad learning-by-doing, we are close to Bretschger (2000). Bretschger enlarges the concept of knowledge formation by proposing that

[1] Goldsmith (1969) is an early contribution to this field. Levine (1997) gives an excellent survey of the literature on financial development and economic growth.

macroeconomic learning is an economy-wide process that is not restricted to a specific sector. In addition, we relate to Krusell (1998) who describes the decline in the relative price of capital in an imperfect competition framework, too. His explanation differs, though: in Krusell (1998), the fall in the relative price of capital is the outcome of investment-specific R&D.

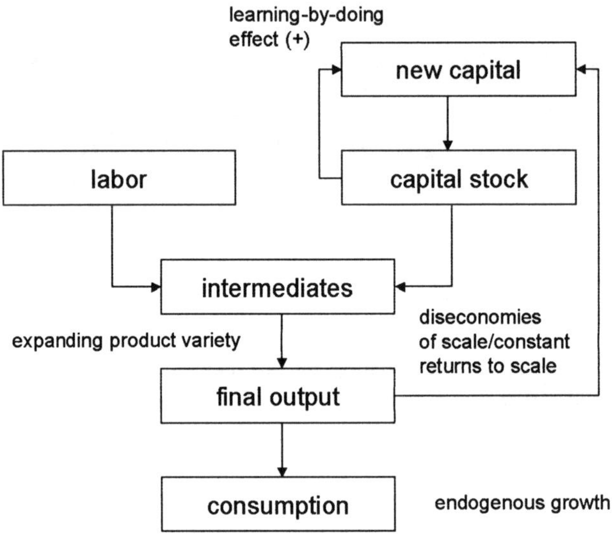

Figure 7.1: A schematic representation of the model.

The plan of this chapter is as follows. In section one, we present the technology that our learning-by-doing model postulates. Section two investigates the model's laissez-faire outcome. Section three yields the social planner's solution. Section four derives policy implications. Section five recapitulates the results.

7.1 Technology

7.1.1 Final Output

The intermediate goods sector's technology is given by the one-to-one production functions, $x_{kt} = l_{kt}$, where $k \in [0, K_t]$. That is, firm k produces x_{kt} units of intermediate k, whereas it employs l_{kt} units of labor. The elasticity of substitution of intermediates is $\epsilon = 1/[1-\alpha]$, where $0 < \alpha < 1$.

Final output's technology is given by the CES aggregate production function

$$Y_t = \left[\int_0^{K_t} x_{kt}^{\alpha} dk \right]^{\frac{\nu}{\alpha}} \tag{7.1}$$

where $0 < \nu \leq 1$. The parameter ν denotes whether there are diseconomies of scale, and if so ($\nu < 1$), their size.[2] The diseconomies of scale affect the economy as a whole, i.e. an individual firm cannot improve its cost structure by shrinking. K_t may be interpreted in three ways: amount of intermediates firm, amount of differentiated intermediates, and size of the economy's capital stock.

Imposing symmetry, the final output production function (7.1) becomes[3]

$$Y_t = \left[K_t^{\frac{1-\alpha}{\alpha}} L \right]^{\nu} = K_t^{\eta} L^{\nu} \tag{7.2}$$

where $\eta \equiv [1 - \alpha]\nu/\alpha$, and $0 < \eta < 1$.[4]

7.1.2 Capital Good

The capital good sector's technology is given by

$$\dot{K}_t = \frac{1}{\omega} S_t I_t \tag{7.3}$$

where $\omega > 0$ is an efficiency parameter that measures the development of an economy's financial intermediaries. A sophisticated financial system promotes capital accumulation by mobilizing savings, allocating resources, exerting corporate control, facilitating risk management, and easing the trading of goods, services, and contracts [cf. Levine (1997)].

[2] Since in the present model, we introduce a broadly-conceived learning-by-doing effect which encompasses cost reduction due to agglomerative effects, we abstract from the possibility of a positive scale effect.

[3] In subsection 7.2.1, we show that the identity of the K_t market shares is implied by intermediates firms' profit-maximization. Notice that production function (7.2) restricts labor's output elasticity to ν. This restriction may be relaxed by the modeling of scale-dependent costs [cf. appendix A]. Pursuing the representation of scale-dependent costs, we obtain an aggregate production function that is given by $Y_t = K_t^{\eta} L^{\nu[1-\phi]}$, where $\phi > 0$.

[4] Notice that $0 < \alpha < 1$ and $0 < \nu \leq 1$ imply $\eta > 0$. For $\alpha = \nu$, final output production function (7.2) reduces to the Cobb-Douglas function $Y_t = L^{\alpha} K_t^{1-\alpha}$. Thus, if we would not introduce learning-by-doing, our economy would be at the aggregate level observationally equivalent to a neoclassical economy with perfect competition and constant returns to scale. It is readily shown that in such an economy with imperfect competition, Cobb-Douglas technology at the aggregate level, and without learning-by-doing, the imperfect competition distortion and the diseconomies-of-scale externality just neutralize, and, thus, laissez-faire is indeed socially optimal.

S_t is the level of social knowledge, i.e. the social knowledge capital stock, and I_t is investment.[5] Hence, the higher the level of social technical knowledge that is available to capital good producers, the higher their productivity in producing capital. For a given level of social technical knowledge, the transformation of final output into capital is proportional, but not necessarily one-to-one.

We assume that the level of social knowledge, S_t, depends on the accumulated physical capital stock, K_t, as follows[6]

$$S_t = K_t^{1-\eta} \tag{7.4}$$

where $0 < \eta < 1$. This specification implies a falling return in the generation of social technical knowledge. The reasoning is that early cost-reducing contributions from learning-by-doing are more significant than later ones. A falling return in the generation of social technical knowledge is in line with the empirical finding of decreasing, convex learning curves.[7]

Moreover, equation (7.4) implies a dependence of learning-by-doing on two properties of the final output technology: the elasticity of substitution between intermediates, and the diseconomies of scale. First, the higher the substitutability between intermediates, the stronger learning-by-doing. Stated differently: the more alike the intermediates are, the more the individual firm benefits from the experience that the economy as a whole has accumulated. Second, strong diseconomies of scale are associated with strong learning-by-doing. This relationship may be illustrated as follows. A human-capital abundant economy is likely to engage in a human-capital intensive production. In human-capital intensive industries, both diseconomies of scale and learning-by-doing are typically strong. E.g., a doubling of software engineers does not double output, while learning-by-doing in the production of software is impressive. A physical-capital abundant economy is likely to produce physical-capital intensively. Physical-capital intensive industries exhibit usually weak diseconomies of scale and weak learning-by-doing. E.g., a doubling of coal and ore doubles the output of steal, while learning-by-doing in the industry is relatively weak.[8]

---

[5]Notice that for $S_t/\omega \neq 1$, investment is not equal to the increase in capital stock.

[6]Notice that equation (7.4) gives a fourth interpretation of K_t: apart from representing the amount of intermediates firms, the amount of differentiated intermediates, and the size of the capital stock, in this model, it works as an index for the amount of accumulated social knowledge, too.

[7]Learning curves with a convex shape are documented by Wright (1936), Sheshinski (1967b), Argote/Epple (1990), Caballero/Lyons (1990, 1992b).

[8]The assumption according to which the learning-by-doing elasticity equals exactly $[1-\eta]$ may be perceived as stark. However, the assumption has to be drawn in order to make the economy exhibiting balanced growth. If the elasticity were below $[1-\eta]$, growth would peter out.

7.2 Laissez-faire Outcome

7.2.1 Intermediate Market

By symmetry, total cost may be stated as $C_Y(p_{xt}, L) = p_{xt}L$. Perfect competition in the market for final output implies that the price of final output, p_{Yt}, is the ratio of aggregate cost over aggregate output. We set $p_{Yt} = 1$ for all t, and obtain

$$p_{xt} = L^{-[1-\nu]}K_t^{\eta} \tag{7.5}$$

For $\nu < 1$, i.e. diseconomies of scale, the intermediates' price decreases with a larger labor force.

The intermediates suppliers' profit rates at time t are given by

$$\pi_{kt} = p_{x_k t}(x_{kt})x_{kt} - w_t x_{kt} \tag{7.6}$$

where $p_{x_k t}$ denotes the price of the intermediate k, where $k \in [0, K_t]$. A pricing given by $p_{x_k t} = w_t/\alpha$ is profit-maximizing. Moreover, it implies a symmetric solution. Thus, we may indeed use production function (7.2) and intermediates price (7.5). Inserting price equation (7.5) into profit equation (7.6) yields

$$\pi_t = [1-\alpha]L^{\nu}K_t^{-[1-\eta]} \tag{7.7}$$

Profit equation (7.7) shows that the launch of an additional intermediate lowers the profit, i.e. as in the Ramsey model with imperfect competition, here, too, the market-saturation effect dominates the productivity effect.

7.2.2 Asset Market

The claim to a unit of capital may be acquired in one of two ways. First, an individual can purchase a claim in the assets market at value v_t. Second, an individual may produce a unit of capital at cost p_{Kt}. Individuals are willing to produce a unit of capital as long as the discounted flow of future profits that arise from this unit is at least equal to the per unit cost, i.e. as long as $v_t \geq p_{Kt}$. If $v_t < p_{Kt}$, there is no investment. Moreover, in a competitive economy, $v_t > p_{Kt}$ is not admissible: if the value were to exceed the cost, additional firms would immediately enter the market. Thereby, they would drive down profit rate and, thus, capital value. This process would continue until $v_t = p_{Kt}$. Accordingly, the condition of a free entry into the production of intermediates is given by $v_t \leq p_{Kt}$, with $v_t = p_{Kt}$ whenever investment takes place. Capital's production function (7.3) together with function (7.2) yields $p_{Kt} = \omega K_t^{-[1-\eta]}p_{Yt}$. We obtain the free-entry condition as

$$v_t \leq \omega K_t^{-[1-\eta]} \tag{7.8}$$

with equality whenever $\dot{K}_t > 0$.

7.2.3 Steady-State Growth

Profit equation (7.7) yields

$$\frac{\dot{\pi}_t}{\pi_t} = -[1-\eta]\frac{\dot{K}_t}{K_t}$$

Thus, the profit of the representative firm falls with a rising K_t due to market saturation. The faster capital is accumulated, the faster the decrease of the profit. The rate of decrease goes up with a higher elasticity of substitution of intermediates, and with stronger diseconomies of scale. Since the growth rate is constant, i.e. $\dot{c}_t/c_t = \eta\dot{K}_t/K_t \equiv \gamma$, the steady-state evolution of the profit can be written as

$$\frac{\dot{\pi}}{\pi} = -\left[\frac{1-\eta}{\eta}\right]\gamma \tag{7.9}$$

The steady-state evolution of the value of capital follows from free-entry condition (7.8) together with equation (7.4) as

$$\frac{\dot{v}}{v} = -\left[\frac{1-\eta}{\eta}\right]\gamma \tag{7.10}$$

The rate of capital depreciation is negatively linked to the rate of capital accumulation: the faster capital is accumulated, the more learning-by-doing, and therefore the faster capital's depreciation. The depreciation rate increases with a stronger learning-by-doing effect, $[1-\eta]$. Equations (7.9) and (7.10) imply a constant dividend, given by

$$\frac{\pi}{v} = \frac{1}{\omega}[1-\alpha]L^{\nu} \tag{7.11}$$

Thus, the economy exhibits endogenous growth.[9]

Inserting dividend (7.11) and the capital value's equation of motion (7.10) into Keynes/Ramsey rule $\dot{c}_t/c_t = \sigma\left[\pi_t/v_t + \dot{v}_t/v_t - \rho\right]$), where $\rho, \sigma > 0$, we obtain the laissez-faire steady-state growth rate

$$\gamma = \frac{\sigma\left[\frac{1}{\omega}[1-\alpha]L^{\nu} - \rho\right]}{1+\sigma\frac{1-\eta}{\eta}} \tag{7.12}$$

where for a positive growth rate, i.e. $\gamma > 0$, $[1-\alpha]L^{\nu}/\omega > \rho$ has to be met. The transversality condition implies $\rho > [\sigma - 1]\gamma/\sigma$. The economy is immediately in the steady state. Growth goes up for a higher productivity in producing capital, i.e. a more developed financial system. Moreover, a

[9] A way to check this finding is to revise capital's production function (7.2) to $\dot{K}_t = s_t L^{\nu} K_t/\omega$, where s_t is the savings rate, defined as $s_t \equiv I_t/Y_t$. The production of capital exhibits constant returns to capital itself. Constant returns to the reproducible factor is a necessary condition for endogenous growth.

lower elasticity of substitution of intermediates, lower diseconomies of scale, a larger labor force, a lower rate of time preference, and a higher intertemporal elasticity of substitution increase growth.[10]

7.3 Social Planner's Solution

To evaluate the social desirability of laissez-faire, we investigate the social planner's solution. The preferences of the representative individual are given by equations (3.21) and (3.22). From production functions (7.2) and (7.3) follows the technology constraint $\dot{K}_t = K_t^{1-\eta}\left[L^\nu K_t^\eta - c_t L\right]/\omega$. Hence, the intertemporal maximization problem can be stated in terms of the following current-value Hamiltonian

$$H = u(c_t) + \lambda_t \frac{1}{\omega} K_t^{1-\eta}\left[L^\nu K_t^\eta - c_t L\right]$$

The first-order conditions for an optimum consumption path yield an equation of motion for the shadow price of capital in the steady state as follows[11]

$$\frac{\dot{\lambda}}{\lambda} = \frac{u''(c)\dot{c}}{u'(c)} - \left[\frac{1-\eta}{\eta}\right]\gamma_S = -\left[\frac{1}{\sigma} + \frac{1-\eta}{\eta}\right]\gamma_S \tag{7.13}$$

Deviating from the Ramsey model with imperfect competition, the decrease in the shadow price of capital depends not only on the intertemporal elasticity of substitution, but also on the size of the learning-by-doing effect: the stronger learning-by-doing, the faster the depreciation in the shadow price of capital. A further equation of motion for the shadow price of capital can be stated as

$$\frac{\dot{\lambda}_t}{\lambda_t} = -\left[\frac{1}{\omega}\{L^\nu - [1-\eta]c_t L K_t^{-\eta}\} - \rho\right] \tag{7.14}$$

Solving the technology constraint for $c_t L K_t^{-\eta}$, and inserting the term into equation (7.14) yields a second steady-state equation of motion for the shadow price of capital

$$\frac{\dot{\lambda}}{\lambda} = -\left[\frac{1}{\omega}\eta L^\nu + \frac{1-\eta}{\eta}\gamma_S - \rho\right] \tag{7.15}$$

Equations (7.13) and (7.15) give the social optimum steady-state growth

---

[10] The saving rate follows as $s = I/Y = [\omega/L^\nu]\left[\dot{K}/K\right] = \omega\gamma/[\eta L^\nu]$.

[11] Due to the concavity of the Hamiltonian, the necessary conditions are also sufficient conditions.

rate[12]

$$\gamma_S = \sigma\left[\frac{1}{\omega}\eta L^{\nu} - \rho\right] \tag{7.16}$$

where for a positive growth rate, i.e. $\gamma_S > 0$, $\eta L^{\nu}/\omega > \rho$ applies. The social optimum growth rate increases with a higher productivity in producing capital, a lower elasticity of substitution of intermediates, lower diseconomies of scale, and a larger labor force. Furthermore, a lower rate of time preference, and a higher intertemporal elasticity of substitution increase the rate.[13]

How does laissez-faire growth (7.12) compare to social optimum growth (7.16)? We detect five effects: a business-stealing effect, a specialization effect, a monopoly distortion effect, a congestion effect, and a learning-by-doing effect. First, a *business-stealing effect*: an investor does not account for the loss in business that the existing firms incur due to her new firm. Second, a *specialization effect*: an investor does not account for the surplus that the demanders of the differentiated intermediates enjoy if an additional intermediate is launched. Third, a *monopoly distortion effect*: since the monopoly rent that the intermediates suppliers levy is passed to the demanders of final output, capital is in laissez-faire inefficiently expensive, and, thus, investment is suboptimally low. Fourth, a *congestion effect*: an investor does not regard the decrease in productivity that incumbent firms incur as a result of her investment in an economy that features diseconomies of scale. Fifth, a *learning-by-doing effect*: an investor attaches no weight to the decrease in capital costs that future firms enjoy due to her investment.

We may wonder what sign the net effect of these five externalities bears, i.e. whether laissez-faire growth is below or above the social optimum. It can be shown that in expanding product variety models with CES technology, the negative business-stealing effect and the positive specialization effect neutralize.[14] In turn, we investigate the three remaining externalities: monopoly distortion effect, congestion effect, and learning-by-doing effect. Two of them – monopoly distortion effect and learning-by-doing effect – lead to an inefficiently low laissez-faire growth rate, whereas the congestion effect leads to an inefficiently high laissez-faire growth rate.

---

[12]Social planner's intertemporal allocation of final output is not biased as can be seen from the fact that learning-by-doing enters both equations (7.13) and (7.15). This result is opposed to the laissez-faire outcome. Entrepreneurs do not consider the external effect of their individual investment. Nevertheless, they regard the decline in the value of capital due to aggregate investment [cf. equation (7.10)]. The induced decrease of the private return on investment contributes to the result that the laissez-faire outcome is biased towards today's consumption.

[13]The social optimum saving rate is given by $s_S = \omega\gamma_S/\left[\eta L^{\nu}\right]$. Hence, for $\gamma_S > \gamma$, we obtain $s_S > s$.

[14]Cf. Grossman/Helpman (1991a), pp. 82-83.

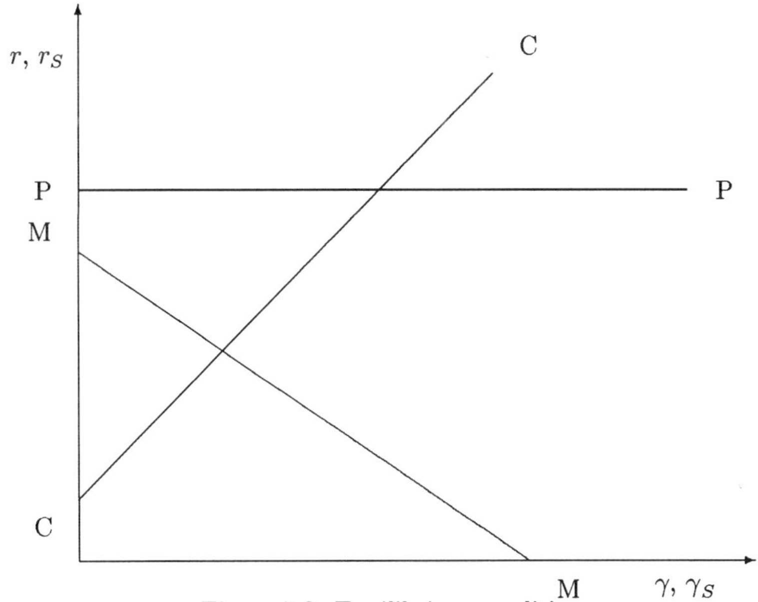

Figure 7.2: Equilibrium conditions.

For our investigation, we employ the steady-state equilibrium conditions. Both decentralized solution and social planner's solution involve condition (CC), given by

$$r = r_S = \rho + \frac{1}{\sigma}\gamma \qquad (CC)$$

where r_S denotes the social optimum steady-state return on capital. The CC graph is upward-sloping in γ-r-space [cf. figure 7.2]. For laissez-faire, the equilibrium condition (MM) follows as [cf. equations (7.10) and (7.11)]

$$r = \frac{1}{\omega}[1-\alpha]L^{\nu} - \left[\frac{1-\eta}{\eta}\right]\gamma \qquad (MM)$$

Social planner's equilibrium condition (PP) is implied by social optimum growth rate (7.16) as

$$r_S = \frac{1}{\omega}\eta L^{\nu} \qquad (PP)$$

Thus, whereas the MM graph is downward-sloping in γ-r-space, the PP graph is a horizontal line.

Equations (CC), (MM), and (PP) show that in real world, it is unlikely that the difference $[\gamma_S - \gamma]$ turns negative, i.e. for reasonable parameter values, the congestion effect does not dominate the monopoly distortion effect and the learning-by-doing effect. Even in an economy with almost perfect competition, say, with an α that approaches one, and with very patient individuals, say, with a ρ that approaches zero, the net effect would only turn negative if the diseconomies of scale were extremely high, i.e. $\nu < 1/[1+\sigma]$. The finding that, in real world economies, excessive growth is an unlikely phenomenon is in line with the evidence that studies on investment externalities document [cf. section 2.3].

7.4 Policy Implications

The model suggests that in an economy in which imperfect competition prevails, and in which learning-by-doing leads to balanced growth, the laissez-faire growth rate is socially inefficient. This result poses the question whether there are policy measures which allow to decentralize the social optimum solution. The after-tax steady-state rate of return may be derived as

$$r_T = \left[\frac{1-t_\pi}{1+t_I}\right]\frac{1}{\omega}[1-\alpha]L^\nu - \left[\frac{1-\eta}{\eta}\right]\gamma \tag{TT}$$

where t_π is a profit tax, t_I is an investment tax, and taxes obey $-1 < t_\pi, t_I < 1$.

Optimal are combinations of subsidies that shift the MM line upwards until it goes trough the intersection of the CC line with the PP line [cf. figure 7.2]. The respective optimum combinations $[t_\pi, t_I]^*$ are given by

$$t_\pi = 1 - [1+t_I]\left[\frac{\eta + \sigma\frac{1-\eta}{\eta}[\eta - \omega\rho L^{-\nu}]}{1-\alpha}\right] \tag{7.17}$$

In turn, we compare this optimum profit subsidy with the respective subsidy in the Ramsey model with imperfect competition, augmented by a scale effect of size ν. We find that optimum profit subsidy (7.17) is equal to the respective subsidy in the augmented Ramsey model, plus the term $\sigma[1+t_I][1-\eta][\eta - \omega\rho L^{-\nu}]/[1-\alpha]\eta$. This term is positive for all admissible parameter values. Apparently, considering learning-by-doing leads ceteris paribus to higher optimum subsidies.

According to equation (7.17), in the learning-by-doing model, the optimum subsidies increase – ceteris paribus – with a lower rate of time preference and with a higher intertemporal elasticity of substitution, i.e. the subsidies rise with the willingness of the representative individual to reduce today's consumption for the sake of tomorrow's consumption. Moreover, the optimum subsidies increase with the productivity in producing capital, i.e. the subsidies depend positively on the magnitude with which tomorrow's consumption increases if the individual forgoes today's consumption.[15] Finally, the optimum subsidies increase in the size of the labor force, i.e. in the size of the economy, since a larger economy benefits from learning-by-doing's scale effect. Thus, compared to a smaller economy, postponing consumption in a larger economy yields higher returns. As in the basic model, for optima, there is a trade-off between subsidizing profit and investment. For $t_I = 0$, the optimum profit subsidy is given by

$$t_\pi^* = -\left[\frac{\eta + \sigma\frac{1-\eta}{\eta}[\eta - \omega\rho L^{-\nu}]}{1-\alpha} - 1\right]$$

For $t_\pi = 0$, the optimum investment subsidy follows as

$$t_I^* = -\left[1 - \frac{1-\alpha}{\eta + \sigma\frac{1-\eta}{\eta}[\eta - \omega\rho L^{-\nu}]}\right]$$

7.5 Discussion

The model pursues a learning-by-doing approach, and represents forward-looking entrepreneurs who maximize profits on imperfectly competitive markets. The model's predictions are consistent with the empirical evidence of, first, a positive relationship between the development of financial intermediaries and economic growth, and, second, a decline in the relative price of capital.

In this imperfect competition framework, for reasonable parameter values, investment's social return exceeds its private return. This result is in line with the finding of empirical studies [cf. section 2.3]. Hence, the model suggests that real world's laissez-faire growth rates are below the social optimum. The policy implications are straightforward: since entrepreneurs disregard the positive external effect of their investment, governments are recommended to set incentives for an increase in capital accumulation.

[15] Reflecting its Janus-faced nature, the impact of the productivity parameter η on the optimum subsidies is ambiguous.

Part IV

R&D Revisited

Chapter 8

R&D's Exhaustion Effect

Decreasing patent-R&D ratios suggest that the costs of R&D are rising. Kortum (1993) presents data according to which, during three decades, the U.S. patent-R&D ratio has steadily decreased: while in the late 1950's, one million 1982-dollars of company-funded research yielded over three patents, by the late 1980's, the same R&D funds produced one patent.[1]

What makes R&D costs rise? Evenson (1984, 1991) argues that the exhaustion of technological opportunities lowers the R&D productivity. Hence, rising R&D costs reflect a negative externality of R&D: as more inventions have already been made, the development of further inventions takes more resources. We will refer to this effect as the exhaustion effect of R&D.

Despite the fact that rising R&D costs lower the profitability of research, R&D investment grows steadily. In the U.S., e.g., the company-funded R&D in constant dollars increased between 1957 and 1989 at an annual rate of 4.9 percent [cf. Kortum (1993)].

What keeps R&D investment up? We argue that besides its negative exhaustion effect, R&D has a positive effect on the profitability of R&D, too: research leads to innovations that, in turn, increase the economy's productivity. As we will see, a higher productivity implies a rise in R&D-related profits. We shall label this effect the productivity effect of R&D. Notice that without this positive effect, it is most likely that growth would have faded due to the negative exhaustion effect.

While some of the more recent growth models capture the exhaustion effect of R&D, they do not represent its productivity effect [cf. Jones (1995a), Kortum (1997), Segerstrom (1998)]. In those models of semi-endogenous

[1] There is a vivid discussion on the appropriateness of patent counts as innovation indicators. Nevertheless, due to the lack of respective data, empirical studies that investigate the appropriateness of patent counts as innovation indicators are rare [see the survey by Encaoua/Hall/Laisney/Mairesse (1998)]. Recently, Duguet/Kabla (1998) have conducted a study based on French data. The study suggests that, although patent counts bear shortcomings, they are helpful indicators to measure at least a part of the innovation activity.

growth, an exogenously given population growth is necessary to keep up R&D investment. Without population growth, R&D investment becomes non-profitable, the economy stops undertaking research efforts, and growth peters out. Contrarily, our model allows for long-run growth in the absence of population growth. Furthermore, it reinstates the essential result of endogenous growth theory according to which policy may affect the long-run growth rate.

Another property in which our model deviates from semi-endogenous growth models is its comprehension of excessive long-run growth. While semi-endogenous growth models allow for transitional excessive growth, laissez-faire long-run growth proves to be unambiguously socially optimal. Aghion/Howitt (1992) find excessive long-run growth to be a possible laissez-faire outcome [cf. IPQ model, chapter 4]. However, since in their quality ladder framework, the business stealing effect is the unique negative R&D externality, this business stealing effect has to be extraordinarily strong relative to the positive R&D externalities in order to turn laissez-faire growth excessive.

The model is a three-sector growth model, consisting of an intermediate goods sector, a final output sector, and an R&D sector [cf. figure 8.1]. The production of final output takes two stages. At the first stage, intermediates are produced. Inputs are labor and R&D capital. At the second stage, intermediates are transformed to final output. Final output can either be consumed or invested in R&D.

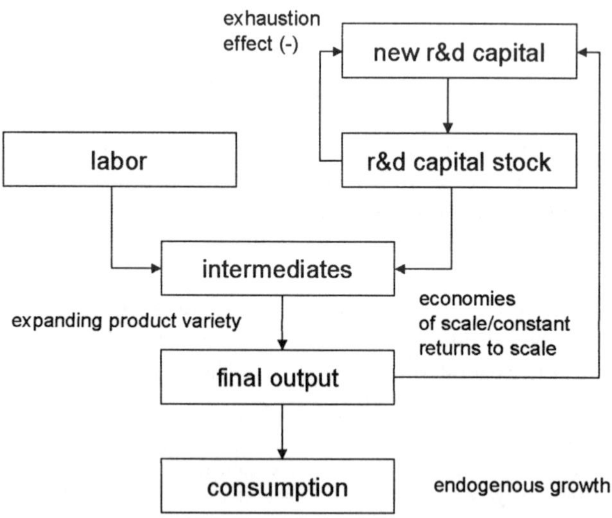

Figure 8.1: A schematic representation of the model.

Notice that the three models of this part are R&D based, and, hence, share shortcomings that are typical for this class of models. In particular, the models are restricted to R&D as the only kind of growth-affecting investment, and, moreover, do not represent the capability of physical capital to differentiate products [cf. first and second point of our critique of the EPV model, chapter 3]. Suggestively, the purpose of this part's focusing on R&D is to investigate the externalities of research comprehensively rather than to play down the severeness of these shortcomings.

Still, the three models of this part address the third and fourth point of our EPV model critique: in the present models, imperfect competition matters for the production of both the consumption and the capital good, and research is assumed to be rather capital-intensive than labor-intensive. Thus, regarding the inputs, our modeling of the R&D sector is close to the "lab equipment specification of R&D" that Rivera-Batiz/Romer (1991) and Aghion/Howitt (1998) employ. Aghion/Howitt provide casual evidence for the capital intensity of research: "Labor is not the only input to research. On the contrary, research in fact uses a great deal of physical capital, in the form of laboratories, offices, plant and equipment needed for constructing and testing pilot models and prototypes, computers and other scientific instruments, particle accelerators, observatories, space vehicles, and so forth." [p. 100].

The present chapter is organized as follows. In section one, we present the technology of our model. Section two investigates the model's laissez-faire outcome. Section three yields the social planner's solution. Section four derives policy implications. Section five gives an appraisal of the model.

8.1 Technology

8.1.1 Final Output

Final output Y_t is produced by an infinite set of firms j, the amount of which is normalized to unity, i.e. $j \in [0, 1]$.[2] Final output is given by the following CES production function

$$Y_t = \left[\int_0^{A_t} x_{at}^{\alpha} da \right]^{\frac{\nu}{\alpha}}$$

where $0 < \alpha < 1$, and $\nu \geq 1$. The inputs x_{at} to the production of final output are differentiated intermediates, where $a \in [0, A_t]$. For $\nu > 1$, the economy exhibits economies of scale. The economies of scale are independent of firm size: an individual firm cannot exploit economies of scale by expanding. We motivate the economies of scale by network effects.

[2] Aggregation implies $Y_t = \int_0^1 Y_{jt} dj$, where Y_{jt} denotes output of firm j. Thus, output of an average firm is given by Y_t.

To open up an intermediates production unit, it takes one unit of R&D capital, i.e. a blueprint. The one-to-one intermediates production functions are given by $x_{at} = l_{at}$, where $a \in [0, A_t]$. The output of production unit a depends on the labor force l_{at} that it employs: one unit of labor is transformed into one unit of the respective intermediate. Imposing full employment, i.e. $\int_0^{A_t} l_{at} da = L$, and symmetry, we obtain $x_{at} = L/A_t \equiv x_t$.[3] Thus, the final output production function may be written as

$$Y_t = A_t^{\eta} L^{\nu} \tag{8.1}$$

where $\eta \equiv [1-\alpha]\nu/\alpha > 1$.[4] A_t is a measure for the amount of intermediates production units that have been opened up before time t. Notice that A_t yields two additional interpretations. First, since A_t denotes the amount of units that produce differentiated intermediates, it denotes the amount of differentiated intermediates itself. Second, since the sum of intermediates production units is just the sum of the economy's blueprints, A_t represents furthermore the size of the accumulated R&D capital stock.

8.1.2 R&D

Semi-endogenous growth models hold an asymmetry: while the production of the consumption good uses the full array of differentiated intermediates, the R&D sector is quite modest – the only input to research is labor.[5] Our model deviates from semi-endogenous growth models with respect to the R&D input. In our model, research uses the same mix of inputs as the production of the consumption good does. We assume that the transformation of final output into new R&D capital, $\dot{A}_t$, is represented by the subsequent production function

$$\dot{A}_t = \frac{1}{\omega} A_t^{-[\eta-1]} I_t \tag{8.2}$$

where $\omega > 0$ reflects the efficiency of the economy's research sector. Input into R&D is that part of final output that is not consumed, i.e. investment I_t. In other words: the input into R&D is a capital good. Notice that with the representation of final output as the input into R&D, this model addresses the fourth point of the critique that we have raised in our discussion of the EPV model [cf. chapter 3]. The present model's capital good can be broadly interpreted: since the good is defined as forgone consumption, it includes both physical capital and human capital components.

[3] In subsection 8.2.1, we show that the identity of the A_t market shares is implied by intermediates firms' profit-maximization.

[4] We draw on the assumption that elasticity η is above unity in order to replicate real world's increasing R&D costs.

[5] It may be claimed that in semi-endogenous growth models, the input to R&D is not labor but human capital. However, considering the fact that the input cannot be accumulated, this interpretation appears to be questionable [cf. Aghion/Howitt (1998), p. 99].

R&D laboratories' productivity is given by $A_t^{-[\eta-1]}/\omega$. With more blueprints already developed, i.e. a higher A_t, the amount of final output that is necessary to develop a further blueprint increases. Furthermore, we argue that the "greater" the inventions in an economy are, the more and more difficult it becomes to add new inventions to the existing ones. There are two criteria for "greatness". First, the longer the distance between a newly invented intermediate and the existing intermediates, i.e. the lower α, the more and more difficult it becomes to develop such new intermediates. Second, the stronger the positive externality of a newly invented intermediate to the existing intermediates combined, i.e. the higher ν, the faster the costs of R&D increase. This reasoning suggests a specification of the R&D technology as in equation (8.2).[6]

To sum up: we observe two effects of R&D on the profitability of R&D. First, a negative exhaustion effect. A blueprint's development becomes more difficult as more blueprints have already been developed. The input into R&D – i.e. the economy's investment – that is required to keep the steady-state innovation rate constant has to grow at rate $\eta\gamma_A$, where γ_A denotes the steady-state innovation rate [cf. R&D production function (8.2)].[7] Second, a positive productivity effect. With a larger amount of blueprints, the economy's labor productivity increases. Production function (8.1) implies that due to this rising labor productivity, in the steady state, final output grows at rate $\eta\gamma_A$. Thus, steady-state investment grows at rate $\eta\gamma_A$, too. Apparently, the exhaustion effect and the productivity effect neutralize.

8.2 Laissez-faire Outcome

8.2.1 Intermediate Market

The market for intermediates is imperfectly competitive. Intermediates suppliers' flow profit rates are given by

$$\pi_{at} = p_{x_a t}(x_{at})x_{at} - w_t x_{at} \tag{8.3}$$

where $p_{x_a t}$ is the price of intermediate a, where $a \in [0, A_t]$.[8] The suppliers maximize their profit rates by charging $p_{x_a t} = w_t/\alpha \equiv p_{xt}$. Since all A_t intermediates suppliers charge a common price, p_{xt}, we obtain a symmetric

[6]The assumption according to which the exhaustion elasticity equals exactly $[\eta - 1]$ may be perceived as stark. However, the assumption has to be drawn in order to make the economy exhibiting balanced growth. If the elasticity were above $[\eta - 1]$, growth would peter out. Notice that, using equation (8.2), a market clearing condition may be stated as $Y_t = c_t L + \omega A_t^{\eta}\left[\dot{A}_t/A_t\right]$. Hence, a higher rate of innovation, $\dot{A}_t/A_t$, implies a higher share of R&D investment in total expenditure.

[7]Notice that the economy jumps immediately to the steady state.

[8]We refer to these profits as R&D-related profits since it takes R&D investment to open up intermediates production units, i.e. to appropriate these profits.

solution where all A_t production units share an output of same size, x_t. Thus, we may use final output production function (8.1).

In order to determine the evolution of relative prices, we derive the cost function of the final output sector. The cost function C_y which is dual to the production function of a final output firm j, where $j \in [0,1]$, is given by[9]

$$C_y(\{p_{x_at}\}_{a=0}^{A_t}, y_{jt}) = \left[\int_0^{A_t} p_{x_at}^{-\left[\frac{\alpha}{1-\alpha}\right]} da\right]^{-\left[\frac{1-\alpha}{\alpha}\right]} y_{jt}$$

y_{jt} is the fictitious output of firm j that we would observe if the economy exhibited no economies of scale, that is $y_{jt} = \left[\int_0^{A_t} x_{jat}^{\alpha} da\right]^{1/\alpha}$, with x_{jat} representing the amount of intermediate a that is used in firm j. Using the symmetry result, total cost may be stated as $C_Y(p_{xt}, L) = p_{xt}L$. Since perfect competition prevails on the market for final output, total revenue equals total cost, and price equals average cost, i.e. $p_{Yt} = AC_{Yt}$. Setting $p_{Yt} = 1$, and solving for p_{xt} yields the intermediates price

$$p_{xt} = A_t^{\eta} L^{\nu-1} \tag{8.4}$$

Price equation (8.4) shows that the intermediates price increases with the accumulation of R&D capital.

Intermediates price (8.4) suggests a revisit of the flow profit rates. The representative firm's profit is given by $\pi_t = [1-\alpha]p_{xt}x_t$ [cf. equation (8.3) together with the markup]. The profit increases with the firms' market power and with the intermediates' price. An increase in the amount of varieties has two opposite effects on the profit rate. First, a positive price effect: it follows from the induced rise in the intermediates price [cf. price equation (8.4)]. Second, a negative market-saturation effect: the intermediate's share of a market the size of which is given by the non-growing population L is negatively related to the number of intermediates. To determine the sign of the overall effect, we insert $x_t = L/A_t$ and equation (8.4) into the profit equation. We obtain the following expression where profit depends on the sizes of R&D capital stock and labor force[10]

$$\pi_t = [1-\alpha]A_t^{\eta-1}L^{\nu} \tag{8.5}$$

Profit equation (8.5) shows that, with $\eta > 1$, the positive price effect dominates the negative market-saturation effect. Hence, the overall effect of the launch of an additional intermediate on the profit rate is positive.

---

[9] The cost function is the solution to the problem $\min\left\{\int_0^{A_t} p_{x_at}x_{jat}da + \mu\left[y_{jt} - \left[\int_0^{A_t} x_{jat}^{\alpha}da\right]^{1/\alpha}\right]\right\}$.

[10] Notice that the factor's shares of gross national product are independent of the sizes of R&D capital stock and labor force: $[1-\alpha]$ depicts R&D capital's income share, and α denotes labor's income share.

8.2.2 Asset Market

In equilibrium, R&D investment implies that the blueprints' value equals their price. If their value were to fall below their price, R&D investment would stop. If their value were to be above their price, an unbounded demand for blueprints would arise. The condition for a free entry into the intermediates production follows as $v_t \leq p_{At}$, with equality whenever R&D is done, i.e. whenever $\dot{A}_t > 0$. v_t denotes the value of a blueprint, and p_{At} its price. R&D capital's production function (8.2) yields free-entry condition

$$v_t \leq \omega A_t^{\eta-1} \tag{8.6}$$

with equality whenever $\dot{A}_t > 0$. Hence, with $\eta > 1$, the launch of additional intermediates raises the costs of R&D.

Thus, we may describe the two effects of R&D on the profitability of R&D – exhaustion effect and productivity effect – in terms of prices, considering blueprints' value [cf. free entry (8.6)] and the R&D-related profit rate [cf. equation (8.5)]. First, in the steady state, with an increasing amount of existing blueprints, the amount of final output that is necessary to develop a further blueprint grows at rate $[\eta - 1]\gamma_A$. Hence, the value of a blueprint grows at this rate, too [cf. free entry (8.6)]. This is the exhaustion effect of R&D. Second, due to R&D, the economy's product variety expands. An increasing product variety boosts the productivity of every differentiated intermediate. Thus, the price of a differentiated intermediate increases at rate $\eta\gamma_A$ [cf. equation (8.4)], and the R&D-related profit rises at rate $[\eta - 1]\gamma_A$ [cf. equation (8.5)]. This is the productivity effect of R&D. Since in the steady state, both the value of a blueprint and the R&D-related profit grow at the same rate, the two effects cancel out, and the dividend π_t/v_t remains constant. Hence, the accumulation of R&D capital does not affect the profitability of R&D investment.

An individual that is willing to postpone consumption may choose from two investment opportunities. First, she may purchase a unit of R&D capital, i.e. a blueprint. Second, she may purchase a bond which yields interest rate r_t. Our setup implies perfect foresight and rules out speculative bubbles. Hence, it is apparent that in equilibrium no-arbitrage holds: the rate of return on a blueprint has to equal the rate of return on a bond.

The return on a blueprint depends on two components: the profit that accrues to a blueprint, π_t, and the change of a blueprint's value, $\dot{v}_t$. Thus, the rate of return is given by $r_t = \pi_t/v_t + \dot{v}_t/v_t$. Using profit rate (8.5) and free entry (8.6), we may derive the following expression for the steady-state rate of return

$$r = \frac{1}{\omega}[1-\alpha]L^{\nu} + \frac{\eta-1}{\eta}\gamma \tag{MM}$$

where γ denotes the laissez-faire steady-state consumption growth rate.

8.2.3 Steady-State Growth

The intertemporal maximization problem of the individual is equivalent to $\max U_t$ subject to flow budget constraint $c_t + \dot{q}_t \leq w_t + r_t q_t$, where q_t is per capita financial assets, w_t is wage rate, and r_t is interest rate. Total income can either be spent on consumption c_t, or saved and invested in $\dot{q}_t$. The solution to the maximization problem is the Keynes/Ramsey rule, $\dot{c}_t/c_t = \sigma\left[r_t - \rho\right]$, where $\sigma > 0$ denotes the intertemporal elasticity of substitution, and $\rho > 0$ represents the time preference rate.

Inserting the steady-state rate of return (MM), we obtain the economy's laissez-faire steady-state growth rate,

$$\gamma = \frac{\sigma\left[\frac{1}{\omega}\left[1-\alpha\right]L^{\nu} - \rho\right]}{1 - \sigma\frac{\eta-1}{\eta}} \tag{8.7}$$

where for a positive growth rate, i.e. $\gamma > 0$, first, $\left[1-\alpha\right]L^{\nu}/\omega > \rho$ must hold, and, second, $1/\sigma > \left[\eta - 1\right]/\eta$ must be fulfilled. The transversality condition implies $\rho > \left[\sigma - 1\right]\gamma/\sigma$. Laissez-faire growth goes up with a higher R&D productivity, a lower elasticity of substitution of intermediates, higher economies of scale, and a larger labor force. A lower rate of time preference and a higher intertemporal elasticity of substitution increase the growth rate, too.[11]

8.3 Social Planner's Solution

The social planner's problem is to max U_t subject to the technology constraint $\dot{A}_t = A_t^{-\left[\eta-1\right]}\left[A_t^{\eta}L^{\nu} - c_t L\right]/\omega$. Simplifying the first-order conditions, the social optimum steady-state growth rate is derived as

$$\gamma_S = \sigma\left[\frac{1}{\omega}\eta L^{\nu} - \rho\right] \tag{8.8}$$

How does laissez-faire growth compare to social optimum growth? We have investigated two countervailing effects of R&D on the profitability of R&D: the exhaustion effect and the productivity effect. Both effects hold externalities. In fact, the *exhaustion effect* is a pure negative externality. The other effect – the productivity effect – holds four externalities. First, a *business stealing effect*: an innovator does not account for the loss in business that the incumbent intermediates suppliers incur due to the extra competition. Second, a *specialization effect*: an innovator does not regard the productivity gain that the existing intermediates enjoy due to the increased diversity. Third, a *monopoly distortion effect*: since the markup on marginal costs in the intermediates sector is passed to the demanders of final output,

[11] Production function (8.1) and growth rate (8.7) imply a saving rate that is given by $s = \omega\gamma/\left[\eta L^{\nu}\right]$.

R&D is in laissez-faire inefficiently expensive, and innovators undertake sub-optimal low R&D efforts. Fourth, a *network effect*: an innovator attaches no weight to the productivity gain that accrues to the existing intermediates as a result of the economy-wide economies of scale.[12]

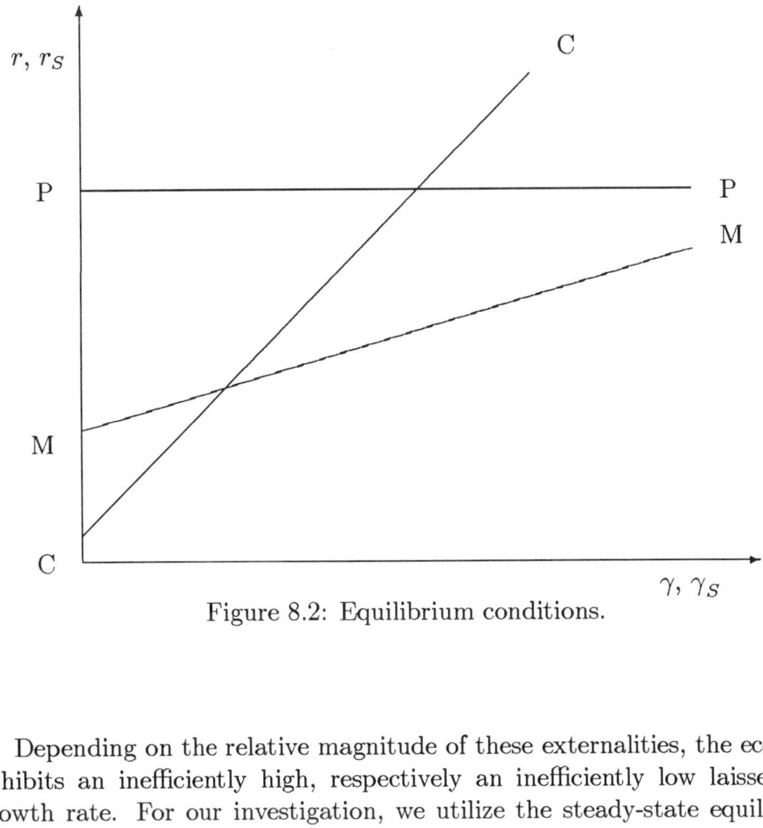

Figure 8.2: Equilibrium conditions.

Depending on the relative magnitude of these externalities, the economy exhibits an inefficiently high, respectively an inefficiently low laissez-faire growth rate. For our investigation, we utilize the steady-state equilibrium conditions. Both decentralized solution and social planner's solution involve condition (CC), given by

$$r = r_S - \rho + \frac{1}{\sigma}\gamma \tag{CC}$$

[12] We may wonder what sign the net externality of these four effects does bear. Recall that in expanding product variety models with CES technology, the negative business stealing effect and the positive specialization effect neutralize [cf. Grossman/Helpman (1991a), pp. 82-83]. Thus, since both the monopoly distortion effect and the network effect are positive externalities, the net effect turns out to be a positive externality, too.

where r_S denotes the social optimum steady-state return on capital. The CC graph is upward-sloping in γ-r-space. The laissez-faire equilibrium condition MM has already been derived [cf. equation (MM)]. Social planner's equilibrium condition (PP) is implied by social optimum growth rate (8.8) as

$$r_S = \frac{1}{\omega}\eta L^{\nu} \qquad (PP)$$

Thus, whereas the MM graph is upward-sloping in γ-r-space, the PP graph is a horizontal line. Equations (CC), (MM), and (PP) suggest that, for reasonable parameter values, the laissez-faire growth rate is below the social optimum [cf. figure 8.2].

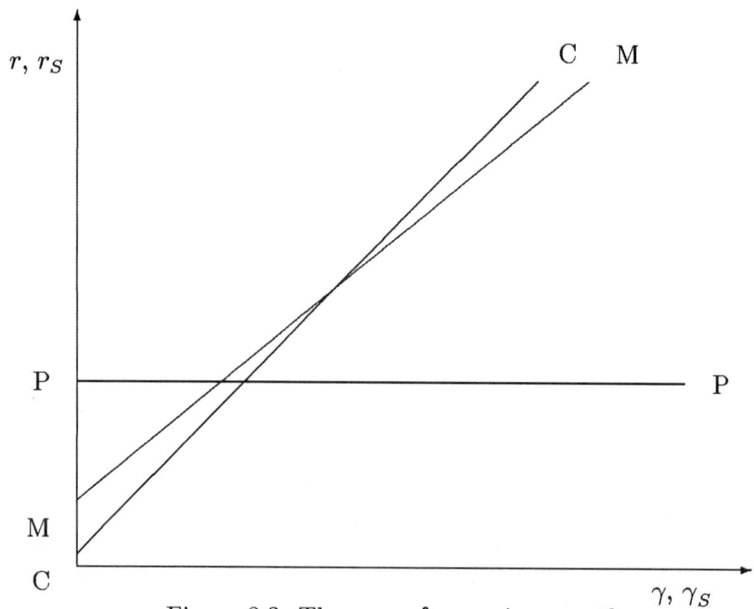

Figure 8.3: The case of excessive growth.

Investigating the steady-state conditions (CC), (MM), and (PP) more carefully, we find two conditions for excessive growth. Taken together, the two conditions are both necessary and sufficient for excessive growth. First, the distance between the intersections of the CC line and the MM line with the y-axis, i.e. $[1-\alpha] L^{\nu}/\omega - \rho$, has to be sufficiently large. Second, the elasticity of intertemporal substitution, σ, is required to be sufficiently close to $\eta/[\eta-1]$, where $\sigma < \eta/[\eta-1]$. The latter condition implies that the slopes of the CC line and the MM line are sufficiently close to each other. If the two conditions are fulfilled, we obtain excessive growth as represented by figure 8.3.

Roughly, excessive growth becomes more likely for parameter values that increase decentralized growth.[13] Recall that Aghion/Howitt (1992) give the somewhat paradoxical result that a laissez-faire growth rate that is already very low is still suspicious to be excessive, whereas a growth rate that is very high is considered to be still below the social optimum [cf. IPQ model, chapter 4]. In the present model, capturing R&D's exhaustion effect, we obtain the opposite result: a higher growth rate is rather excessive than a lower growth rate. What is the reason for our deviating result? In both models, for a lower growth rate, the size of the intertemporal R&D spillover decreases, too. Since in Aghion/Howitt (1992), the intertemporal spillover is positive, a decrease in the growth rate leads to an increase of the relative magnitude of the negative business stealing effect. Ceteris paribus, a lower growth rate has a higher probability to be an excessive one. In the present model, the intertemporal spillover is negative. Thus, by representing the exhaustion effect of research, we obtain the intuitively more appealing result that a high growth rate rather than a low growth rate is excessive.

Considering the fairly restrictive second prerequisite for excessive growth – i.e. σ is required to be sufficiently close to $\eta/[\eta-1]$, where $\sigma < \eta/[\eta-1]$ –, our model implies that, in an expanding product variety framework, it is unlikely that excessive growth is a real world phenomenon.[14] This finding is consistent with the empirical literature on R&D spillovers. Surveying the strand, Griliches (1992) concludes that a number of reasonably done studies suggest that positive R&D spillovers are present [cf. section 2.3]. Recently, Jones/Williams (1999) employ a calibrated model to investigate R&D externalities. They find that, in real world, laissez-faire R&D investment is most likely below the social optimum.

---

[13] Apart from the productivity parameter $\eta \equiv [1-\alpha]\nu/\alpha$, the result holds for both preference and technology parameters. Reflecting its Janus-faced nature, the impact of the productivity parameter η on the relative magnitude of the negative R&D externalities is ambiguous. Nevertheless, for $\sigma > 1$, the impact of η turns unambiguous: then, a higher η increases the relative magnitude of the negative R&D externalities, and for both a lower substitutability between intermediates and stronger economies of scale, excessive laissez-faire growth becomes more probable.

[14] For instance, with $\omega = 1$, $L = 1$, $\nu = 1.1$, $\rho = 0.02$, and $\sigma = 1.1$, the technology parameter α has to be in a range between 0.09 and 0.24, in order to obtain excessive growth. With $\omega = 1$, $L = 1$, $\nu = 1.1$, $\rho = 0.02$, and $\sigma = 1$, the social optimum growth rate is unambiguously above the laissez-faire growth rate, no matter what value the technology parameter α takes.

8.4 Policy Implications

We introduce a profit tax, t_π, a tax on R&D investment, t_I, and a lump-sum tax, T. Taxes obey the condition $-1 < t_\pi, t_I < 1$. The after-tax steady-state rate of return is readily derived as

$$r = \left[\frac{1-t_\pi}{1+t_I}\right]\frac{1}{\omega}\left[1-\alpha\right]L^\nu + \frac{\eta-1}{\eta}\gamma \tag{TT}$$

The optimum combinations of taxes $[t_\pi, t_I]^*$ fulfill the subsequent equation[15]

$$t_\pi = 1 - [1+t_I]\left[\frac{\eta - \sigma\frac{\eta-1}{\eta}[\eta - \omega\rho L^{-\nu}]}{1-\alpha}\right] \tag{8.9}$$

where $\sigma < \eta^2\left[\eta - \omega\rho L^{-\nu}\right]/\left[\eta - 1\right]$. In the case of inefficiently low laissez-faire growth, optimum combinations $[t_\pi, t_I]^*$ shift the MM line upwards until it goes through the intersection of the CC line with the PP line [cf. figure 8.2]. In the case of excessive laissez-faire growth, optimum combinations $[t_\pi, t_I]^*$ shift the MM line downwards until it goes through the intersection of the CC line with the PP line [cf. figure 8.3].

Thus, for $t_I = 0$, the optimum profit tax is given by

$$t_\pi^* = 1 - \left[\frac{\eta - \sigma\frac{\eta-1}{\eta}[\eta - \omega\rho L^{-\nu}]}{1-\alpha}\right]$$

Accordingly, for $t_\pi = 0$, the optimum R&D tax is given by

$$t_I^* = \left[\frac{1-\alpha}{\eta - \sigma\frac{\eta-1}{\eta}\left[\eta - \omega\rho L^{-\nu}\right]}\right] - 1$$

Hence, in the case of excessive growth, the optimum taxes increase with a higher R&D productivity and a larger labor force. Furthermore, a higher intertemporal elasticity of substitution and a lower rate of time preference raise the optimum taxes. The impact of productivity parameter η on the optimum taxes is ambiguous.[16] To balance its budget, the government may use a lump sum transfer.

---

[15] We may compare equation (8.9) with the respective equation in the Ramsey model with imperfect competition. Profit tax (8.9) is equal to the profit tax there, plus the term $\sigma[1+t_I][\eta-1][\eta-\omega\rho L^{-\nu}]/[1-\alpha]\eta$ [cf. equation (5.17)]. Notice that $\eta > \omega\rho L^{-\nu}$ has to hold in order to obtain a positive social optimum growth rate [cf. equation (7.16)]. Hence, in a model without an exhaustion effect of investment, the optimum policy measure is unambiguously a subsidy.

[16] However, for $\sigma > 1$, the impact of η turns unambiguous: a higher η increases the optimum taxes, i.e. for both a lower substitutability between intermediates and stronger economies of scale, the optimum taxes go up.

8.5 Discussion

The present model yields two main results. First, it gives an endogenous explanation of long-run growth using a framework that accounts for negative intertemporal R&D spillovers. Our model reproduces the exhaustion effect of the recent literature on semi-endogenous growth: since R&D exhausts technological opportunities, innovators face rising R&D costs. A key difference between our model and the existing models is that we complement this negative effect by a positive productivity effect: since R&D boosts the productivity of the differentiated products, successful innovators enjoy increasing profits. In the steady state, both the costs of R&D and the R&D-related profits increase at the same rate. Hence, in our model, the profitability of R&D investment is unaffected by research activity, and the economy exhibits endogenous long-run growth.

Second, in the present paper, we derive the result that long-run growth may be excessive even without an extraordinarily strong business stealing effect. Deviating from Aghion/Howitt (1992), our model complements the business stealing effect by a second negative R&D externality: the exhaustion effect. Since this negative R&D externality increases with the growth rate, while the positive effects – i.e. the specialization effect, the monopoly distortion effect, and the network effect – are not growth dependent, we obtain the following relation: the higher the laissez-faire growth is, the more likely it is that this growth is above the social optimum. Apparently, our finding according to which excessive growth is found rather in fast growing than in slowly growing economies is intuitively more appealing than Aghion/Howitt's somewhat paradoxical result according to which low growth is more suspicious to be excessive than high growth. Summarizing our normative findings, though, we conclude that, considering an expanding product variety framework, excessive growth appears to be a fairly unlike real world phenomenon.

Chapter 9

Quality Ladders and Excessive Growth

In the present chapter, we set R&D's exhaustion effect into a quality ladder framework. This permits to investigate comprehensively cases in which the laissez-faire growth rate is above the social optimum. In particular, we capture both the case of excessively slow growth [cf. chapter 4] and the case of excessively fast growth [cf. chapter 8] within one model. Moreover, compared to chapter 8's model, the approach deviates in its representation of the stochastic nature of the innovation process. At the firm level, we assume that a higher level of research activity does not necessarily lead to more innovation, but increases the probability that innovation occurs. The structure of the model is shown by figure 9.1.

The plan of the present chapter is as follows. In section one, we present the technology of our model. Section two investigates the model's laissez-faire outcome. Section three yields the social planner's solution. Section four derives policy implications. Section five summarizes.

9.1 Technology

9.1.1 Final Output

Final output Y_t is produced by an infinite set of firms j, the amount of which is normalized to unity, i.e. $j \in [0,1]$. The aggregate technology is given by

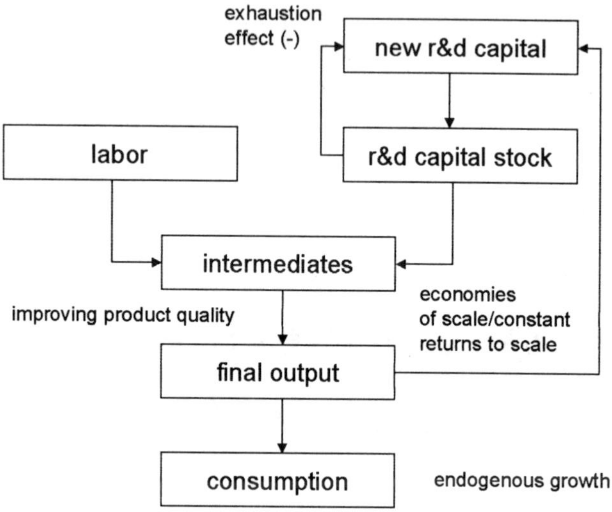

Figure 9.1: A schematic representation of the model.

the subsequent CES production function

$$Y_t = \left[\int_0^1 A_{it} x_{it}^{\alpha} di \right]^{\frac{\nu}{\alpha}} \tag{9.1}$$

where $0 < \alpha < 1$, and $\nu > 0$. x_{it} denotes the quantity of intermediate i that is used in the production of final output at time t, where $i \in [0,1]$. A_{it} represents the level of technical knowledge that is used in the production of intermediate i: a higher A_{it} increases the intermediate's product quality, i.e. the productivity of the specific intermediate in producing final output. Since $0 < \alpha < 1$, the intermediates market is imperfectly competitive. For $\nu > 1$, the economy exhibits economies of scale.

The intermediate goods sector's technology is given by production functions $x_{it} = l_{it}/A_{it}$, where $i \in [0,1]$. l_{it} denotes the labor force that is used in the production of intermediate i. The technology implies that the production of intermediates that incorporate a more recent technology, i.e. a higher A_{it}, are more resource-intensively produced. That is, the higher the quality of a product is, the higher is its cost of production.[1] Notice that the index i serves to count the intermediates firms, the differentiated intermediates themselves, and the niches of the intermediates market.

With regard to research externalities, we represent strong intersectoral spillovers: as described in chapter 4, the qualities of the differentiated products increase in a symmetric manner. This implies that there is at every

[1] The formulation of a resource-intensifying intermediates production is owed to Aghion/Howitt [cf. Aghion/Howitt (1998), pp. 94-95]. Notice that the present model's findings do not hinge on this assumption.

point in time a common level of technical knowledge across the economy, i.e. $A_{it} = A_t$, where $i \in [0,1]$. Accordingly, imposing symmetry on the sizes of the intermediates firms, the intermediates sector's technology may be written as $x_t = L/A_t$, whereas the final output production function (9.1) becomes[2]

$$Y_t = A_t^{\eta} L^{\nu} \tag{9.2}$$

where $\eta \equiv [1-\alpha]\nu/\alpha > 0$.[3]

9.1.2 R&D

The expenditure that flows into the research laboratories that target niche i is denoted by e_{it}. We assume that the sequence of innovations in market niche i is a random process that follows a Poisson distribution with parameter $\psi e_{it}/A_{it}^{\eta}$, where $\psi > 0$. Thus, product improvement becomes more difficult as the quality of the state-of-the-art product is already fairly advanced. That is, for a given R&D expenditure flow, with each innovation, it takes longer to come up with a further innovation. Moreover, our formulation implies that other things equal, the stronger the positive externality of the newly invented product is – i.e. the higher ν, and, thus, the higher η –, the faster increases the expected cost of an innovation.[4]

Apart from the Poisson arrival rate, $\psi e_{it}/A_{it}^{\eta}$, the evolution of the technology parameter A_{it} depends on the innovation size, $\delta > 0$. Hence, the expected value of the growth rate of intermediate i's product quality, $\dot{A}_{it}/A_{it}$, is given by the expected amount of innovation steps that occur in a unit-time interval, $\psi e_{it}/A_{it}^{\eta}$, premultiplied by the innovation size, δ, i.e.

$$E\left(\frac{\dot{A}_{it}}{A_{it}}\right) = \delta\psi\frac{e_{it}}{A_{it}^{\eta}} \tag{9.3}$$

Imposing symmetry on the sizes of the research niches, we obtain $e_{it} = e_t = I_t$.[5] That is, the normalization of the amount of differentiated intermediates to unity implies that I_t represents, first, the economy's total investment, $\int_0^1 e_{it}di$, and, second, the R&D expenditure that is undertaken in the representative niche of the intermediates market, e_t. Since there is an infinite number of market niches i, the economy performs an infinite number of research projects i. Applying the symmetry of technical progress, i.e. $A_{it} = A_t$,

[2] In subsection 9.2.1, we show that the common size of the A_t intermediates firms is implied by their profit-maximization.

[3] Notice that $0 < \alpha < 1$ and $\nu > 0$ imply $\eta > 0$.

[4] The assumption according to which the exhaustion elasticity equals exactly η may be perceived as stark. However, the assumption has to be drawn in order to make the economy exhibiting balanced growth. If the elasticity were above η, growth would peter out.

[5] In subsection 9.2.2, we show that the identity of the sizes of the A_t research niches follows from the absence of arbitrage opportunities in the capital market.

we find that the technology parameter A_t grows steadily, and the economy's innovation process is deterministic.[6]

Summing up the assumptions that concern the economy's R&D sector, we may formulate the subsequent production function

$$\frac{\dot{A}_t}{A_t} = \delta\psi\frac{I_t}{A_t^\eta} \tag{9.4}$$

The formulation reflects the two countervailing effects that research has on the profitability of R&D. First, a negative exhaustion effect. Product improvement becomes more difficult as the quality of existing products is already fairly advanced. That is: with a higher level of knowledge already attained, the costs that have to be incurred in order to push the technological frontier even further increase. In the steady state, the input into R&D – i.e. the economy's investment – that is required to keep the innovation rate constant has to grow at rate $\eta\gamma_A$, where γ_A denotes the steady-state innovation rate [cf. R&D production function (9.4)].[7] Second, a positive productivity effect. With better products at hand, the economy's labor productivity increases. Production function (9.2) implies that due to this rising labor productivity, in the steady state, final output grows at rate $\eta\gamma_A$. Thus, the steady-state investment grows at rate $\eta\gamma_A$, too. Apparently, the exhaustion effect and the productivity effect cancel out.

9.2 Laissez-faire Outcome

9.2.1 Intermediate Market

The flow profit rates of the suppliers of differentiated intermediates at time t are given by

$$\pi_{it} = p_{x_it}(x_{it})x_{it} - w_tA_{it}x_{it}$$

where p_{x_it} denotes the price of the intermediate i, and $i \in [0,1]$. With $A_{it} = A_t$, the profit-maximizing price is given by $p_{x_it} = w_tA_t/\alpha$, implying a common intermediates price, i.e. $p_{x_it} = p_{xt}$, a common intermediates output, i.e. $x_{it} = x_t$, and a common production labor force, i.e. $l_{it} = l_t$, where $i \in [0,1]$. Thus, we find indeed symmetry for the intermediates firms' sizes.

[6] The variance of the Poisson distributed random variable $\dot{A}_{it}/A_{it}$ is given by $var\left(\dot{A}_{it}/A_{it}\right) = \delta\psi e_{it}/A_t^\eta = \delta\psi I_t/A_t^\eta$ [cf. equation (9.3)]. Hence, for an infinite number of research projects i, we obtain $var\left(\dot{A}_t/A_t\right) = 0$.

[7] Notice that the economy jumps immediately to the steady state.

The cost function that is dual to production function (9.1) is given by[8]

$$C_y(\{p_{x_it}\}_{i=0}^{1}, y_{jt}) = \left[\int_0^1 A_{it}^{\frac{1}{1-\alpha}} p_{x_it}^{-\left[\frac{\alpha}{1-\alpha}\right]} di\right]^{-\left[\frac{1-\alpha}{\alpha}\right]} y_{jt}$$

where y_{jt} is the fictitious output of firm j that we would observe if the economy exhibited no economies of scale. By symmetry, total cost can be stated as $C_Y(p_{xt}, L) = p_{xt}L$. Since revenue equals cost, the price of final output, p_{Yt}, is equal to aggregate cost over aggregate output. Thus, setting $p_{Yt} = 1$ for all t, we obtain the intermediates price[9]

$$p_{xt} = A_t^{\eta+1} L^{\nu-1} \tag{9.5}$$

Applying intermediates price (9.5), and $x_t = L/A_t$, a modified profit equation which depends only on R&D capital stock and production labor force may be derived as

$$\pi_t = [1-\alpha] A_t^{\eta} L^{\nu} \tag{9.6}$$

We obtain an unambiguous result: quality improvements increase the profit rate of the representative intermediates firm.

9.2.2 Asset Market

The value of blueprint i, v_{it}, equals the discounted expected stream of future profits that are bound to this blueprint. The stream starts at time t and ends with the obsolence of the innovation. Hence,

$$v_{it} = \int_t^{\infty} e^{-R_{ts} - \psi e_{is}/A_{is}^{\eta}} \pi_s ds \tag{9.7}$$

where $R_{ts} \equiv \int_t^s r_u du$ denotes the cumulative discount factor from time t to time s. The flow probability $\psi e_{it}/A_{it}^{\eta}$ is the arrival rate for a complete capital loss that a firm incurs when it is replaced by a new innovator.

With free entry into the market niches i, where $i \in [0,1]$, the blueprints share a common value, i.e. $v_{it} = v_t$. The reasoning is straightforward. If the R&D expenditures in market niche i were relatively small, i.e. $e_{it} < I_t$, the flow probability that market niche i's most recent innovator incurs a complete capital loss would be relatively low, i.e. $\psi e_{it}/A_t^{\eta} < \psi I_t/A_t^{\eta}$. Accordingly, by equation (9.7), the value of an innovation in the respective niche would be relatively high, i.e. $v_{it} > v_t$. Hence, we find a strong incentive for investors

[8] The cost function is the solution to the problem $\min\left\{\int_0^1 p_{x_it} x_{jit} di + \mu\left[y_{jt} - \left[\int_0^1 A_{it} x_{jit}^{\alpha} di\right]^{1/\alpha}\right]\right\}$, where x_{jit} represents the amount of intermediate i that is used in final output firm j.

[9] Intermediates price (9.5) implies a wage rate given by $w_t = \alpha A_t^{\eta} L^{\nu-1}$.

to turn research expenditures towards to market niche i. We may conclude that in equilibrium, blueprints share a common value, i.e. $v_{it} = v_t$, and the sectoral R&D expenditures as the sectoral innovation arrival rates are the same, i.e. $e_{it} = I_t$, and $\psi e_{it}/A_t^\eta = \psi I_t/A_t^\eta$, where $i \in [0,1]$. Notice that, applying our two results on symmetry, we may indeed use production functions (9.2) and (9.4). Moreover, the value of the representative blueprint follows as

$$v_t = \int_t^\infty e^{-R_{ts} - \psi I_s[s-t]/A_t^\eta} \pi_s ds \tag{9.8}$$

Since the flow probability of an innovation is $\psi I_t/A_t^\eta$, in steady state, for a constant arrival rate, research expenditure has to grow at rate $\eta\gamma_A$.

With free entry into the production of intermediates, the value of the representative blueprint cannot exceed its price. Hence, $v_t \leq p_{At}$, where p_{At} is the price of the representative blueprint. R&D capital's production function (9.4) yields price equation $p_{At} = A_t^\eta/\psi$. The expected cost of developing a blueprint increases with a lower probability that research is successful and a higher level of technical knowledge. The free-entry condition follows as

$$v_t \leq \frac{1}{\psi} A_t^\eta \tag{9.9}$$

with equality whenever research is performed, i.e. $\dot{A}_t > 0$.

Thus, we may describe the two effects of R&D on the profitability of R&D – exhaustion effect and productivity effect – in terms of prices, considering blueprints' value [cf. free entry (9.9)] and the R&D-related profit rate [cf. equation (9.6)]. First, in the steady state, with an increasing product quality, the amount of final output that is required to improve product quality further grows at rate $\eta\gamma_A$. Hence, the value of a blueprint grows at this rate, too [cf. free entry (9.9)]. This is the exhaustion effect of R&D. Second, due to R&D, the economy's product quality improves. An increasing product quality boosts the productivity of every differentiated intermediate. Thus, the price of a differentiated intermediate increases at rate $[\eta + 1]\,\gamma_A$ [cf. equation (9.5)], and the R&D-related profit rises at rate $\eta\gamma_A$ [cf. equation (9.6)]. This is the productivity effect of R&D. Since in the steady state, both the value of a blueprint and the R&D-related profit grow at the same rate, the two effects cancel out, leaving the dividend π_t/v_t unaffected. Hence, the accumulation of R&D capital has no impact on the profitability of R&D investment.

9.2.3 Steady-State Growth

The solution to the intertemporal utility maximization problem is the Keynes/Ramsey rule, $\dot{c}_t/c_t = \sigma\,[r_t - \rho]$, where $\sigma, \rho > 0$. Differentiating equation (9.8) with respect to time, and dividing the resulting equation by the value of a blueprint, we obtain no-arbitrage condition $\pi_t/v_t + \dot{v}_t/v_t - \psi I_t/A_t^\eta =$

r_t. Substituting for r_t in the Keynes/Ramsey rule yields the laissez-faire steady-state growth rate

$$\gamma = \frac{\sigma\left\{[1-\alpha]\,\psi L^{\nu} - \rho\right\}}{1-\sigma\left[1-\frac{1}{\delta\eta}\right]} \tag{9.10}$$

where for a positive growth rate, i.e. $\gamma > 0$, first, $[1-\alpha]\,\psi L^{\nu} > \rho$ must hold, and, second, $1/\sigma > 1-1/\delta\eta$ must be met. Moreover, for a bounded attainable utility, $\rho > [\sigma-1]\,\gamma/\sigma$ has to be fulfilled. Laissez-faire growth increases with a higher probability that research is successful, a higher innovation size, a lower elasticity of substitution of intermediates, higher economies of scale, and a larger labor force. A lower rate of time preference and a higher intertemporal elasticity of substitution increase the growth rate, too.[10]

9.3 Social Planner's Solution

The social planner's problem is to max U_t subject to the technology constraint $\dot{A}_t = \delta\psi A_t^{-[\eta-1]}\,[A_t^{\eta}L^{\nu} - c_t L]$. The social optimum steady-state growth rate is readily derived as

$$\gamma_S = \sigma\,[\delta\psi\eta L^{\nu} - \rho] \tag{9.11}$$

where for a positive growth rate, i.e. $\gamma_S > 0$, $\delta\psi\eta L^{\nu} > \rho$ has to be fulfilled.

Appraising the laissez-faire outcome, we have found two countervailing effects of R&D on the profitability of research: the exhaustion effect and the productivity effect. Whereas the *exhaustion effect* is a pure negative externality, the productivity effect holds four externalities. First, a *business stealing effect*: an innovator does not account for the loss in business that the intermediates supplier incurs that the innovator drives out of the respective market niche. Second, a *product improvement effect*: an innovator does not regard the productivity gain that the existing intermediates enjoy due to the increased level of technical knowledge. Third, a *monopoly distortion effect*: since the monopoly rent that the intermediates suppliers levy is passed to the demanders of final output, R&D is in laissez-faire inefficiently expensive, and innovators undertake suboptimal low R&D efforts. Fourth, a *network effect*: an innovator attaches no weight to the productivity gain that accrues to the existing intermediates as a result of the economy-wide economies of scale.

---

[10] It is straightforward to derive the saving rate as $s = \gamma/\,[\delta\psi\eta L^{\nu}]$.

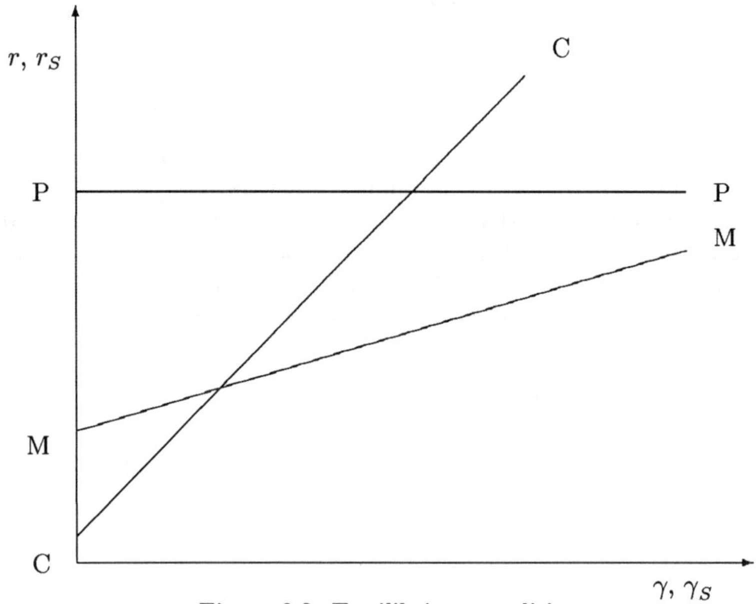

Figure 9.2: Equilibrium conditions.

For our normative analysis, we employ the steady-state equilibrium conditions. Both decentralized solution and social planner's solution involve condition (CC), given by

$$r = r_S = \rho + \frac{1}{\sigma}\gamma \qquad (CC)$$

where r_S denotes the social optimum steady-state return on capital. The CC graph is upward-sloping in γ-r-space. For laissez-faire, the equilibrium condition (MM) follows as

$$r = [1-\alpha]\psi L^{\nu} + \left[1 - \frac{1}{\delta\eta}\right]\gamma \qquad (MM)$$

Social planner's equilibrium condition (PP) is implied by social optimum growth rate (9.11) as

$$r_S = \delta\psi\eta L^{\nu} \qquad (PP)$$

Thus, whereas the MM graph's slope is ambiguous, the PP graph is horizontal. Equations (CC), (MM), and (PP) imply that, for reasonable parameter values, the laissez-faire growth rate is below the social optimum [cf. figure 9.2].

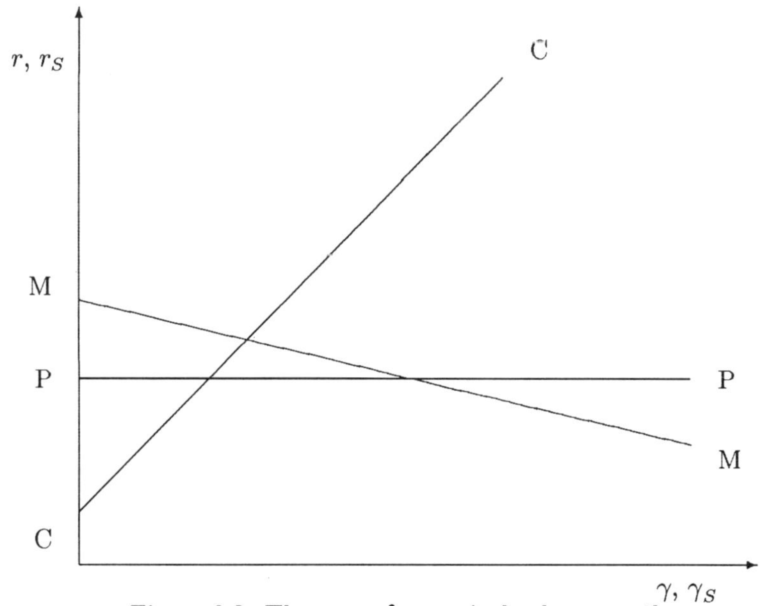

Figure 9.3: The case of excessively slow growth.

Investigating equations (CC), (MM), and (PP) more carefully, we find two different cases of excessive growth. First, we obtain a case of excessively slow growth. It is implied by the association of a low decentralized growth rate to a low innovation size [cf. equation (9.10)]. This case resembles the one that we are familiar with from our analysis of the IPQ model [cf. chapter 4]. It is represented by figure 9.3.

Second, we obtain a case of excessively fast growth. This case is analogous to the one that we have investigated in the preceding chapter. Again, excessive growth becomes more likely for parameter values that increase decentralized growth. The latter result holds for both technology parameters and preference parameters, i.e. for a higher innovation arrival rate, larger economies of scale, a larger labor force, a higher intertemporal elasticity of substitution, and a lower time preference rate. For an arbitrary elasticity

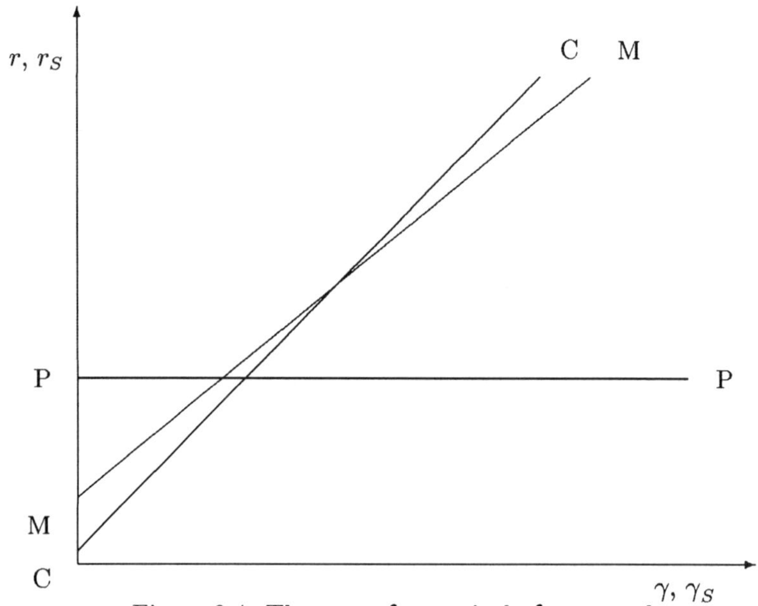

Figure 9.4: The case of excessively fast growth.

of intertemporal substitution, the impact of the elasticity of substitution of intermediates is ambiguous. For a logarithmic instantaneous utility function, i.e. $\sigma = 1$, its impact turns unambiguous: then, a lower elasticity of substitution makes excessive growth more likely. The case of excessively fast growth is shown in figure 9.4.

Recall that the IPQ model gives the somewhat paradoxical result that a laissez-faire growth rate that is already very low is still suspicious to be excessive, whereas a growth rate that is very high is considered to be still below the social optimum [cf. Aghion/Howitt (1992)]. In the present model, considering R&D's exhaustion effect, we complement this case of excessively slow growth by a case of excessively fast growth. Nevertheless, appraising equations (CC), (MM), and (PP), it appears to be quite unlikely that real world economies actually exhibit excessive growth.

9.4 Policy Implications

We introduce a profit tax, t_π, a tax on R&D investment, t_I, and a lump-sum tax, T. Taxes obey the condition $-1 < t_\pi, t_I < 1$. The after-tax steady-state rate of return is readily derived as

$$r_T = \left[\frac{1-t_\pi}{1+t_I}\right][1-\alpha]\psi L^\nu + \left[1-\frac{1}{\delta\eta}\right]\gamma \qquad (TT)$$

In the case of inefficiently low laissez-faire growth, optimum combinations $[t_\pi, t_I]^*$ shift the MM line upwards until it goes through the intersection of the CC line with the PP line [cf. figure 9.2]. In the case of excessive growth, optimum combinations shift the MM line downwards until it goes through the intersection of the CC line with the PP line [cf. figures 9.3 and 9.4].

To keep expressions handy, in the remainder of this chapter, we base the derivation of the optimum policy measures on the assumption of a logarithmic instantaneous utility function, i.e. $\sigma = 1$. Hence, the optimum combinations of taxes $[t_\pi, t_I]^*$ fulfill the subsequent equation

$$t_\pi = 1 - [1+t_I]\left[\frac{1}{1-\alpha} + \frac{[\delta\eta - 1]\rho}{[1-\alpha]\delta\psi\eta L^\nu}\right]$$

where $\delta > \delta_L = \rho/\eta[\psi L^\nu + \rho]$. Thus, for $t_I = 0$, the optimum profit tax is given by

$$t_\pi^* = -\left[\frac{\alpha}{1-\alpha} + \frac{[\delta\eta - 1]\rho}{[1-\alpha]\delta\psi\eta L^\nu}\right] \qquad (9.12)$$

Accordingly, for $t_\pi = 0$, the optimum R&D tax follows as

$$t_I^* = -\left[\frac{\alpha\delta\psi\eta L^\nu + [\delta\eta - 1]\rho}{\delta\psi\eta L^\nu + [\delta\eta - 1]\rho}\right] \qquad (9.13)$$

Hence, for $\delta \longrightarrow \delta_L$, the optimum taxes (9.12) and (9.13) turn positive.

9.5 Discussion

The present model is a merger of the improving product quality framework [cf. chapter 4] with an approach that represents R&D's exhaustion externality [cf. chapter 8]. The result is a model that encompasses the case of excessively slow growth as well as the case of excessively fast growth. Thus, it provides a comprehensive representation of excessive growth cases. Considering realistic parameter values, we suggest that neither slowly growing economies nor fast growing economies experience excessive growth. In the light of the present model, laissez-faire growth in real world is most likely below the social optimum.

Chapter 10

Growth without Scale Effects

The total quantity of rents that successful entrepreneurs have in prospect increases with the size of the economy. That is because a larger population increases aggregate demand, sales per investment, and, thus, the profit prospects of investors. Hence, in larger economies, investment shares are higher, and, in turn, economic growth rates are higher. These are the scale effects of growth.

In the present model, these scale effects are suppressed by an imitation process. Here, a larger labor force induces, apart from a higher aggregate demand, an imitation process that leads to a broader differentiation of market niches. Since the aggregate demand and the amount of market niches increase at the same rate, the demand per market niche is constant. Moreover, sales per investment and profit prospects of investors remain unchanged. Hence, in this model, investment shares and economic growth rates do not depend on the scale of the economy.

With the present model, we relate to the recent debate on "growth with or without scale effects" [cf. Jones (1999)]. The literature on growth without scale effects may be divided into two strands. First, there is the strand of semi-endogenous growth models [Jones (1995a), Kortum (1997), Segerstrom (1998)]. Whereas these models capture the exhaustion effect of research, they propose a growth rate that is linearly dependent on the population growth rate. Second, there is the strand of endogenous non-scale growth models [cf. endogenous growth III, i.e. Aghion/Howitt (1998, ch. 3), Dinopoulos/Thompson (1998), Peretto (1998), Young (1998)]. Whereas these models feature an endogenously determined growth rate, they do not consider the exhaustion effect of research.

In this chapter, we set forth a non-scale growth model that combines the representation of R&D's exhaustion effect with an endogenously determined growth rate. The idea to dampen the scale effect by a scale-dependent imitation process is owed to the strand of recent endogenous non-scale growth models. Our model represents a two-dimensional product differentiation: whereas vertically, products are differentiated as the result of innovation, horizontally, products are differentiated due to imitation.

The model deviates from previous chapter's models in, first, the absence of scale effects, and, second, the capturing of population growth. Notice that in endogenous growth models with scale effects, a positive population growth rate implies exploding growth. The present model is a three-sector growth model, consisting of an intermediate goods sector, a final output sector, and an R&D sector [cf. figure 10.1].

In terms of the empirics, the absence of scale effects is far from being clear [cf. chapter 1]. Hence, the purpose of this chapter is rather to investigate what mechanics may dampen the evidence of growth' scale effects than to suggest that economic growth does not exhibit scale effects.

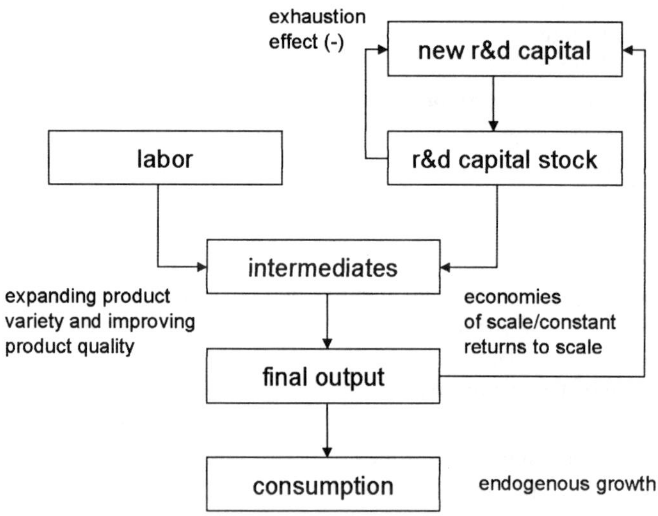

Figure 10.1: A schematic representation of the model.

This chapter is organized as follows. In section one, we present the technology of our model. Section two investigates the model's laissez-faire outcome. Section three yields the social planner's solution. Section four derives policy implications. Section five gives an discussion of the model.

10.1 Technology

10.1.1 Final Output

The technology of final output is given by

$$Y_t = \left[Q_t^{-[1-\alpha]} \int_0^{Q_t} A_{qt} x_{qt}^{\alpha} dq \right]^{\frac{\nu}{\alpha}} \tag{10.1}$$

where $0 < \alpha < 1$, and $\nu > 0$. x_{qt} denotes the quantity of intermediate q that is used in the production of final output at time t, where $q \in [0, Q_t]$. Hence, Q_t denotes the amount of differentiated intermediates. A_{qt} represents the level of technical knowledge that is used in the production of intermediate q: a higher A_{qt} increases the intermediate's product quality, i.e. the productivity of the specific intermediate in producing final output. α determines the elasticity of substitution of intermediates, i.e. $\epsilon = 1/[1-\alpha]$. ν determines the sign and the size of the economies of scale.

In the present subsection, we analyze the economy's horizontal product differentiation, i.e. the imitation process. The amount of horizontally differentiated intermediates, Q_t, depends on the size of the economy's population, L_t: a larger population features a more differentiated demand, i.e. $\partial Q_t / \partial L_t > 0$. In the present model, the process of horizontal product differentiation deviates substantially from the respective process in the models that we have investigated. There, the differentiation is the result of investment. It reflects a process of innovation, and the social return to product differentiation is positive. In the present model, product differentiation is induced by mere population growth. It represents a process of imitation where imitations just happen, i.e. in order to imitate, no resources have to be spent. Hence, it is suggestive to set the social return to product differentiation equal to zero.[1]

We specify the dependence of product variety on population size, i.e. $\partial Q_t / \partial L_t > 0$, in the following manner

$$Q_t = \frac{1}{\iota} L_t^{\nu}$$

where $\iota \equiv L_t^{\nu} / Q_t$ is a constant parameter. It reflects the economy's imitation propensity: for a lower ι, a population of same size induces a higher product diversity. The population growth rate is given by $\dot{L}_t / L_t = \gamma_L$. Notice that our formulation of product variety's evolution deviates from Aghion/Howitt (1998). There, product differentiation is assumed to follow a Poisson process.[2]

---

[1] Cf. Aghion/Howitt (1998), p. 106, footnote 24.

[2] If we were to obtain a semi-endogenous growth model, we would turn the constant parameter $\iota \equiv L_t^{\nu} / Q_t$ into the time-varying variable $\iota_t \equiv L_t^{\nu} / Q_t$. Moreover, we would describe the imitation process by $\dot{Q}_t = \varphi L_t^{\nu}$, where φ denotes the Poisson-distributed

The intermediate goods sector's technology is given by production functions $x_{qt} = l_{qt}/A_{qt}$, where $q \in [0, Q_t]$. l_{qt} denotes the labor force that is used in the production of intermediate q. The technology implies that the production of intermediates that incorporate a more recent technology, i.e. a higher A_{qt}, are more resource-intensively produced. That is, the higher the quality of a product is, the higher is its cost of production. Notice that the index q serves to count the intermediates firms, the differentiated intermediates themselves, and the niches of the intermediates market.

With regard to research externalities, we represent strong intersectoral spillovers. In our model, the qualities of the differentiated products increase in a symmetric manner. This implies that there is at every point in time a common level of technical knowledge across the economy, i.e. $A_{qt} = A_t$, where $q \in [0, Q_t]$. Accordingly, imposing symmetry on the sizes of the intermediates firms, the intermediates sector's technology may be written as $x_t = L_t/A_tQ_t$, whereas the final output production function (10.1) becomes[3]

$$Y_t = A_t^\eta L_t^\nu \tag{10.2}$$

where $\eta \equiv [1-\alpha]\nu/\alpha > 0$.[4]

10.1.2 R&D

In this subsection, we investigate the economy's vertical product differentiation, i.e. the innovation process. Recall that the emergence of a horizontally differentiated market niche q is the result of imitation. As soon as a new market niche has been opened up, inside this niche, an R&D race takes place. These R&D races, in turn, lead to the improvement of product qualities, i.e. to a vertical product differentiation. Whereas the imitation process does not contribute to aggregate growth, the innovation process does: it is the sustained flow of innovations that propels aggregate growth.

The R&D expenditure that is devoted to niche q is represented by e_{qt}. We assume that the sequence of innovations in market niche q is a random process that follows a Poisson distribution with parameter $\psi e_{qt}/A_{qt}^\eta$, where $\psi > 0$. Thus, for a given R&D expenditure flow, with each innovation, it takes longer to come up with a further innovation. Moreover, our formulation implies that other things equal, the stronger the positive externality of the newly invented product is – i.e. the higher ν, and, thus, the higher η –, the faster increases the expected cost of an innovation.[5]

---

imitation arrival rate. In the resulting semi-endogenous growth model, the differential equation that drives the variable ι_t is given by $\dot{\iota}_t = \nu\gamma_L\iota_t - \varphi\iota_t^2$. The variable ι_t converges asymptotically to its steady state value, given by $\iota = \nu\gamma_L/\varphi$. Thus, without population growth, i.e. $\gamma_L = 0$, the steady-state value of the variable ι_t is zero, i.e. $\iota = 0$.

[3] In subsection 10.2.1, we show that the identity of the sizes of the A_t intermediates firms is implied by their profit-maximization.

[4] Notice that $0 < \alpha < 1$ and $\nu \geq 0$ imply $\eta > 0$.

[5] The assumption according to which the exhaustion elasticity equals exactly η may

Apart from the innovation arrival rate, $\psi e_{qt}/A_{qt}^{\eta}$, the evolution of the technology parameter A_{qt} depends on the innovation size, $\delta > 0$. Hence, the expected value of the growth rate of intermediate q's product quality, $\dot{A}_{qt}/A_{qt}$, is given by the expected amount of innovation steps that occur in a unit-time interval, $\psi e_{qt}/A_{qt}^{\eta}$, premultiplied by the innovation size, δ, i.e.

$$E\left(\frac{\dot{A}_{qt}}{A_{qt}}\right) = \delta\psi\frac{e_{qt}}{A_{qt}^{\eta}} \tag{10.3}$$

Imposing symmetry on the sizes of the market niches, we obtain $e_{qt} = e_t = I_t/Q_t$.[6] That is, the R&D expenditure that is invested in the representative niche, e_t, decreases with an expanding product variety, i.e. with an increasing amount of market niches. Since there is an infinite number of market niches q, the economy performs an infinite number of research projects q, where $q \in [0, Q_t]$. Applying the symmetry of technical progress, i.e. $A_{qt} = A_t$, we find that the technology parameter A_t grows steadily, and the economy's innovation process is deterministic.[7]

Summing up the assumptions that concern the economy's R&D sector, we may formulate the subsequent production function

$$\frac{\dot{A}_t}{A_t} = \delta\psi\frac{I_t}{A_t^{\eta}Q_t} \tag{10.4}$$

Defining the saving rate $s_t \equiv I_t/Y_t$, we may rearrange terms as $\dot{A}_t/A_t = s_t\delta\iota\psi$. Accordingly, for a constant saving rate, the economy exhibits sustained innovation.[8] Moreover, a higher saving rate implies a higher innovation rate.

10.2 Laissez-faire Outcome

10.2.1 Intermediate Market

The flow profit rates of the suppliers of differentiated intermediates at time t are given by

$$\pi_{qt} = p_{x_q t}(x_{qt})x_{qt} - w_t A_{qt} x_{qt}$$

be perceived as stark. However, the assumption has to be drawn in order to make the economy exhibiting balanced growth. If the elasticity were above η, growth would peter out.

[6] In subsection 10.2.2, we show that the identity of the sizes of the A_t research niches follows from the absence of arbitrage opportunities in the capital market.

[7] The variance of the Poisson distributed random variable $\dot{A}_{qt}/A_{qt}$ is given by $var\left(\dot{A}_{qt}/A_{qt}\right) = \delta\psi e_{qt}/A_t^{\eta} = \delta\psi I_t/A_t^{\eta}$ [cf. equation (10.3)]. Hence, for an infinite number of research projects q, we obtain $var\left(\dot{A}_t/A_t\right) = 0$.

[8] Notice that the economy jumps immediately to the steady state.

where p_{x_qt} denotes the price of the intermediate q, where $q \in [0, Q_t]$. With $A_{qt} = A_t$, the profit-maximizing price is given by $p_{x_qt} = w_tA_t/\alpha$, implying a common intermediates price, i.e. $p_{x_qt} = p_{xt}$, a common intermediates output, i.e. $x_{qt} = x_t$, and a common production labor force, i.e. $l_{qt} = l_t$, where $i \in [0, 1]$.

The cost function that is dual to production function (10.1) is given by[9]

$$C_y(\{p_{x_it}\}_{i=0}^1, y_{jt}) = \left[\int_0^{Q_t} A_{qt}^{\frac{1}{1-\alpha}} p_{x_qt}^{-\left[\frac{\alpha}{1-\alpha}\right]} dq\right]^{-\left[\frac{1-\alpha}{\alpha}\right]} Q_t^{\frac{1-\alpha}{\alpha}} y_{jt}$$

where y_{jt} is the fictitious output of final output firm j that we would observe if there were no economies of scale. By symmetry, total cost can be stated as $C_Y(p_{xt}, L_t) = p_{xt}L_t/A_t$. Since revenue equals cost, the price of final output, p_{Yt}, is equal to aggregate cost over aggregate output. Thus, setting $p_{Yt} = 1$ for all t, we obtain the intermediates price[10]

$$p_{xt} = A_t^{\eta+1}L_t^{\nu-1} \tag{10.5}$$

Applying the intermediates price (10.5), and $x_t = L_t/A_tQ_t$, a modified profit equation which depends on the R&D capital stock and the ratio $\iota \equiv L_t^\nu/Q_t$ may be derived as

$$\pi_t = [1-\alpha]\iota A_t^\eta \tag{10.6}$$

We obtain an unambiguous result: quality improvements increase the profit rate of the representative intermediates firm.

10.2.2 Asset Market

With free entry into the market niches q, where $q \in [0, Q_t]$, the differentiated blueprints share a common value, i.e. $v_{qt} = v_t$. If the value of an innovation in the niche q were relatively high, i.e. $v_{qt} > v_t$, there would be a strong incentive for investors to turn research expenditure towards the respective market niche. Thereby, investors would drive down the value, until $v_{qt} = v_t$ would hold. Accordingly, in equilibrium, the sectoral R&D expenditures are at a common level, i.e. $e_{qt} = I_t/Q_t$, and the incumbent intermediates suppliers share a common replacement probability, given by $\psi e_{qt}/A_t^\eta = \psi I_t/A_t^\eta Q_t$, where $q \in [0, Q_t]$. Notice that, thus, we may indeed use production functions (10.2) and (10.4). Moreover, the value of the representative blueprint follows as

$$v_t = \int_t^\infty e^{-R_{ts}-\psi I_s[s-t]/A_t^\eta Q_t}\pi_s ds \tag{10.7}$$

[9] The cost function is the solution to the problem $\min\left\{\int_0^{Q_t} p_{x_qt}x_{jqt}dq + \mu\left[y_{jt} - \left[\int_0^{Q_t} Q_t^{-[1-\alpha]}A_{qt}x_{jqt}^\alpha dq\right]^{1/\alpha}\right]\right\}$, where x_{jqt} represents the amount of intermediate q that is used in final output firm j.

[10] Intermediates price (10.5) implies a wage rate given by $w_t = \alpha A_t^\eta L_t^{\nu-1}$.

where $R_{ts} \equiv \int_t^s r_u du$ denotes the cumulative discount factor from t to time s. Since the flow probability of an innovation is $\psi I_t / A_t^\eta Q_t$, in steady state, for a constant arrival rate, research expenditure has to grow at rate $\eta\gamma_A + \nu\gamma_L$.

With free entry into the production of intermediates, in an equilibrium with R&D performance, the value of the representative blueprint is equal to its price. That is, $v_t \leq p_{At}$, where p_{At} is the price of the representative blueprint. R&D capital's production function (10.4) yields price equation $p_{At} = A_t^\eta / \psi$. Hence, the free-entry condition follows as

$$v_t \leq \frac{1}{\psi} A_t^\eta \tag{10.8}$$

with equality whenever R&D investment is positive, i.e. $\dot{A}_t > 0$.

Thus, we may describe the two effects of R&D on the profitability of R&D – exhaustion effect and productivity effect – in terms of prices, considering blueprints' value [cf. free entry (10.8)] and the R&D-related profit rate [cf. equation (10.6)]. First, in the steady state, with an increasing product quality, the amount of final output that is required to improve product quality further grows at rate $\eta\gamma_A$. Hence, the value of a blueprint grows at this rate, too [cf. free entry (10.8)]. This is the exhaustion effect of R&D. Second, due to R&D, the economy's product quality improves. An increasing product quality boosts the productivity of every differentiated intermediate. Thus, the price of a differentiated intermediate increases at rate $[\eta + 1]\,\gamma_A$ [cf. equation (10.5)], and the R&D-related profit rises at rate $\eta\gamma_A$ [cf. equation (10.6)]. This is the productivity effect of R&D. Since in the steady state, both the value of a blueprint and the R&D-related profit grow at the same rate, the two effects cancel out, leaving the dividend π_t / v_t unaffected. Accordingly, the accumulation of R&D capital has no impact on the profitability of R&D investment.

10.2.3 Steady-State Growth

The solution to the intertemporal utility maximization problem is the Keynes/Ramsey rule, $\dot{c}_t / c_t = \sigma [r_t - \rho]$, where $\sigma, \rho > 0$. Differentiating equation (10.7) with respect to time, and dividing the resulting equation by the value of a blueprint, we obtain no-arbitrage condition $\pi_t / v_t + \dot{v}_t / v_t - \psi I_t / A_t^\eta Q_t = r_t$. Substituting for r_t in the Keynes/Ramsey rule yields the per-capita laissez-faire steady-state growth rate

$$\gamma = \frac{\sigma \{[1-\alpha]\,\psi\iota - \rho\}}{1 - \sigma\left[1 - \frac{1}{\delta\eta}\right]} \tag{10.9}$$

where for a positive growth rate, i.e. $\gamma > 0$, first, $[1-\alpha]\,\psi\iota > \rho$ must hold, and, second, $1/\sigma > 1 - 1/\delta\eta$ must be met. Furthermore, for a bounded attainable utility, $\rho > [\sigma - 1]\,\gamma / \sigma$ is required.[11] Laissez-faire growth increases

[11] Notice that the saving rate is readily derived as $s = \gamma / [\delta\iota\psi\eta]$.

with a higher innovation size, a lower elasticity of substitution of intermediates, higher economies of scale, a lower rate of time preference and a higher intertemporal elasticity of substitution. Moreover, growth accelerates for a higher ι, i.e. a lower imitation propensity.[12]

In the present model, the per-capita laissez-faire growth rate is independent from the size of the labor force, L_t [cf. equation (10.9)]. Hence, we deviate from endogenous growth models that feature scale effects. Moreover, in our model, the per-capita laissez-faire growth rate is not affected by the population growth rate, $\gamma_L \equiv \dot{L}_t/L_t$. This finding differentiates the present model from the literature on semi-endogenous growth. There, the steady-state growth rate depends linearly on the population growth rate. That dependence implies that without population growth, the long-run growth rate of the economy is necessarily zero. In our model, the long-run growth rate to be positive does not require a positive population growth rate.[13]

10.3 Social Planner's Solution

The social planner's problem is to max U_t subject to the technology constraint $\dot{A}_t = \delta\iota\psi A_t^{-[\eta-1]} L_t^{-\nu} [A_t^\eta L_t^\nu - c_t L_t]$. The social optimum steady-state growth rate is readily derived as

$$\gamma_S = \sigma \{\delta\iota\psi\eta + [\nu - 1]\gamma_L - \rho\} \tag{10.10}$$

where for a positive growth rate, i.e. $\gamma_S > 0$, $\delta\iota\psi\eta + [\nu - 1]\gamma_L > \rho$ has to be fulfilled.

How does laissez-faire growth compare to social optimum growth? Apart from the five externalities that we have investigated before – exhaustion effect, business stealing effect, product improvement effect, monopoly distortion effect, and network effect – we detect a further externality, which we refer to as the *dynamic network effect.* The size of this effect increases for stronger economies of scale, ν, and a higher population growth rate, γ_L.

---

[12] If we were to have a semi-endogenous growth model, where, in the long run, ι converges to $\nu\gamma_L/\varphi$, we would find that laissez-faire growth increases for a stronger network externality, a higher population growth rate, and a lower imitation arrival rate.

[13] In our model, the growth rate of aggregate output is affected by the population growth rate. Recall that the economy's total output is given by $Y_t = A_t^\eta L_t^\nu = c_t L_t$ [cf. equation (10.2)]. Accordingly, the laissez-faire steady-state growth rate of aggregate output follows as $\gamma_Y = \gamma + \gamma_L$. That is, a higher population growth rate, γ_L, increases the growth rate of aggregate output, γ_Y. Moreover, the per-capita laissez-faire growth rate γ may be stated as $\gamma = \eta\gamma_A + [\nu - 1]\gamma_L$.

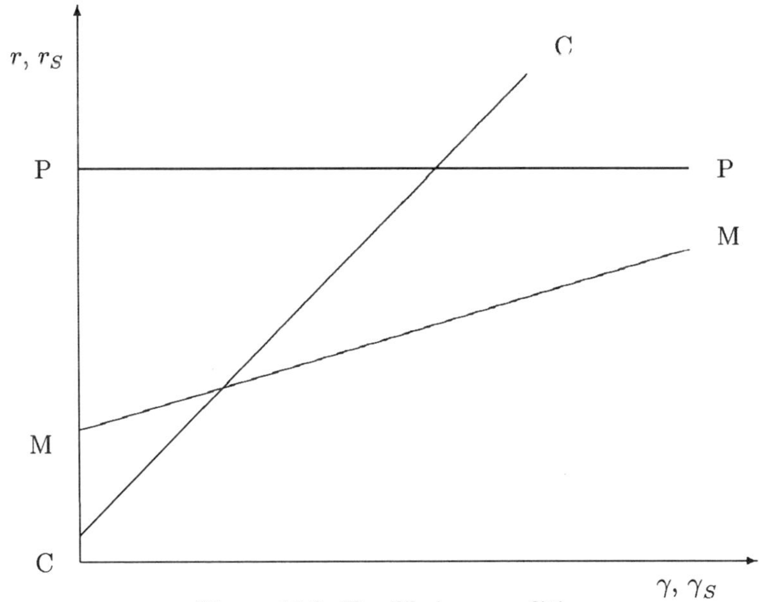

Figure 10.2: Equilibrium conditions.

For our investigation of the desirability of laissez-faire, we utilize the steady-state equilibrium conditions. Both decentralized solution and social planner's solution involve condition (CC), given by

$$r = r_S = \rho + \frac{1}{\sigma}\gamma \tag{CC}$$

where r_S denotes the social optimum steady-state return on capital. The CC graph is upward-sloping in γ-r-space [cf. figure 10.2]. For laissez-faire, the equilibrium condition (MM) follows as

$$r = [1-\alpha]\iota\psi + \left[1 - \frac{1}{\delta\eta}\right]\gamma \tag{MM}$$

Social planner's equilibrium condition (PP) is implied by social optimum growth rate (10.10) as

$$r_S = \delta\iota\psi\eta + [\nu - 1]\gamma_L \tag{PP}$$

Thus, the MM graph's slope is ambiguous, and the PP graph is horizontal. Equations (CC), (MM), and (PP) suggest that whereas we may construe cases of excessive growth, they are probably not real world phenomena [cf. figure 10.2].[14]

[14] The analysis is analogous to the investigation in the model of the preceding chapter.

10.4 Policy Implications

We introduce a profit tax, t_π, a tax on R&D investment, t_I, and a lump-sum tax, T. Taxes obey the condition $-1 < t_\pi, t_I < 1$. The after-tax steady-state rate of return is readily derived as

$$r_T = \left[\frac{1-t_\pi}{1+t_I}\right][1-\alpha]\iota\psi + \left[1-\frac{1}{\delta\eta}\right]\gamma \tag{TT}$$

Optimum combinations $[t_\pi, t_I]^*$ shift the MM line in a way so that it goes through the intersection of the CC line with the PP line [cf. figure 10.2].

To keep expressions handy, in the remainder of this chapter, we base the derivation of the optimum policy measures on the assumption of a logarithmic instantaneous utility function, i.e. $\sigma = 1$. Hence, the optimum combinations $[t_\pi, t_I]^*$ fulfill the subsequent equation

$$t_\pi = 1 - [1+t_I]\left[\frac{1}{1-\alpha} + \frac{[\nu-1]\,\gamma_L + [\delta\eta - 1]\,\rho}{[1-\alpha]\,\delta\iota\psi\eta}\right]$$

where $\delta > \delta_L = \{\rho - [\nu-1]\,\gamma_L\}/\eta\,[\iota\psi+\rho]$. Hence, for $t_I = 0$, the optimum profit tax is given by

$$t_\pi^* = -\left[\frac{\alpha}{1-\alpha} + \frac{[\nu-1]\,\gamma_L + [\delta\eta-1]\,\rho}{[1-\alpha]\,\delta\iota\psi\eta}\right] \tag{10.11}$$

Accordingly, for $t_\pi = 0$, the optimum R&D tax follows as

$$t_I^* = -\left[\frac{\alpha\delta\iota\psi\eta + [\nu-1]\,\gamma_L + [\delta\eta-1]\,\rho}{\delta\iota\psi\eta + [\nu-1]\,\gamma_L + [\delta\eta-1]\,\rho}\right] \tag{10.12}$$

Hence, for $\delta \longrightarrow \delta_L$, the optimum taxes (10.11) and (10.12) turn positive.

10.5 Discussion

In this chapter, we present a growth model that combines the capturing of R&D's exhaustion effect with the representation of an endogenously determined growth rate. Moreover, the model describes growth without scale effects, and, hence, allows for a growing labor force.

The model captures an innovation and an imitation process. The innovation process leads to an improving product quality. The imitation process implies an expanding product variety, i.e. a diversification of market niches. Since the innovation process features an exhaustion effect, and the pace of the imitation process is linked to the size of the population, we obtain the result that even with growing R&D expenditure and a growing population, the rate of innovation both at the level of market niches and at the aggregate level does not increase. Particularly, in the present model, the scale effect is eliminated by the utilization of a scale-dependent imitation process.

Again, we obtain two cases of excessive growth: a case of excessively slow growth and a case of excessively fast growth.

Part V

Two-Stage Input Differentiation

Chapter 11

R&D and Physical Capital

The capability of R&D to differentiate products has been acknowledged, at the latest, since Paul Romer presented his seminal paper on "Growth based on increasing returns due to specialization" at the AEA meeting of December 1986.[1] His application of Dixit/Stiglitz' imperfect competition to economic growth triggered the vast body of literature on R&D-based growth [cf. endogenous growth II, endogenous growth III]. R&D-based growth models suggest that long-run growth is determined primarily by the amount of R&D that is undertaken.

This chapter considers the empirical phenomenon that product differentiation is not restricted to investment in R&D. Apart from R&D's capability to differentiate products, our model represents the capability of physical capital investment to differentiate products, too. Entrepreneurs may invest either in R&D or in physical capital. Thus, the economy exhibits a two-stage product differentiation. The model sheds light on the complementarity of capital accumulation and innovation. It suggests that growth is more than mere R&D. Hence, the paper shares its motivation – extending product-differentiating investment beyond R&D – with the models of part II. There, entrepreneurs invest in a homogenous capital stock, and the economy exhibits a one-stage product differentiation. The present model deviates in its separate treatment of R&D and physical capital investment.

Hence, with the present model, we address all four points of critique that we have raised in our discussion of the EPV model [cf. chapter 3]. First, the model leaves the narrow research focus of R&D-based growth models. Here, physical capital accumulation is growth-affecting, too. Second, physical capital's capability to differentiate products, and, in turn, to provide monopoly power, is considered. Third, the model represents an economy in which imperfectly competitive markets are present in both the production of consumption goods and capital goods. Fourth, the model shows an economy

[1] Cf. Romer (1987).

in which research is assumed to be, consistently with empirical studies, rather capital-intensive than labor-intensive.

The present model has been inspired by both theoretical and empirical work. On the theoretical side, many authors – e.g. Schmookler (1966) – express the view that capital accumulation and innovation are complementary processes, and that a proper understanding of this complementarity may contribute to the understanding of economic growth. Bental/Peled (1996) employ a search theoretic approach to investigate the feedback between physical capital accumulation and technical change. In their model, phases of investment and phases of research alternate.

On the empirical side, there is evidence for the complementarity of R&D and physical capital. Mohnen (1990) surveys studies on R&D and productivity growth. Appraising the literature, he concludes that "R&D and physical capital are generally estimated to be complements" [p. 27]. More recently, Aghion/Howitt (1998) stress the importance of the complementarity of capital accumulation and innovation, stating that "neither process could take place in the long run without the other" [p. 99].

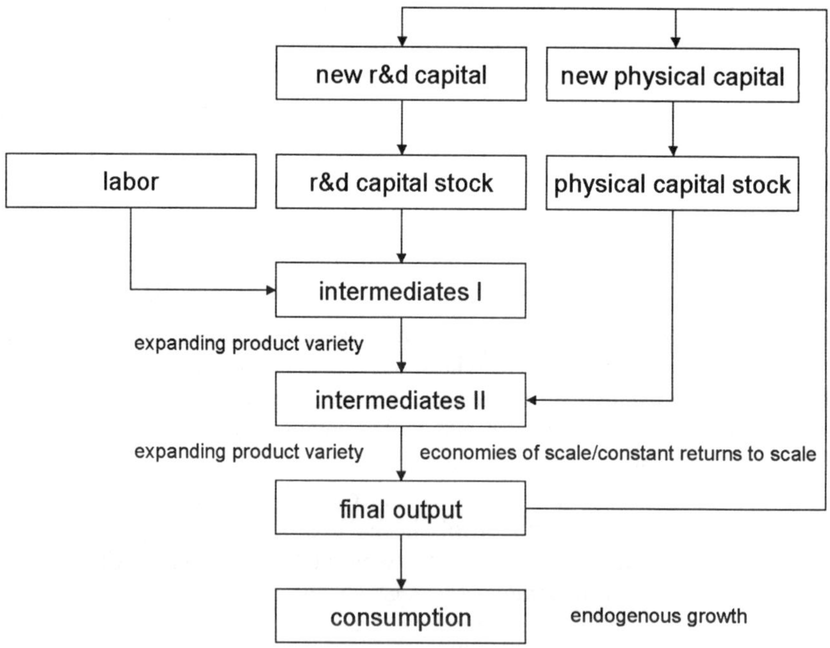

Figure 11.1: A schematic representation of the model.

The model presented here is a five-sector growth model, consisting of two intermediate goods sectors, a final output sector, an R&D sector, and a physical capital good sector [cf. figure 11.1]. The production of final output takes three stages. At the first stage, intermediates I are produced. Inputs are labor and R&D capital. At the second stage, intermediates II are produced. Inputs are intermediates I and physical capital. At the third stage, with the use of intermediates II, final output is produced. Final output can either be consumed or transformed into capital – either R&D capital or physical capital.

The three-stage production process that the model represents may be illustrated as follows. Software firms are at the first stage of the economy. Apart from labor services, the software firms necessitate blueprints as inputs. The software firms purchase these blueprints from the economy's R&D sector. At the second stage of the economy, we find factories. Their input is software as well as hardware. Whereas the software comes from the software firms, the hardware is provided by the economy's capital good sector. The factories produce differentiated goods. At the third stage, these differentiated goods are utilized to produce the economy's final output.

This chapter is organized as follows. In section one, we present the economy's technology. Section two investigates the laissez-faire outcome. Section three yields the social planner's solution. Section four derives policy implications. Section five summarizes the essential results of the model.

11.1 Technology

11.1.1 Final Output

We will present the production technologies of the economy's five sectors one after the other. First, we turn to the final output sector. Final output Y_t is produced by an infinite set of firms j, the amount of which is normalized to unity, i.e. $j \in [0, 1]$. The technology of the final output sector is given by the following CES production function

$$Y_t = \left[\int_0^{K_t} z_{kt}^{\beta} dk \right]^{\frac{\nu}{\beta}} \tag{11.1}$$

where $0 < \beta < 1$, and $\nu \geq 1$. The inputs into the production of final output are the differentiated intermediates II, z_{kt}, where $k \in [0, K_t]$. The parameter β determines the elasticity of substitution of intermediates II, i.e. $\epsilon_z = [1 - \beta] / \beta$. $\nu \geq 1$ implies that the economy may experience positive economies of scale.

The second sector we present is the second-stage intermediates sector. It takes a unit of physical capital to open up an intermediates II production unit. The firm k faces the following CES production function

$$z_{kt} = \left[\int_0^{A_t} x_{kat}^{\alpha} da \right]^{\frac{1}{\alpha}} \tag{11.2}$$

where $0 < \alpha < 1$, and $k \in [0, K_t]$. The inputs into the production of intermediates II are the differentiated intermediates I. Their index is a, where $a \in [0, A_t]$. The quantity of intermediate a that is used to produce intermediate k is denoted by x_{kat}. The elasticity of substitution of intermediates I, i.e. $\epsilon_x = [1 - \alpha] / \alpha$, depends on the parameter α.

Equations (11.1) and (11.2) may be combined to the subsequent final output production function

$$Y_t = \left[\int_0^{K_t} \left[\int_0^{A_t} x_{kat}^{\alpha} da \right]^{\frac{\beta}{\alpha}} dk \right]^{\frac{\nu}{\beta}}$$

The third sector we present is the first-stage intermediates sector. A unit of R&D capital constitutes an intermediates I production unit. The one-to-one production functions are given by $x_{at} = L_{at}$, where $a \in [0, A_t]$. The output of production unit a – which is denoted by x_{at} – depends on the labor force L_{at} that it employs: one unit of labor is transformed into one unit of the respective intermediate.

Notice that A_t and K_t allow each for three interpretations. With regard to A_t, three interpretations are suggested. First, A_t represents the amount of intermediates I production units. Second, since A_t denotes the amount of production units that produce differentiated intermediates I, it denotes the amount of differentiated intermediates I itself. Third, since it takes a blueprint to open up an intermediates I production unit, we may interpret the amount of units, A_t, as the size of the economy's accumulated R&D capital stock. Turning, to K_t, we obtain three interpretations, too: amount of intermediates II production units, amount of differentiated intermediates II, and size of the accumulated physical capital stock.

In the remainder of this subsection, we impose full employment and symmetry.[2] Thus, we obtain the following intermediates I production function[3]

$$x_{At} = \frac{L}{A_t} \tag{11.3}$$

where x_{At} denotes the output of the representative intermediates I production unit. Equation (11.2) allows to give the subsequent intermediates II

[2] In subsection 11.2.1, we show that intermediates firms' profit maximization implies identical market shares at production process' first stage, respectively at production process' second stage.

[3] The index' capital letter denotes that there is one common output quantity for all A_t intermediates I production units. In the remainder, for further symmetric quantities, the notation will be analogous.

production function

$$z_{Kt} = A_t^{\frac{1-\alpha}{\alpha}} \frac{L}{K_t} \tag{11.4}$$

where z_{Kt} denotes the output of a representative intermediates II production unit. Hence, the productivity of intermediates II production units in terms of the labor force that is incorporated in intermediates I increases with an expanding product variety of intermediate I.

Equations (11.1) and (11.4) imply the subsequent final output production function

$$Y_t = \left[A_t^{\frac{1-\alpha}{\alpha}} K_t^{\frac{1-\beta}{\beta}} L \right]^{\nu} \tag{11.5}$$

We assume that $[1-\alpha]/\alpha + [1-\beta]/\beta = 1/\nu$. Thus, the economy is characterized by a trade-off: the higher the substitutability between intermediates is, the stronger are the economies of scale, i.e. the more alike the intermediates are, the stronger are the network effects. In other word: when the goods that are produced within the economy differ very much, the positive externalities spilling from one firm to the other are relatively weak.[4] We define $\eta \equiv [1-\alpha]\nu/\alpha = 1 - [1-\beta]\nu/\beta$, where $0 < \eta < 1$.[5] Restating production function (11.5) yields

$$Y_t = A_t^{\eta} K_t^{1-\eta} L^{\nu} \tag{11.6}$$

11.1.2 R&D and Capital Good

The fourth sector we present is the R&D sector. We assume that the transformation of final output into R&D capital A_t is proportional, but not necessarily one-to-one. Thus,

$$\dot{A}_t = \frac{1}{\omega_A} u_t I_t \tag{11.7}$$

where ω_A is R&D unit input requirement. I_t represents total investment, i.e. $I_t \equiv Y_t - c_t L$, where $I_t \geq 0$. The part of total investment which is spent on R&D is denoted by u_t, where $0 \leq u_t \leq 1$. Hence, apart from imposing a constraint of nonnegative total investment, we rule out negative R&D investment, respectively negative physical capital investment.[6]

[4] The assumption according to which $[1-\alpha]/\alpha + [1-\beta]/\beta = 1/\nu$ may be perceived as stark, but it is necessary to make the economy exhibiting balanced growth. If $[1-\alpha]/\alpha + [1-\beta]/\beta < 1/\nu$ were to hold, growth would peter out.

[5] Notice that $0 < \alpha < 1$, $0 < \beta < 1$, and $\nu \geq 1$ imply $0 < \eta < 1$.

[6] Notice that for $\omega_A \neq 1$, R&D investment is not equal to the increase in R&D capital stock. ω_A may be interpreted as a measure for the efficiency of an economy's R&D laboratories.

The fifth sector we present is the physical capital good sector. The economy's physical capital stock is denoted by K_t. Again, we assume a proportional production technology. It is given by

$$\dot{K}_t = \frac{1}{\omega_K} [1 - u_t] I_t \tag{11.8}$$

where ω_K is physical capital unit input requirement. $[1 - u_t]$ is the part of total investment which is spent on investment in physical capital.[7]

11.2 Laissez-faire Outcome

11.2.1 Input Markets

There are two markets which are imperfectly competitive: the market for intermediates I and the market for intermediates II. We will investigate the profit maximizations of both the suppliers of intermediates I and the suppliers of intermediates II.

First, we turn to the intermediates I sector. Firms' profit rates at time t are given by

$$\pi_{at} = p_{x_a t}(x_{at})x_{at} - AC_{x_a t}x_{at} \tag{11.9}$$

where $p_{x_a t}$ is the price of the intermediate a, and $AC_{x_a t}$ is the average cost that firm a faces, where $a \in [0, A_t]$. The suppliers maximize their flow profit rates by charging

$$p_{x_a t} = \frac{MC_{x_a t}}{\alpha} \tag{11.10}$$

where $MC_{x_a t}$ is the marginal cost that firm a faces. Since $MC_{x_a t} = AC_{x_a t} = w_t$, we obtain $p_{xt} = w_t/\alpha$.[8] Hence, the output quantities of all A_t production units are of same size. Thus, we may indeed use production function (11.3).

Second, we investigate the profit maximization of intermediates II suppliers. Firms' profit rates at time t are given by

$$\pi_{kt} = p_{z_k t}(z_{kt})z_{kt} - AC_{z_k t}z_{kt} \tag{11.11}$$

where $p_{z_k t}$ is the price of the intermediate k, and $AC_{z_k t}$ is the average cost that firm k faces, where $k \in [0, K_t]$. The suppliers maximize their flow profit rates by charging

$$p_{z_k t} = \frac{MC_{z_k t}}{\beta}$$

[7]Notice that for $\omega_K \neq 1$, investment in physical capital is not equal to the increase in physical capital stock. ω_K may be interpreted as a measure for the efficiency of an economy's capital good production. Moreover, production functions (11.7) and (11.8) imply $Y_t = c_t L + \omega_A \dot{A}_t + \omega_K \dot{K}_t$ as the market-clearing condition for final output.

[8]The missing of index a denotes that there is one common price for all A_t differentiated intermediates I. In the remainder, for further symmetric quantities, prices, and costs, the notation will be analogous.

where $MC_{z_k t}$ is the marginal cost that firm k faces. Since the individual firm cannot exploit economies of scale, marginal cost equals average cost, and this cost is the same to all K_t firms, i.e. $MC_{z_k t} = AC_{z_k t} = AC_{zt}$. Thus, $p_{zt} = AC_{zt}/\beta$. Accordingly, the output quantities of all K_t production units are of same size, and, in the remainder, we may use production functions (11.4), (11.5), and (11.6).

In order to determine the evolution of prices, we derive the cost functions of the final output sector and the intermediates II sector. First, we turn to the final output sector. The cost function C_y which is dual to the production function of a final output firm j, where $j \in [0,1]$, is given by[9]

$$C_y(\{p_{z_k t}\}_{k=0}^{K_t}, y_{jt}) = \left[\int_0^{K_t} p_{z_k t}^{-\left[\frac{\beta}{1-\beta}\right]} dk\right]^{-\left[\frac{1-\beta}{\beta}\right]} y_{jt}$$

where y_{jt} is the fictitious output of firm j that we would observe if the economy exhibited no scale effect. By symmetry, total cost C_Y may be stated as

$$C_Y(p_{zt}, L) = p_{zt} A_t^{\frac{1-\alpha}{\alpha}} L \tag{11.12}$$

The average cost of producing final output is aggregate cost (11.12) over aggregate output (11.6), i.e.[10]

$$AC_{Yt} = p_{zt} A_t^{-\left\{\eta - \left[\frac{1-\alpha}{\alpha}\right]\right\}} K_t^{-[1-\eta]} L^{-[\nu-1]} \tag{11.13}$$

Since perfect competition prevails on the market for final output, total revenue equals total cost, and price equals average cost, i.e. $p_{Yt} = AC_{Yt}$. Solving for p_{zt}, and setting $p_{Yt} = 1$, for all t,[11] yields the intermediates price

$$p_{zt} = A_t^{\eta - \left[\frac{1-\alpha}{\alpha}\right]} K_t^{1-\eta} L^{\nu-1} \tag{11.14}$$

---

[9] The cost function is the solution to the problem $\min\left\{\int_0^{K_t} p_{z_k t} z_{jkt} dk + \mu\left[y_{jt} - \left[\int_0^{K_t} z_{jkt}^{\beta} dk\right]^{1/\beta}\right]\right\}$, where z_{jkt} represents the amount of intermediate k that is used in final output firm j.

[10] The result that the average cost of producing final output decreases with an expanding product variety of intermediate II [cf. cost function (11.13)] corresponds to the finding that the productivity in producing final output increases with an expanding product variety of intermediate II [cf. production function (11.6)]. The dependence of the average cost (11.13) on R&D capital stock and labor force hinges on a mere scale effect.

[11] The choice of numéraire is arbitrary. Taking p_{Yt} as numéraire yields, as long as physical capital is accumulated, a steady rise of both intermediates prices and the wage rate, i.e. an inflationary effect. If we took p_{xt} or p_{zt} as numéraire, we would obtain a steady fall in p_{Yt}, i.e. a deflation in the price of final output. With either choice, an expanding variety of intermediate II lowers the relative price between final output and both types of intermediates.

Second, we investigate the intermediates II sector. The cost function C_z which is dual to production function (11.2) is given by[12]

$$C_z(\{p_{x_a t}\}_{a=0}^{A_t}, z_{kt}) = \left[\int_0^{A_t} p_{x_a t}^{-\left[\frac{\alpha}{1-\alpha}\right]} da\right]^{-\left[\frac{1-\alpha}{\alpha}\right]} z_{kt}$$

By symmetry, total cost C_Z may be stated as

$$C_Z(p_{xt}, L) = p_{xt} L \qquad (11.15)$$

The average cost of producing intermediates II is derived by dividing aggregate cost (11.15) by aggregate output [cf. equation (11.4)]. We obtain[13]

$$AC_{zt} = p_{xt} A_t^{-\left[\frac{1-\alpha}{\alpha}\right]} \qquad (11.16)$$

The suppliers of intermediates II put a mark-up $1/\beta$ on average cost (11.16). Hence,

$$p_{zt} = \frac{1}{\beta} p_{xt} A_t^{-\left[\frac{1-\alpha}{\alpha}\right]} \qquad (11.17)$$

Solving equation (11.17) for the price of intermediates I yields

$$p_{xt} = \beta p_{zt} A_t^{\frac{1-\alpha}{\alpha}} \qquad (11.18)$$

Inserting equation (11.14) into equation (11.18) gives

$$p_{xt} = \beta A_t^{\eta} K_t^{1-\eta} L^{\nu-1} \qquad (11.19)$$

Applying $w_t = \alpha p_{xt}$, we obtain the subsequent wage rate

$$w_t = \alpha\beta A_t^{\eta} K_t^{1-\eta} L^{\nu-1} \qquad (11.20)$$

How do the relative prices depend on the market powers of suppliers of intermediates I and II? Price equation (11.14) shows that the price of intermediates II is not affected by suppliers' markups. Price equation (11.19) implies that the larger the markup of intermediates II suppliers is, the lower is the price of intermediates I. Wage equation (11.20) suggests that the larger the markups of suppliers of intermediates I and II are, the lower is the wage rate. Part of this result is as expected: an increase in the markup of intermediates

[12]The cost function is the solution to the problem $\min\left\{\int_0^{A_t} p_{x_a t} x_{kat} da + \mu\left[z_{kt} - \left[\int_0^{A_t} x_{kat}^{\alpha} da\right]^{1/\alpha}\right]\right\}$.

[13]The result that the average cost of producing intermediates II decreases with an expanding product variety of intermediate I [cf. cost function (11.16)] corresponds to the finding that the productivity in producing intermediates II increases with an expanding product variety of intermediate I [cf. production function (11.4)].

II suppliers raises the relative price of intermediates II to intermediates I as well as to labor service. Furthermore, an increase in the markup of intermediates I suppliers raises the relative price of intermediates I to labor service. What might come as a surprise is the finding that an increase in the markup of intermediates I suppliers does not raise the relative price of intermediates I to intermediates II.

To conclude: while physical capital investors (suppliers of intermediates II) are able to influence the relative price of intermediates II to intermediates I, p_{zt}/p_{xt}, R&D investors (suppliers of intermediates I) lack this ability. The reason for this asymmetry is the sequence of input differentiation in our model. Since the differentiation due to physical capital investment comes on the production process' second stage, physical capital investors have the capability to raise the relative price of intermediates II to intermediates I by putting a markup on their marginal cost p_{xt}. In turn, since R&D-related input differentiation is on the first stage of the production process, R&D investors are unable to influence this relative price. Actually, it is this asymmetry in the pricing capabilities that contributes to the inefficiency of laissez-faire that we will investigate shortly.

How does the evolution of prices depend on the accumulation of R&D capital and physical capital? In order to abstract from any scale effect, we assume for a moment that constant returns to scale were to prevail, i.e. $\nu = 1$. Price equation (11.14) shows that the price of intermediates II increases with the accumulation of physical capital. Price equation (11.19) implies that the price of intermediates I increases with the accumulation of both R&D capital and physical capital. The wage rate's evolution is analogous to the price of intermediates I's evolution [cf. wage rate (11.20)].

The prices that we have just derived suggest a revisit of our flow profits. First, we restate the flow profit of the representative intermediates I firm. Its profit rate is given by [cf. equations (11.9) and (11.10)][14]

$$\pi_{At} = [1 - \alpha] p_{xt} x_{At} \tag{11.21}$$

The profit of a representative intermediates I firm increases with its market power and with the intermediate I's price. An increase in the amount of varieties of intermediate II has an unambiguous positive effect on profit (11.21) through an increase in intermediates I price [cf. price equation (11.19)]. In turn, an increase in the amount of varieties of intermediate I itself has two opposite effects on profit (11.21). First, a positive productivity effect: it follows from the induced rise in the intermediates' price [cf. price equation (11.19)]. Second, a negative market-saturation effect: the intermediate's share of a market the size of which is given by the non-growing population L is negatively related to the amount of intermediates [cf. production function (11.3)].

[14]The index' capital letter denotes that there is one common profit rate for all A_t intermediates I production units. In the remainder, for further symmetric profit rates, the notation will be analogous.

To determine the sign of the overall effect, we insert equations (11.3) and (11.19) into profit equation (11.21). We obtain the following profit equation which depends only on labor and the stocks of R&D capital and physical capital.

$$\pi_{At} = [1-\alpha]\beta \left[\frac{K_t}{A_t}\right]^{1-\eta} L^{\nu} \tag{11.22}$$

Profit equation (11.22) shows that the negative market-saturation effect dominates the positive productivity effect. Hence, the overall effect of the launch of an additional intermediate I on profits of intermediates I suppliers is negative. Equation (11.22) implies that the flow profit of an intermediates I firm increases with the relative abundance of physical capital to R&D capital. With production function (11.6) follows

$$\pi_{At} = [1-\alpha]\beta A_t^{-1} Y_t \tag{11.23}$$

Second, the flow profit of the representative intermediates II firm may be written as [cf. equation (11.11)]

$$\pi_{Kt} = [1-\beta] p_{zt} z_{Kt} \tag{11.24}$$

The profit of a representative intermediates II firm increases with its market power and with the intermediate II's price. An increase in the amount of varieties of intermediate I has an unambiguously positive effect on profit (11.24). While the intermediates II price is – apart from a positive scale effect – not affected [cf. price equation (11.14)], the quantity of intermediates II that is produced per production unit rises [cf. production function (11.4)].[15] In turn, an increase in the number of varieties of intermediate II itself has two opposite effects on profit (11.24). First, a positive productivity effect [cf. price equation (11.14)]. Second, a negative market-saturation effect [cf. production function (11.4)].

By symmetry, we insert equations (11.4) and (11.14) into profit rate (11.24). The profit rate changes to

$$\pi_{Kt} = [1-\beta] \left[\frac{A_t}{K_t}\right]^{\eta} L^{\nu} \tag{11.25}$$

Profit equation (11.25) shows that the overall effect of the launch of an additional intermediate II on profits of intermediates II suppliers is negative. Equation (11.25) implies that the flow profit of an intermediates II firm increases with the relative abundance of R&D capital to physical capital. Considering production function (11.6) yields

$$\pi_{Kt} = [1-\beta] K_t^{-1} Y_t \tag{11.26}$$

[15] To state it differently: an expanding product variety of intermediate I raises the intermediates II profit even when constant returns to scale prevail since the expanding variety lowers the intermediates II average cost [cf. cost function (11.16)].

Production function (11.6) allows furthermore to restate wage rate (11.20) as

$$w_t = \alpha\beta L^{-1} Y_t \tag{11.27}$$

Two things are remarkable. First, profits (11.22) and (11.25) illustrate neatly the complementarity of physical capital accumulation and innovation. Investment in physical capital stimulates innovation by raising the profits of intermediates I suppliers, just as innovation stimulates investment in physical capital by raising the profits of intermediates II suppliers. Without physical capital accumulation, diminishing profits to intermediates I suppliers would choke off innovation, and without innovation, the diminishing profits to intermediates II suppliers would choke off investment in physical capital. In order to prevent profits (11.22) and (11.25) from decreasing (respectively increasing), the R&D capital stock and the physical capital stock have to grow at the same rate.

Second, the factor's shares of gross national product are independent of the sizes of R&D capital stock, physical capital stock, and labor force: $[1-\alpha]\beta$ depicts R&D capital's income share, $[1-\beta]$ is physical capital's income share, and $\alpha\beta$ denotes labor's income share [cf. equations (11.23), (11.26), and (11.27)].

11.2.2 Asset Market

In equilibrium, investment activity implies that the value of a unit of R&D capital and the value a unit of physical capital equal the respective prices. If the values were to fall below the prices, investment would stop. If the values were to be above the prices, with free entry, an unbounded demand for capital would arise. Applying R&D capital's production function (11.7), the condition for a free entry into the production of intermediates I follows as

$$v_{At} \leq \omega_A \tag{11.28}$$

with equality whenever $\dot{A}_t > 0$. v_{At} denotes the value of a blueprint. Analogous reasoning yields a condition for a free entry into the production of intermediates II. Physical capital's production function (11.8) implies free-entry condition

$$v_{Kt} \leq \omega_K \tag{11.29}$$

The condition must hold with equality, if there is to be some aggregate physical capital investment at all, i.e. if $\dot{K}_t > 0$. v_{Kt} denotes the value of a unit of physical capital.

An individual that is willing to postpone consumption may choose from three investment opportunities. First, she may purchase a unit of R&D capital, i.e. a blueprint. Second, she may purchase a unit of physical capital.

Third, she may purchase a bond which yields interest rate r_t. Our setup implies perfect foresight. Thus, we rule out speculative bubbles. It is apparent that in steady-state equilibrium, for no-arbitrage's sake, the return on a bond has to equal both the return on a blueprint and the return on a unit of physical capital. First, we investigate the return on a blueprint. It depends on two components: the profit that accrues to a blueprint, π_{At}, and the change in the blueprint's value, $\dot{v}_{At}$. Thus,

$$\frac{\pi_{At}}{v_{At}} + \frac{\dot{v}_{At}}{v_{At}} = r_t \tag{11.30}$$

Second, we address the return on a share of physical capital, for which we derive an analogous result, i.e.

$$\frac{\pi_{Kt}}{v_{Kt}} + \frac{\dot{v}_{Kt}}{v_{Kt}} = r_t \tag{11.31}$$

We proceed by equating no-arbitrage conditions (11.30) and (11.31). We insert profits (11.23) and (11.26) as well as free-entry conditions (11.28) and (11.29). Thus, the laissez-faire steady-state allocation of savings on R&D capital and physical capital follows as

$$\frac{A_t}{K_t} = \frac{\omega_K}{\omega_A}\frac{[1-\alpha]\beta}{1-\beta} \equiv \bar{\kappa} \tag{11.32}$$

The laissez-faire steady-state R&D capital/physical capital ratio $\bar{\kappa}$ increases with the relative productivity of the R&D sector, ω_K/ω_A. A higher market power of intermediates I suppliers raises $\bar{\kappa}$, while a higher market power of intermediates II suppliers lowers $\bar{\kappa}$. The laissez-faire steady-state R&D capital/physical capital ratio $\bar{\kappa}$ is constant over time.[16]

11.2.3 Steady-State Growth

Applying no-arbitrage (11.31) yields the Keynes/Ramsey rule $\dot{c}_t/c_t = \sigma\left[\pi_{Kt}/v_{Kt} + \dot{v}_{Kt}/v_{Kt} - \rho\right]$, where $\rho, \sigma > 0$. ρ denotes the time preference rate, σ represents the intertemporal elasticity of substitution. Inserting profit rate (11.25) and free entry (11.29), and considering equation (11.32), we obtain the subsequent laissez-faire steady-state growth rate[17]

$$\gamma = \sigma\left[\left[\frac{[1-\alpha]\beta}{\omega_A}\right]^{\eta}\left[\frac{1-\beta}{\omega_K}\right]^{1-\eta} L^{\nu} - \rho\right] \tag{11.33}$$

[16] Thus, the steady-state share of R&D expenditures in total investment is constant over time, too. Using production functions (11.7) and (11.8) yields $\bar{u} = \bar{\kappa}/\left\{\bar{\kappa} + [\omega_K/\omega_A]\right\}$.

[17] Alternatively, we may insert no-arbitrage (11.30) into the Keynes/Ramsey rule. Inserting profit rate (11.22) and free entry (11.28), and using equation (11.32) leads to steady-state growth rate (11.33), too.

We require two conditions: first, for a positive growth rate, $\{[1-\alpha]\beta/\omega_A\}^{\eta}\{[1-\beta]/\omega_K\}^{1-\eta}L^{\nu} > \rho$, and, second, for a bounded attainable utility, $\rho > [\sigma-1]\gamma/\sigma$. Growth goes up with higher productivities in both R&D and physical capital production. The respective elasticities are η and $[1-\eta]$. Furthermore, a larger labor force, a lower rate of time preference, and a higher intertemporal elasticity of substitution increase growth.[18]

11.2.4 Equilibrium Dynamics

In the beginning, the economy is endowed with capital stocks A_0 and K_0. Suppose that the ratio $\kappa_0 \equiv A_0/K_0$ deviates from the value given by equation (11.32). In order to investigate the equilibrium dynamics of our model, we employ two variables: apart from the ratio of R&D capital stock over physical capital stock, i.e. $\kappa_t \equiv A_t/K_t$, we define the ratio of consumption over physical capital stock as $\chi_t \equiv c_t L/K_t$. In the steady state, these two variables are constant.

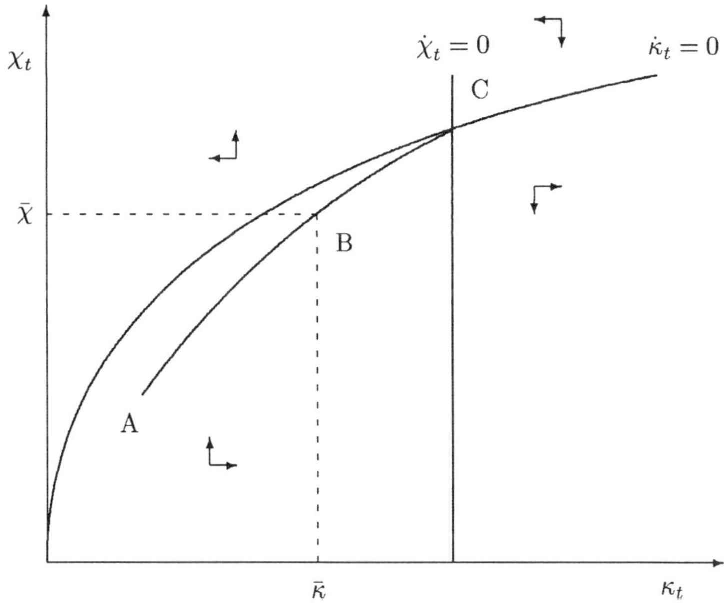

Figure 11.2: Equilibrium dynamics, case I.

[18]The steady-state saving rate may be derived as $\bar{s} = I/Y = \omega_A\gamma[\kappa+\omega_K/\omega_A]/[\eta\kappa^{\eta}L^{\nu}]$.

First, we analyze the case in which physical capital's relative abundance is above its steady state level, i.e. $\kappa_0 = A_0/K_0 < \kappa$. We will refer to this scenario as case I. Since in this case, the R&D-related dividend exceeds the dividend that corresponds to physical capital investment, we require $\dot{K}_t = 0$ and $\dot{A}_t = Y_t - c_t L$.[19] By the same token, the value of a unit of physical capital is below its production cost, i.e. $v_{Kt} < \omega_K$, whereas $v_{At} = \omega_A$.

Our dynamic system consists of two differential equations. Growth rate (11.33) implies a first equation of motion, given by

$$\frac{\dot{\chi}_t}{\chi_t} = \sigma \left\{ \frac{1}{\omega_A} [1-\alpha] \beta \kappa_t^{-[1-\eta]} L^\nu - \rho \right\} \tag{11.34}$$

$\dot{\chi}_t = 0$ implies

$$\bar{\kappa}_I = \left[\frac{[1-\alpha] \beta L^\nu}{\omega_A \rho} \right]^{\frac{1}{1-\eta}} \tag{11.35}$$

where $\bar{\kappa}_I$ denotes the steady-state value of κ that is implied by differential equation (11.34). Accordingly, the $\dot{\chi}_t = 0$-locus is a vertical line in κ-χ-space. A value of κ_t to the left of this line corresponds to $\dot{\chi}_t > 0$, a value of κ_t to the right of this line corresponds to $\dot{\chi}_t < 0$.

Moreover, $\dot{A}_t = Y_t - c_t L$ and $\dot{K}_t = 0$ imply a second equation of motion, denoted by

$$\frac{\dot{\kappa}_t}{\kappa_t} = \kappa_t^{-[1-\eta]} L^\nu - \frac{\chi_t}{\kappa_t} \tag{11.36}$$

$\dot{\kappa}_t = 0$ requires

$$\chi_t = \kappa_t^\eta L^\nu \tag{11.37}$$

Hence, the $\dot{\kappa}_t = 0$-locus is an upward-sloping concave curve. A value of χ_t above the curve corresponds to $\dot{\kappa}_t < 0$, a value of χ_t below the curve corresponds to $\dot{\kappa}_t > 0$. Equations (11.35) and (11.37) imply the existence of a steady-state equilibrium.[20]

Figure 11.2 shows the phase diagram for case I. The curve ABC depicts the stable saddle path.[21] Point A is associated to the economy's initial R&D

[19] Notice that during transition, no-arbitrage conditions (11.30) and (11.31) hold, too. In case I, i.e. $\kappa_0 < \kappa$, the relatively high R&D-related dividend, i.e. $\pi_{At}/v_{At} > \pi_{Kt}/v_{Kt}$, is offset by the evolution of the values of R&D capital and physical capital: in an R&D capital-intensifying economy, the value of a unit of R&D capital decreases, whereas the value of a unit of physical capital increases, i.e. $\dot{v}_{At}/v_{At} < 0 < \dot{v}_{Kt}/v_{Kt}$. Thus, the economy offers no arbitrage opportunities, i.e. the condition given by $\pi_{At}/v_{At} + \dot{v}_{At}/v_{At} = \pi_{Kt}/v_{Kt} + \dot{v}_{Kt}/v_{Kt} = r_t$ holds.

[20] In appendix C, we show that the dynamic system that represents case I is stable.

[21] It may be shown that the curvature of the saddle path ABC in figure 11.2 depends on the relative magnitude of the elasticity of intertemporal substitution, σ. For $\sigma < \omega_A / [1-\alpha] \beta$, the saddle path is, as in figure 11.2 represented, concave, and the speed of convergence is low. For $\sigma = \omega_A / [1-\alpha] \beta$, the trajectory is linear. For $\sigma > \omega_A / [1-\alpha] \beta$, the saddle path has a convex shape, and the system converges rapidly.

capital/physical capital ratio, i.e. κ_0. Point B corresponds to the economy's steady-state R&D capital/physical capital ratio, i.e. $\bar{\kappa}$ [cf. equation (11.32)]. Point C is related to the steady-state R&D capital/physical capital ratio that is implied by differential equation (11.34), i.e. $\bar{\kappa}_I$. Thus, figure 11.2 indicates that, along the stable saddle path ABC, both χ_t and κ_t rise monotonically. Although the economy heads towards point C, it reaches point B in finite time, and stops there.[22] The reason is straightforward: in point B, the economy has attained its steady-state R&D capital/physical capital ratio. Since in point B, the R&D-related dividend and the dividend that is associated with physical capital investment are of same size, the constraint of nonnegative investment in physical capital becomes nonbinding, and, thus, the capital stocks A_t and H_t grow with the same constant, positive rate.

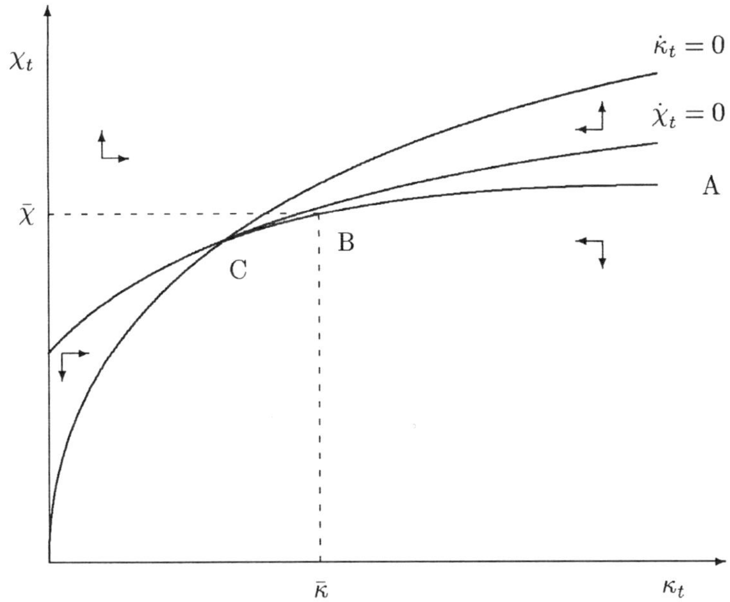

Figure 11.3: Equilibrium dynamics, case II.

[22]Notice that since $\dot{c}_t/c_t > 0$, $\rho < \{[1-\alpha]\beta/\omega_A\}^{\eta}\{[1-\beta]/\omega_K\}^{1-\eta}L^{\nu}$, and, in turn, $\bar{\kappa} < \bar{\kappa}_I$ [cf. equations (11.32), (11.33), and (11.35)].

Second, we investigate the case in which R&D capital is relative abundant, i.e. $\kappa_0 = A_0/K_0 > \kappa$. We will refer to this scenario as case *II*. In this case, the dividend that corresponds to physical capital investment exceeds the R&D-related dividend. Accordingly, we require $\dot{A}_t = 0$ and $\dot{K}_t = Y_t - c_t L$.[23] By the same token, the value of a unit of R&D capital is below its production cost, i.e. $v_{At} < \omega_A$, while $v_{Kt} = \omega_K$.

Again, our dynamic system encompasses two differential equations. From growth rate (11.33) together with $\dot{K}_t = Y_t - c_t L$, we obtain a first equation of motion as

$$\frac{\dot{\chi}_t}{\chi_t} = \sigma \left\{ \frac{1}{\omega_K} [1-\beta] \kappa_t^{\eta} L^{\nu} - \rho \right\} + \frac{\dot{\kappa}_t}{\kappa_t} \tag{11.38}$$

$\dot{\chi}_t = 0$ implies

$$\chi_t = \left\{ 1 - \sigma \frac{1}{\omega_K} [1-\beta] \right\} \kappa_t^{\eta} L^{\nu} + \sigma\rho \tag{11.39}$$

Accordingly, for $\sigma < \omega_K / [1-\beta]$, the $\dot{\chi}_t = 0$-locus is an upward-sloping concave curve in κ-χ-space.[24] A value of χ_t above this curve corresponds to $\dot{\chi}_t > 0$, a value of χ_t below this curve corresponds to $\dot{\chi}_t < 0$.

Moreover, $\dot{K}_t = Y_t - c_t L$, and $\dot{A}_t = 0$ imply a second equation of motion given by

$$\frac{\dot{\kappa}_t}{\kappa_t} = -\kappa_t^{\eta} L^{\nu} + \chi_t \tag{11.40}$$

$\dot{\kappa}_t = 0$ requires equation (11.37) to hold. Hence, the $\dot{\kappa}_t = 0$-locus is an upward-sloping concave curve. Opposed to case *I*, here, a value of χ_t above the curve corresponds to $\dot{\kappa}_t > 0$, whereas a value of χ_t below the curve implies $\dot{\kappa}_t < 0$. Equations (11.37) and (11.39) imply the existence of a steady-state equilibrium.[25]

Figure 11.3 shows the phase diagram for case *II*. The curve *ABC* represents the stable saddle path.[26] Point *A* is associated to the economy's initial

[23] Notice that in case *II*, i.e. $\kappa_0 > \kappa$, the relatively low R&D-related dividend, i.e. $\pi_{At}/v_{At} < \pi_{Kt}/v_{Kt}$, is offset by the evolution of the values of R&D capital and physical capital: in a physical capital-intensifying economy, the value of a unit of R&D capital increases, whereas the value of a unit of physical capital decreases, i.e. $\dot{v}_{Kt}/v_{Kt} < 0 < \dot{v}_{At}/v_{At}$. Accordingly, the economy offers no arbitrage opportunities, i.e. the condition given by $\pi_{At}/v_{At} + \dot{v}_{At}/v_{At} = \pi_{Kt}/v_{Kt} + \dot{v}_{Kt}/v_{Kt} = r_t$ holds.

[24] Notice that for $\sigma = \omega_K / [1-\beta]$, the $\dot{\chi}_t = 0$-locus is a horizontal line, and for $\sigma > \omega_K / [1-\beta]$, the $\dot{\chi}_t = 0$-locus is a downward-sloping convex curve [cf. appendix D].

[25] In appendix C, we show that the dynamic system that represents case *II* is stable.

[26] As the curvature of the $\dot{\chi}_t = 0$-locus, the curvature of the stable saddle path depends on the relative magnitude of the elasticity of intertemporal substitution, σ. For $\sigma < \omega_K / [1-\beta]$, the saddle path is an upward-sloping concave curve as in figure 11.3. In this case, the system converges slowly. Analogously, for $\sigma = \omega_K / [1-\beta]$, the trajectory is a horizontal line, and for $\sigma > \omega_K / [1-\beta]$, the saddle path has a downward-sloping convex shape. In the latter case, the speed of convergence is high. In appendix D, we investigate the cases in which $\sigma \geq \omega_K / [1-\beta]$ holds in detail.

R&D capital/physical capital ratio, i.e. κ_0. Point B corresponds to the economy's steady-state R&D capital/physical capital ratio, i.e. $\bar{\kappa}$ [cf. equation (11.32)]. Point C is related to the steady-state R&D capital/physical capital ratio that is implied by differential equation (11.38), i.e. $\bar{\kappa}_{II}$. Thus, for $\sigma < \omega_K / [1-\beta]$, figure 11.3 indicates that, along the stable saddle path ABC, both χ_t and κ_t fall monotonically. Although the economy heads towards point C, it reaches point B in finite time, and stops there.[27] In point B, both investment opportunities – that is, R&D and physical capital investment – yield the same dividend. Hence, in point B, the constraint of nonnegative investment in R&D capital becomes nonbinding, and, thus, the capital stocks A_t and H_t grow with the same constant, positive rate.

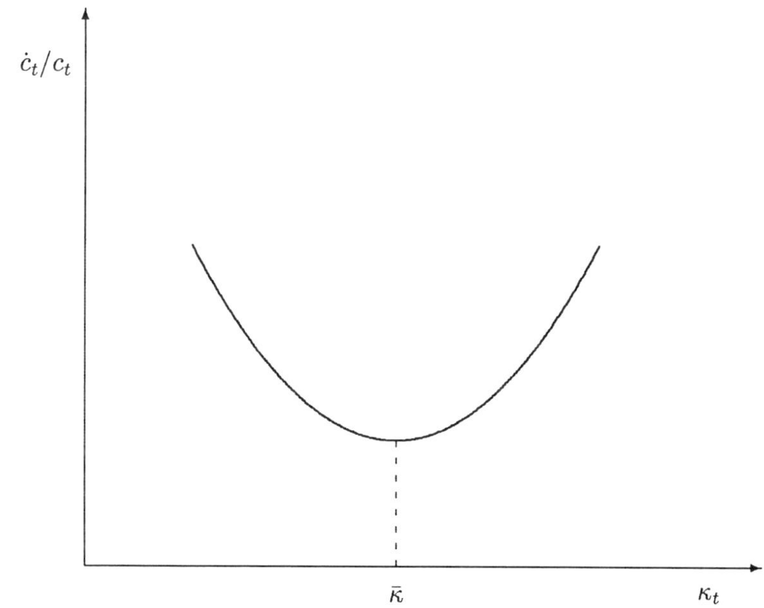

Figure 11.4: The imbalance effect.

[27] $\bar{\kappa}_{II}$ follows from equation (11.38) as $\{\omega_K \rho / [1-\beta] L^{\nu}\}^{1/\eta}$. Notice that since $\dot{c}_t/c_t > 0$, $\rho < \{[1-\alpha]\beta/\omega_A\}^{\eta} \{[1-\beta]/\omega_K\}^{1-\eta} L^{\nu}$, and, in turn, $\bar{\kappa}_{II} < \bar{\kappa}$ [cf. equations (11.32) and (11.33)].

The analysis implies the our model exhibits convergence in the sense that economic growth declines monotonically over time. The closer the economy gets to its steady-state R&D capital/physical capital ratio, $\bar{\kappa}$, the lower becomes its growth rate. Stated differently: whereas the minimal growth rate corresponds to the steady-state R&D capital/physical capital ratio $\bar{\kappa}$, on either side of the steady state, the growth rate increases symmetrically with the magnitude of the gap between κ_t and $\bar{\kappa}$. The association between $\dot{c}_t/c_t$ and κ_t shows an imbalance effect: the greater the imbalance, i.e. the longer the distance between κ_t and its steady-state value $\bar{\kappa}$, the higher the economic growth [cf. figure 11.4].

The present model's convergence property permits to describe the growth performance of postwar economies quite intuitively. Whereas wars destroy physical capital at large scale, R&D capital tends to be left intact. Hence, postwar economies are often characterized by a relative scarce endowment with physical capital. Our model predicts that in such postwar economies, output grows at a rate well above the steady-state growth rate. Hence, the casual evidence of Germany and Japan is consistent with this prediction of our model. Both countries exhibited in their level of economic activity a fairly impressive catching up.

11.3 Social Planner's Solution

After having analyzed the laissez-faire outcome, we investigate the social planner's solution. The preferences of the representative individual are given by equations (3.21) and (3.22). The technology constraints are given by $\dot{A}_t = u_t I_t/\omega_A$, and $\dot{K}_t = [1-u_t] I_t/\omega_K$. Accordingly, the intertemporal maximization problem may be stated in terms of a current-value Hamiltonian by

$$H = u(c_t) + \lambda_{At}\frac{1}{\omega_A}u_t I_t + \lambda_{Kt}\frac{1}{\omega_K}\left[1-u_t\right] I_t$$

The first-order conditions for an optimum consumption path are given by

$$\frac{\partial H}{\partial c_t} = 0 \tag{11.41}$$

$$\frac{\partial H}{\partial u_t} = 0 \tag{11.42}$$

$$\dot{A}_t = \frac{\partial H}{\partial \lambda_{At}}$$

$$\dot{K}_t = \frac{\partial H}{\partial \lambda_{Kt}}$$

$$\dot{\lambda}_{At} = \rho\lambda_{At} - \frac{\partial H}{\partial A_t} \tag{11.43}$$

and

$$\dot{\lambda}_{Kt} = \rho\lambda_{Kt} - \frac{\partial H}{\partial K_t} \tag{11.44}$$

The transversality conditions are

$$\lim_{t\to\infty} [e^{-\rho t}\lambda_{At}A_t] = 0$$

and

$$\lim_{t\to\infty} [e^{-\rho t}\lambda_{Kt}K_t] = 0$$

Condition (11.42) implies that for an optimum allocation of final output, the marginal productivity of final output in the production of R&D capital times the shadow price of a blueprint has to be equal to the marginal productivity of final output in the production of physical capital times the shadow price of a unit of physical capital, i.e.

$$\frac{1}{\omega_A}\lambda_{At} = \frac{1}{\omega_K}\lambda_{Kt} \tag{11.45}$$

Thus, the shadow prices of both types of capital evolve at the same rate, i.e.

$$\frac{\dot{\lambda}_{At}}{\lambda_{At}} = \frac{\dot{\lambda}_{Kt}}{\lambda_{Kt}} = \frac{\dot{\lambda}_t}{\lambda_t} \tag{11.46}$$

Condition (11.41) implies that for an optimum consumption path, the marginal utility of consumption has to equate the marginal productivity of final output in the production of either kind of capital times the shadow price of the respective kind of capital. This equation yields a first equation of motion for the shadow prices

$$\frac{\dot{\lambda}_t}{\lambda_t} = \frac{u''(c_t)\dot{c}_t}{u'(c_t)} = -\frac{1}{\sigma}\frac{\dot{c}_t}{c_t} \tag{11.47}$$

Condition (11.43) yields a second equation of motion for the shadow prices, using equations (11.45) and (11.46)

$$\frac{\dot{\lambda}_t}{\lambda_t} = -\left[\frac{1}{\omega_A}\eta A_t^{-1}Y_t - \rho\right] \tag{11.48}$$

Condition (11.44) gives a third equation of motion for the shadow prices

$$\frac{\dot{\lambda}_t}{\lambda_t} = -\left[\frac{1}{\omega_K}[1-\eta] K_t^{-1}Y_t - \rho\right] \tag{11.49}$$

Comparing laissez-faire with social optimum, we will find a double suboptimality. First, the level of total investment is too low. Second, the allocation of the too low total investment is biased: there is too little R&D investment relative to investment in physical capital. First, we turn to the inefficiency that is due to the suboptimal level of total investment. Using equations (11.47) and (11.48), we derive the social optimum steady-state growth rate as[28]

$$\gamma_S = \sigma \left[\left[\frac{1-\alpha}{\alpha \omega_A} \right]^{\eta} \left[\frac{1-\beta}{\beta \omega_K} \right]^{1-\eta} \nu L^{\nu} - \rho \right] \tag{11.50}$$

Growth increases with higher productivities in both R&D and physical capital production. As before, growth goes up for a larger labor force, a lower rate of time preference, and a higher intertemporal elasticity of substitution.

Both the laissez-faire outcome and the social optimum solution involve a steady-state equilibrium condition (CC), given by

$$r = r_S = \rho + \frac{1}{\sigma}\gamma \tag{CC}$$

The laissez-faire equilibrium condition (MM) follows as

$$r = \left[\frac{[1-\alpha]\beta}{\omega_A} \right]^{\eta} \left[\frac{1-\beta}{\omega_K} \right]^{1-\eta} L^{\nu} \tag{MM}$$

It social optimum counterpart (PP) may be derived as

$$r_S = \frac{\nu}{\alpha^{\eta}\beta} \left[\frac{[1-\alpha]\beta}{\omega_A} \right]^{\eta} \left[\frac{1-\beta}{\omega_K} \right]^{1-\eta} L^{\nu} \tag{PP}$$

Whereas the CC line is upward-sloping, the graphs that are given by conditions (MM) and (PP) are horizontal in γ-r-space [cf. figure (11.5)]. We find that the social optimum rate of return is unambiguously above the private laissez-faire rate of return, that is $r_S = \nu r / [\alpha^{\eta}\beta]$, where $\nu / [\alpha^{\eta}\beta] > 1$. Hence, the laissez-faire growth is unambiguously below the social optimum, i.e. $\gamma < \gamma_S$. The difference between the two growth rates increases with higher degrees of imperfectness of competition in the intermediates markets. Furthermore, it increases with stronger economies of scale.[29]

---

[28] Instead of equation (11.48), we could utilize equation (11.49), too. The equations prove to be equivalent.

[29] If the economy exhibited constant returns to scale, i.e. $\nu = 1$, and the intermediates markets were perfectly competitive, i.e. $\alpha = \beta = 1$, the inefficiency that is due to the too low level of total investment would vanish. If the intermediates markets were perfectly competitive, entrepreneurs would invest neither in R&D nor in physical capital.

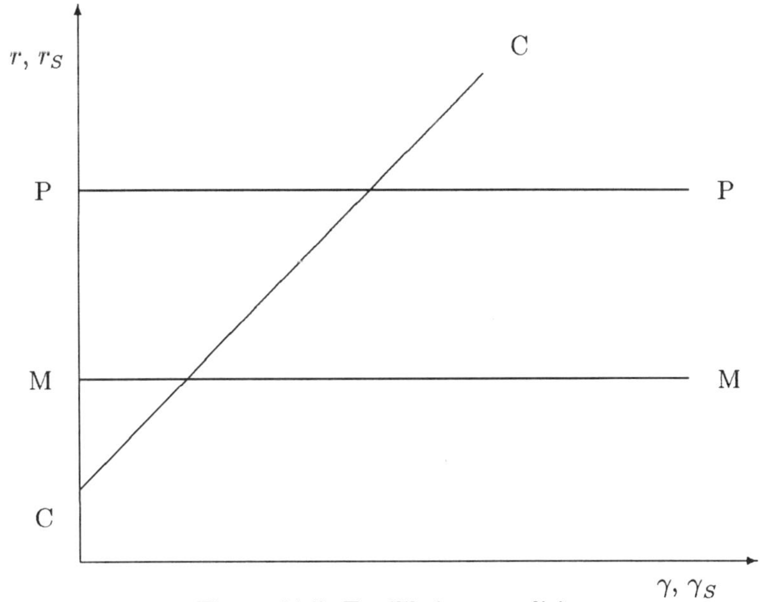

Figure 11.5: Equilibrium conditions.

Second, we investigate the inefficiency that is the result of the biased allocation of total investment. Equations (11.48) and (11.49) imply for the steady-state social optimum R&D capital/physical capital ratio κ_S the subsequent equation

$$\frac{A_t}{K_t} = \frac{\omega_K}{\omega_A}\frac{[1-\alpha]\beta}{\alpha[1-\beta]} = \frac{\omega_K}{\omega_A}\frac{\eta}{1-\eta} \equiv \bar{\kappa}_S \tag{11.51}$$

The ratio increases with R&D's relative productivity. A lower substitutability of intermediates I and a higher substitutability of intermediates II raise the ratio. As its laissez-faire counterpart, the social optimum steady-state R&D capital/physical capital ratio is constant.

A comparison of laissez-faire ratio (11.32) and social optimum ratio (11.51) shows that with laissez-faire, the steady-state ratio of R&D capital stock to physical capital stock is unambiguously too low, i.e. $\bar{\kappa} < \bar{\kappa}_S$. Stated differently: the steady-state share of total investment that is spent on R&D is too small, i.e. $u < u_S$, where $\bar{u}_S$ is the steady-state social optimum R&D share of total investment. The inefficiency increases with a lower substitutability between intermediates I.[30] Notice that the inefficiency in the allocation of investment results from the economy's structure, i.e. the

[30] If the intermediates I market were perfectly competitive, i.e. $\alpha = 1$, the inefficiency

assumption that first-stage intermediates I are differentiated due to R&D, while second-stage intermediates II are differentiated due to physical capital investment.[31]

11.4 Policy Implications

We introduce a government which faces the following flow budget constraint

$$\begin{aligned} & t_\pi \left[\pi_{At} A_t + \pi_{Kt} K_t\right] + t_I I_t \\ & + t_{\pi_A} \pi_{At} A_t + t_{I_A} u_t I_t \\ & + t_{\pi_K} \pi_{Kt} K_t + t_{I_K} \left[1 - u_t\right] I_t \\ + T_t L \;=\; & 0 \end{aligned} \tag{11.52}$$

where t_π is a general profit tax, t_I is a general investment tax, t_{π_A} is a tax on profits that intermediates I suppliers incur, t_{I_A} is a tax on R&D, t_{π_K} is a tax on profits that accrue to intermediates II suppliers, t_{I_K} is a tax on physical capital investment, and T_t is a lump-sum tax. Taxes obey the condition $-1 < t_\pi, t_I, t_{\pi_A}, t_{I_A}, t_{\pi_K}, t_{I_K} < 1$. To obtain a balanced budget, as soon as one tax is positive, at least one tax has to turn negative. A negative tax is a subsidy.

The after-tax intermediates I profit rate is given by [cf. equation (11.23)]

$$\pi_{At} = \left[1 - t_\pi\right]\left[1 - t_{\pi_A}\right][1 - \alpha]\beta A_t^{-1} Y_t$$

The intermediates I free-entry condition changes to [cf. condition (11.28)]

$$v_{At} \leq [1 + t_I][1 + t_{I_A}]\omega_A$$

with equality whenever $\dot{A}_t > 0$. The after-tax intermediates II profit rate may be stated as [cf. equation (11.26)]

$$\pi_{Kt} = \left[1 - t_\pi\right]\left[1 - t_{\pi_K}\right][1 - \beta] K_t^{-1} Y_t$$

The intermediates II free-entry condition becomes [cf. condition (11.29)]

$$v_{Kt} \leq [1 + t_I][1 + t_{I_K}]\omega_K$$

with equality whenever $\dot{K}_t > 0$.

that is due to the biased allocation of total investment would vanish, while no R&D would be undertaken. If the intermediates II market were perfectly competitive, i.e. $\beta = 1$, the physical capital good sector would collapse, and the inefficiency in the allocation of investment would vanish, too.

[31] If we reversed this sequence, we would reverse the bias of the laissez-faire outcome, too: if intermediates I were differentiated due to physical capital investment, while intermediates II were differentiated due to R&D, the laissez-faire ratio of R&D capital stock to physical capital stock would be inefficiently high. Nevertheless, it is suggestive to assume that the input differentiation due to R&D is at the first stage of the production process.

First, we derive optimum policy measures to tackle the inefficiency that is due to the too low level of investment. The after-tax steady-state rate of return may be derived as

$$r_T = \frac{1-t_\pi}{1+t_I}\left[\frac{[1-t_{\pi_A}]}{[1+t_{I_A}]}\frac{[1-\alpha]\beta}{\omega_A}\right]^\eta\left[\frac{[1-t_{\pi_K}]}{[1+t_{I_K}]}\frac{1-\beta}{\omega_K}\right]^{1-\eta}L^\nu \tag{TT}$$

Hence, optimum combinations of subsidies, $[t_\pi, t_I]^*$, which close the gap between growth rates (11.33) and (11.50) obey the condition

$$t_\pi = 1-[1+t_I]\frac{\nu}{\alpha^\eta\beta} \tag{11.53}$$

Investment subsidization and profit subsidization prove to be substitutes. The stronger the economies of scale, and the lower the substitutabilities of both types of intermediates, the higher – ceteris paribus – the optimum subsidies. For $t_I^* = 0$, equation (11.53) implies the optimum profit subsidy $t_\pi^* = 1 - \{\nu/[a^\eta\beta]\}$. For $t_\pi^* = 0$, we obtain the optimum investment subsidy $t_I^* = \{[a^\eta\beta]/\nu\} - 1$.

Second, we investigate optimum policy measures to address the inefficiency that is due to the biased allocation of investment. In order to rule out an interference with the intertemporal allocation of final output, the economy's rate of return must not be affected by these policy measures. Optimum combinations of subsidies on R&D activity and taxes on physical capital investment, $[t_{\pi_A}, t_{I_A}, t_{\pi_K}, t_{I_K}]^*$, are given by the subsequent equations

$$t_{\pi_A} = -\left[[1+t_{I_A}]\,\alpha^{-[1-\eta]}-1\right]$$

and

$$t_{\pi_K} = 1-[1+t_{I_K}]\,\alpha^\eta$$

We find a trade-off between subsidies, respectively taxes, on profits and investment. A subsidy on intermediates I profits may be substituted by a direct subsidy on R&D, i.e. $dt_{\pi_A}/dt_{I_A} = -\alpha^{-[1-\eta]}$. Analogously, a tax on intermediates II profits may be replaced by a tax on physical capital investment, i.e. $dt_{\pi_K}/dt_{I_K} = -\alpha^\eta$.

For $t_{I_A}^* = t_{I_K}^* = 0$, we obtain the following optimum combination of a subsidy on R&D-related profits, and a tax on profits that physical capital investors incur[32]

$$[t_{\pi_A}, t_{\pi_K}]^* = \left[-\left[\alpha^{-[1-\eta]}-1\right], 1-\alpha^\eta\right]$$

Alternatively, for $t_{\pi_A}^* = t_{\pi_K}^* = 0$, the static inefficiency may be corrected by a direct subsidy on R&D and a tax on investment in physical capital. The

[32] It is readily shown that the optimum overall tax on profits related to physical capital investment is negative, i.e. $t_{\pi_K}^{overall*} = -\{[\nu/\beta]-1\}$.

respective optimum subsidy-tax-combination may be stated as[33]

$$[t_{I_A}, t_{I_K}]^* = \left[-\left[1-\alpha^{1-\eta}\right], \alpha^{-\eta}-1\right]$$

To balance its budget (11.52), the government may impose a lump sum tax: it has effects neither on R&D activity, nor on physical capital accumulation, nor on income distribution.

11.5 Discussion

In this chapter, we present a growth model with forward-looking entrepreneurs who may invest either in R&D or in physical capital. Thereby, they spread a two-stage product differentiation. The complementarity of capital accumulation and innovation sets off the market saturation effect, which otherwise would lead to a slowing-down of investment, and eventually, to a petering-out of growth.

The model suggests that growth is more than mere R&D: while innovation triggers investment in physical capital by raising the profits that accrue to physical capital investment, the stimulus works the other way round, too: investment in physical capital triggers innovation by raising the profits incurred by researchers. It is apparent that in the long run, neither innovation nor physical capital accumulation were to sustain without the other.

Comparing the model's laissez-faire outcome with the social optimum reveals a double suboptimality. First, we find that the level of total investment is inefficiently low. This implies that the processes of both capital accumulation and innovation are too slow. This inefficiency rises with lower substitutabilities of both types of intermediates. Stronger economies of scale increase this inefficiency, too.

Second, we reveal a biased allocation of total investment. We show that R&D activity relative to physical capital investment is inefficiently low. This inefficiency increases with a lower substitutability between intermediates that are differentiated due to R&D. Contrarily, it is not affected by the degree of substitutability between intermediates the differentiation of which is the result of physical capital investment. This second finding – which proposes that R&D activity is inefficiently low – replicates the result of many of the more recent growth models. Nevertheless, the explanation is innovative: in our model, the inefficiency is not the result of an outstanding nature of R&D spillovers, but a consequence of the economy's structure.

The policy implications are readily derived. To address the inefficiently low level of total investment, non-discriminatory, investment-encouraging policy measures are suggested. Since entrepreneurs disregard the positive external effect of their investment, governments ought to promote en-

[33]The optimum overall tax on physical capital investment is negative, i.e. $t_{I_K}^{overall*} = -\{1-[\beta/\nu]\}$.

trepreneurial activity, i.e. set incentives for an increase in both capital accumulation and innovation. The model recommends supply side policies that strengthen the incentive to invest: either subsidizing profits, or cheapening R&D and physical capital investment through transfers.

To address the biased allocation of total investment, discriminatory policies are appropriate. Optimum measures that set incentives to raise the share of R&D expenditures are easily found. Nevertheless, in real world, correcting the allocation inefficiency may be difficult. First, the government faces an information problem. While all industries will claim that they are the R&D-intensive ones, the government has to detect the really R&D-intensive industries. Second, inefficiencies due to rent-seeking lure.

In turn, a non-discriminatory, investment-encouraging policy to tackle the inefficiently low level of total investment is quite readily implemented. Nevertheless, tax regimes in many countries still hamper investment: far from subsidizing profits or investment, governments put quite significant taxes on entrepreneurial activity. Our model suggests that the policy of taxing entrepreneurs has high social costs: it pushes long-run growth further below the social optimum. Thus, taxes on profits and investment ought to be decreased.

Chapter 12

Skilled Workers: Schooling and Specialization

In the current chapter, we present a growth model in which individuals may invest in human capital, i.e. in skills, and physical capital, i.e. in firms: whereas schooling leads to skill differentiation, investment in physical capital leads to product differentiation [cf. figure 12.1]. Hence, our model deviates from human capital growth models that stand in the tradition of Uzawa (1965) and Lucas (1988) in its comprehensive representation of imperfect competition: both the labor market and the intermediates market are imperfectly competitive.

Moreover, our model differs from existing growth models with respect to the input into human capital production, i.e. with respect to the *schooling input.* Whereas in Uzawa/Lucas-type models labor is the input into schooling, in our model the schooling input is a capital good. This capital good is to be broadly interpreted: since the good is defined as forgone consumption, it comprises both human capital and physical capital components. It is apparent that in today's schools and universities, education is human capital and physical capital intensive rather than labor intensive. The picture is not much different if we turn to the past: casual evidence suggests that the production of human capital has always been capital intensive. The libraries of convents, monasteries and early universities, for instance, represented impressive capital stocks that are in their relative importance comparable to the computer labs of today's educational institutions.

Apart from the comprehensive representation of imperfect competition and the capturing of education's capital intensity, the model deviates from existing growth models in a further essential property: in the present model, the long-run growth rate does not depend on the schooling share. We define the level parameter *schooling share* as the share of the schooling input that is actually devoted to schooling, i.e. the share of the schooling input that is not used for the production of other kinds of goods. Uzawa/Lucas-type models are quite optimistic when it comes to the impact of schooling on economic growth: with an increase in the schooling share, the long-run growth rate is predicted to increase unambiguously. The empirical studies by Levine/Renelt (1992) and Sala-i-Martin (1997) cast serious doubts whether an increase in the schooling share does actually raise economic growth, though. Furthermore, it has been shown that a number of developing countries have expanded education efforts without a subsequent increase in their economic growth [cf. Temple (1999, p. 140)]. In our model, an increase in the schooling share does not necessarily lead to an increase in the long-run growth rate.

In addition, the present model features a thorough investigation of the complementarity of schooling and capital. In an economy with a relative abundance of physical capital, the skill premia are high, and, in turn, there is a strong incentive to invest in schooling. In contrast, in an economy that is relatively human capital abundant, the returns on physical capital are high, and, hence, physical capital investment is very profitable. The long-run growth rate is positive, since the complementarity of human capital and physical capital sets off the market-saturation effect, which otherwise would lead to a petering-out of growth. We find that in the long run, neither schooling nor capital accumulation were to sustain without the other.

The plan of the present chapter is as follows. In section one, we present the economy's technology. Section two investigates the laissez-faire outcome. Section three yields the social planner's solution. Section four derives policy implications. Section five gives a recapitulation.

12.1 Technology

12.1.1 Final Output

Through schooling, a worker appropriates a skill h. Thus, she is able to supply a differentiated labor service l_{ht}, where $h \in [0, H_t]$. Hence, we take the skill space to be continuous, assuming an infinite set of skills. The variable H_t allows for three interpretations. First, H_t represents the amount of skills that are available at time t. Second, since H_t denotes the amount of skills, it denotes the amount of differentiated labor services, too. Third, it is suggestive to interpret the amount of skills as the economy's accumulated human capital stock. The elasticity of substitution between skills may be derived as $\epsilon_l = 1/[1-\alpha]$, where $0 < \alpha < 1$. For $\alpha \to 0$, the skills become complements,

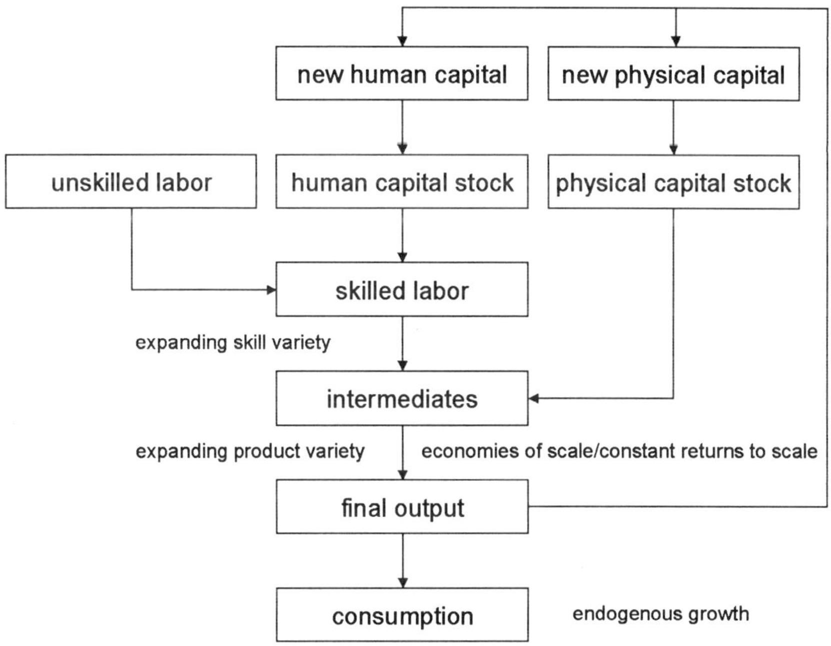

Figure 12.1: A schematic representation of the model.

and skilled workers enjoy maximum market power. For $\alpha \to 1$, the labor market becomes perfectly competitive.

Skilled labor is input into the production of intermediates. Intermediates are differentiated. To open up an intermediates production unit, it takes a unit of physical capital. The firm k faces the following CES production function

$$x_{kt} = \left[\int_0^{H_t} l_{kht}^{\alpha} dh \right]^{\frac{1}{\alpha}} \tag{12.1}$$

The output of intermediates production unit k is denoted by x_{kt}, where $k \in [0, K_t]$. The quantity of labor service h that is used to produce intermediate k is denoted by l_{kht}. Notice that K_t allows for three interpretations, too: amount of intermediates production units, amount of differentiated intermediates, accumulated physical capital stock. The elasticity of substitution between intermediates is given by $\epsilon_x = 1/[1-\beta]$, where $0 < \beta < 1$.

The differentiated intermediates are input into the production of final output. Final output Y_t is produced by an infinite set of firms j, the amount of which is normalized to unity, i.e. $j \in [0, 1]$. The technology is given by the subsequent CES production function

$$Y_t = \left[\int_0^{K_t} x_{kt}{}^{\beta} dk \right]^{\frac{\nu}{\beta}} \tag{12.2}$$

where $\nu \geq 1$. Thus, the economy may exhibit positive economies of scale.

Imposing full employment and symmetric quantities of labor services and intermediates, equations (12.1) and (12.2) imply the subsequent final output production function[1]

$$Y_t = \left[H_t^{\frac{1-\alpha}{\alpha}} K_t^{\frac{1-\beta}{\beta}} L \right]^{\nu} \tag{12.3}$$

where final output depends on the labor force, and the stocks of both human capital and physical capital. We assume that $[1-\alpha]/\alpha + [1-\beta]/\beta = 1/\nu$. Thus, the economy is characterized by a trade-off: the higher the substitutability between skills is, and the higher the substitutability between intermediates is, the stronger are the economies of scale. Stated differently: the more alike skills and intermediates are, the stronger are the network effects.[2] We define $\eta \equiv [1-\alpha]\nu/\alpha = 1 - [1-\beta]\nu/\beta$, where $0 < \eta < 1$.[3] Restating production function (12.3) yields

$$Y_t = H_t^{\eta} K_t^{1-\eta} L^{\nu} \tag{12.4}$$

12.1.2 Schooling and Capital Good

With respect to schooling's technology, we assume that the transformation of final output into human capital H_t is proportional. Thus,

$$\dot{H}_t = \frac{1}{\omega_H} u_t I_t \tag{12.5}$$

where ω_H is the schooling unit input requirement. I_t represents total investment, i.e. $I_t = Y_t - c_t L$, where $I_t \geq 0$. The part of total investment which is spent on schooling is denoted by u_t, where $0 \leq u_t \leq 1$. We will refer to u_t as the schooling share.[4]

The capital good sector is represented by a proportional production technology, too. It is given by

$$\dot{K}_t = \frac{1}{\omega_K} [1 - u_t] I_t \tag{12.6}$$

---

[1] In subsection 12.2.1, we show that the symmetry property is implied by the assumptions of the present model.

[2] The assumption according to which $[1-\alpha]/\alpha + [1-\beta]/\beta = 1/\nu$ may be perceived as stark, but it is necessary to make the economy exhibiting balanced growth. If $[1-\alpha]/\alpha + [1-\beta]/\beta < 1/\nu$ were to hold, growth would peter out.

[3] Notice that $0 < \alpha < 1$, $0 < \beta < 1$, and $\nu \geq 1$ imply $0 < \eta < 1$.

[4] Notice that for $\omega_H \neq 1$, human capital investment is not equal to the increase in human capital stock. ω_H may be interpreted as a measure for the efficiency of an economy's schooling sector.

where ω_K is capital unit input requirement. $[1 - u_t]$ is the part of total investment which is spent on investment in physical capital.[5]

12.2 Laissez-faire Outcome

12.2.1 Input Markets

There are two markets which are imperfectly competitive: the labor market and the intermediates market. First, we turn to the labor market. The wage rate of unskilled labor is denoted by w_{Ut}.[6] An unskilled worker may invest in her schooling, and, thus, appropriate skills. As soon as the economy's human capital stock is positive, all individuals own a positive amount of skills.[7] Thus, all workers are skilled. The wage rate of differentiated labor service h, w_{ht}, is the sum of the wage rate of unskilled labor, w_{Ut}, and the skill premium rate per unit of labor, π_{ht}/l_{ht}, i.e. $w_{ht} = w_{Ut} + \pi_{ht}/l_{ht}$. Hence, the premium rate to skill h is given by

$$\pi_{ht} = w_{ht}(l_{ht})l_{ht} - w_{Ut}l_{ht} \tag{12.7}$$

where $h \in [0, H_t]$. Workers maximize their skill premium rates by charging[8]

$$w_{ht} = \frac{w_{Ut}}{\alpha} = w_t \tag{12.8}$$

The greater workers' market power, the higher the markup $1/\alpha$. Equation (12.8) represents a symmetric solution with one common wage rate w_t, where all H_t labor services are of same size $l_t = L/H_t$.

Second, we investigate the intermediates market, i.e. the profit maximization of intermediates suppliers. Since the individual firm cannot exploit economies of scale, marginal cost equals average cost. Firms' profit rates at time t are given by

$$\pi_{kt} = p_{x_k t}(x_{kt})x_{kt} - AC_{x_k t}x_{kt} \tag{12.9}$$

where $p_{x_k t}$ is the price of intermediate k, and $AC_{x_k t}$ is the average cost that firm k faces, where $k \in [0, K_t]$. The suppliers maximize their flow profit rates by charging

$$p_{x_k t} = \frac{MC_{x_k t}}{\beta} \tag{12.10}$$

---

[5] Notice that for $\omega_K \neq 1$, investment in physical capital is not equal to the increase in physical capital stock. ω_K may be interpreted as a measure for the efficiency of an economy's capital good production. Production functions (12.5) and (12.6) imply a market-clearing condition for final output as $Y_t = c_t L + \omega_H \dot{H}_t + \omega_K \dot{K}_t$.

[6] Notice that the homogeneity of unskilled labor implies a common wage rate.

[7] A zero human capital stock would imply a final output of zero [cf. equation (12.4)].

[8] The missing of index h denotes that there is a common wage rate for all H_t labor services. In the remainder, for further symmetric quantities, prices, and costs, the notation will be analogous.

The greater firms' market power, the higher the markup $1/\beta$. Since marginal cost is equal to average cost, and average cost is the same to all K_t firms, i.e. $MC_{x_kt} = AC_{x_kt} = AC_{xt}$, we obtain $p_{xt} = AC_{xt}/\beta$. The common price is p_{xt}, and the output quantities of all K_t production units are of same size, i.e. $x_t = H_t^{[1-\alpha]/\alpha} L/K_t$. Thus, we may indeed use production functions (12.3) and (12.4).

In order to determine the evolution of prices, we derive the cost functions of the final output sector and the intermediates sector. First, we turn to the final output sector. The cost function C_y that is dual to the production function of final output firm j, where $j \in [0,1]$,is given by[9]

$$C_y(\{p_{x_kt}\}_{k=0}^{K_t}, y_{jt}) = \left[\int_0^{K_t} p_{x_kt}^{-\left[\frac{\beta}{1-\beta}\right]} dk\right]^{-\left[\frac{1-\beta}{\beta}\right]} y_{jt}$$

where y_{jt} is the fictitious output of firm j that we would observe if the economy exhibited no scale effect. By symmetry, total cost may be stated as

$$C_Y(p_{xt}, L) = p_{xt} H_t^{\frac{1-\alpha}{\alpha}} L \tag{12.11}$$

The average cost of producing final output is aggregate cost (12.11) over aggregate output (12.4), i.e.[10]

$$AC_{Yt} = p_{xt} H_t^{-\left\{\eta - \left[\frac{1-\alpha}{\alpha}\right]\right\}} K_t^{-[1-\eta]} L^{-[\nu-1]} \tag{12.12}$$

Since perfect competition prevails on the market for final output, total revenue equals total cost, and price equals average cost, i.e. $p_{Yt} = AC_{Yt}$. Solving for p_{xt}, and setting $p_{Yt} = 1$ for all t, yields the intermediates price

$$p_{xt} = H_t^{\eta - \left[\frac{1-\alpha}{\alpha}\right]} K_t^{1-\eta} L^{\nu-1} \tag{12.13}$$

Second, we investigate the intermediates sector. The cost function C_x which is dual to production function (12.1) is given by[11]

$$C_x(\{w_{ht}\}_{h=0}^{H_t}, x_{kt}) = \left[\int_0^{H_t} w_{ht}^{-\left[\frac{\alpha}{1-\alpha}\right]} dh\right]^{-\left[\frac{1-\alpha}{\alpha}\right]} x_{kt}$$

[9] The cost function is the solution to the problem $\min\left\{\int_0^{K_t} p_{x_kt} x_{jkt} dk + \mu\left[y_{jt} - \left[\int_0^{K_t} x_{jkt}^{\beta} dk\right]^{1/\beta}\right]\right\}$, where x_{jkt} represents the amount of intermediate k that is used in final output firm j.

[10] The result that the average cost of producing final output decreases with an expanding product variety [cf. cost function (12.12)] corresponds to the finding that the productivity in producing final output increases with an expanding product variety [cf. production function (12.4)]. The dependence of the average cost (12.12) on the skill variety and the labor force hinges on a mere scale effect.

[11] The cost function is the solution to the problem $\min\left\{\int_0^{H_t} w_{ht} l_{kht} dh + \mu\left[x_{kt} - \left[\int_0^{H_t} l_{kht}^{\alpha} dh\right]^{1/\alpha}\right]\right\}$.

Using the symmetry results, total cost may be denoted as

$$C_X(w_t, L) = w_t L \tag{12.14}$$

The average cost of producing intermediates is derived by dividing aggregate cost (12.14) by aggregate output [cf. equation (12.1)]. We obtain[12]

$$AC_{xt} = w_t H_t^{-\left[\frac{1-\alpha}{\alpha}\right]} \tag{12.15}$$

The suppliers of intermediates put a markup $1/\beta$ on average cost. Hence,

$$p_{xt} = \frac{1}{\beta} w_t H_t^{-\left[\frac{1-\alpha}{\alpha}\right]} \tag{12.16}$$

Solving equation (12.16) for the wage rate of skilled labor yields

$$w_t = \beta p_{xt} H_t^{\frac{1-\alpha}{\alpha}} \tag{12.17}$$

Inserting equation (12.13) into equation (12.17) gives[13]

$$w_t = \beta H_t^{\eta} K_t^{1-\eta} L^{\nu-1} \tag{12.18}$$

Equations (12.13) and (12.18) imply that firms may influence the intermediates price relative to the wage rate, i.e. p_{xt}/w_t, by varying their markup. Contrarily, workers lack this ability. This asymmetry in the pricing capabilities is implied by the sequence of input differentiation.

The prices that we have just derived suggest a revisit of the skill premium rate and the flow profit rate. First, we restate the skill premium rate as [cf. equations (12.7) and (12.8)][14]

$$\pi_{Ht} = [1-\alpha] w_t l_t \tag{12.19}$$

The premium to the representative skill decreases with skills' substitutability and increases with the wage rate. An increase in the product variety has an unambiguously positive effect on premium (12.19) through an increase in the wage rate [cf. equation (12.18)]. In turn, an increase in the skill variety has two opposite effects on premium (12.19). First, a positive productivity effect: it follows from the induced rise in the wage rate [cf. equation (12.18)]. Second, a negative market-saturation effect: the skill's share of total labor service L is negatively related to the amount of skills.

[12] The result that the average cost of producing intermediates decreases with an expanding skill variety [cf. cost function (12.15)] corresponds to the finding that the productivity in producing intermediates increases with an expanding skill variety [cf. production function (12.1)].

[13] Thus, equations (12.8) and (12.18) imply a wage rate of unskilled labor given by $w_{Ut} = \alpha\beta H_t^{\eta} K_t^{1-\eta} L^{\nu-1}$.

[14] The index' capital letter denotes that there is one common premium rate for all H_t skills. In the remainder, for symmetric profit rates, the notation will be analogous.

To determine the sign of the overall effect, we insert equation (12.18) into premium (12.19). We obtain the following equation in which the premium to the representative skill depends only on labor and the stocks of human capital and physical capital.

$$\pi_{Ht} = [1-\alpha]\beta \left[\frac{K_t}{H_t}\right]^{1-\eta} L^{\nu} \tag{12.20}$$

Premium rate (12.20) shows that the negative market-saturation effect dominates the positive productivity effect. Hence, the overall effect of the launch of an additional skill on skills' premium is negative. Equation (12.20) implies that the premium increases with the relative abundance of physical capital to human capital.

Second, the flow profit rate may be written as [cf. equations (12.9) and (12.10)]

$$\pi_{Kt} = [1-\beta] p_{xt} x_t \tag{12.21}$$

The profit of the representative intermediates firm increases with its market power and with the intermediates price. An increase in the skill variety has an unambiguously positive effect on profit (12.21). While the intermediates price is – apart from a positive scale effect – not affected [cf. price equation (12.13)], the quantity of intermediates that is produced per production unit rises [cf. production function (12.1)].[15] In turn, an increase in the product variety has two opposite effects on profit (12.21). First, a positive productivity effect [cf. price equation (12.13)]. Second, a negative market-saturation effect [cf. production function (12.1)].

Using equations (12.1) and (12.13), profit equation (12.21) may be written as

$$\pi_{Kt} = [1-\beta] \left[\frac{H_t}{K_t}\right]^{\eta} L^{\nu} \tag{12.22}$$

Profit equation (12.22) shows that the overall effect of the launch of an additional intermediate on the profit of the representative firm is negative. Equation (12.22) implies that the flow profit increases with the relative abundance of human capital to physical capital.

Premium rate (12.20) and profit rate (12.22) illustrate neatly the complementarity of schooling and capital accumulation. Investment in physical capital stimulates schooling by raising the premium on skilled labor, just as schooling stimulates investment in physical capital by raising the profit rate. Without the accumulation of physical capital, a diminishing premium on skilled labor would choke off schooling, and without schooling, a diminishing profit rate would choke off investment in physical capital. In order

[15] To state it differently: an expanding skill variety raises the profit even when constant returns to scale prevail since the expanding skill variety lowers the intermediates average cost [cf. cost function (12.15)].

to prevent premium rate (12.20) and profit rate (12.22) from decreasing (respectively increasing), the stocks of human capital and physical capital have to grow at the same rate.

The input factors' shares of gross national product are independent of the sizes of human capital stock, physical capital stock, and labor force: β depicts skilled labor's income share, and $[1-\beta]$ represents physical capital's income share. Thus, β is the economy's distribution parameter: the higher the degree of imperfectness of competition in the intermediates market is, the higher is the share of total income that is appropriated by the owners of physical capital. Nevertheless, since the representative individual is both skilled worker and capitalist, parameter β may not affect the interpersonal distribution of income. Notice that the income distribution between input factors is not affected by the degree of imperfectness of competition in the labor market.

12.2.2 Asset Market

In equilibrium, investment activity implies that the value of a unit of human capital, i.e. a skill, and the value a unit of physical capital, i.e. a share, are equal to the respective costs of production, i.e. their prices. If the values were to fall below the prices, investment would stop. If the values were to be above the prices, with free entry, an unbounded demand for schooling, respectively for shares would arise. The condition of free entry into schooling follows as $v_{Ht} \leq p_{Ht}$, with equality whenever schooling takes place, i.e. whenever $\dot{H}_t > 0$. v_{Ht} denotes the value of a skill, and p_{Ht} its price. Human capital's production function (12.5) yields $p_{Ht} = \omega_H p_{Yt}$. With our normalization, i.e. $p_{Yt} = 1$, we obtain the subsequent free-entry condition

$$v_{Ht} \leq \omega_H \tag{12.23}$$

with equality whenever $\dot{H}_t > 0$. Analogous reasoning yields a condition for a free entry into the intermediates production. Capital good's production function (12.6) implies the following free-entry condition

$$v_{Kt} \leq \omega_K \tag{12.24}$$

with equality whenever investment takes place, i.e. whenever $\dot{K}_t > 0$. v_{Kt} denotes the value of a share.

An individual that is willing to postpone consumption may choose from three investment opportunities. First, appropriating a skill. Second, purchasing a share. Third, purchasing a bond. A bond yields interest rate r_t. Our setup implies perfect foresight and rules out speculative bubbles. It is apparent that in steady state, for no-arbitrage's sake, the return on a bond has to equal both the return on a share and the return on a skill. First, we investigate the return on a share. It depends on two components: the profit hat accrues to a share, π_t, and the change in the value of a share, $\dot{v}_{Kt}$. Thus,

$$\frac{\pi_{Kt}}{v_{Kt}} + \frac{\dot{v}_{Kt}}{v_{Kt}} = r_t \tag{12.25}$$

Second, we address the return on a skill, for which we derive an analogous result, i.e.

$$\frac{\pi_{Ht}}{v_{Ht}} + \frac{\dot{v}_{Ht}}{v_{Ht}} = r_t \tag{12.26}$$

We proceed by equating no-arbitrage conditions (12.25) and (12.26). We insert premium (12.20) and profit (12.22) as well as free entries (12.23) and (12.24). Thus, the steady-state laissez-faire allocation of savings on human capital and physical capital follows as

$$\frac{H_t}{K_t} = \frac{\omega_K}{\omega_H} \frac{[1-\alpha]\beta}{[1-\beta]} \equiv \bar{\kappa} \tag{12.27}$$

The steady-state laissez-faire human capital/physical capital ratio $\bar{\kappa}$ increases with the relative productivity of the schooling sector, ω_K/ω_H. A lower substitutability between skills raises $\bar{\kappa}$, while a lower substitutability between intermediates lowers $\bar{\kappa}$. The steady-state laissez-faire human capital/physical capital ratio $\bar{\kappa}$ is constant over time.[16]

12.2.3 Steady-State Growth

Applying no-arbitrage (12.25), the laissez-faire consumption path may be derived as $\dot{c}_t/c_t = \sigma\left[\pi_{Kt}/v_{Kt} + \dot{v}_{Kt}/v_{Kt} - \rho\right]$, where $\rho, \sigma > 0$. Inserting profit rate (12.22) and free entry (12.24), and using equation (12.27), we obtain the subsequent steady-state laissez-faire growth rate[17]

$$\gamma = \sigma\left[\left[\frac{[1-\alpha]\beta}{\omega_H}\right]^{\eta}\left[\frac{1-\beta}{\omega_K}\right]^{1-\eta} L^{\nu} - \rho\right] \tag{12.28}$$

We require $\{[1-\alpha]\beta/\omega_H\}^{\eta}\{[1-\beta]/\omega_K\}^{1-\eta} L^{\nu} > \rho > [\sigma-1]\gamma/\sigma$. Growth goes up for higher productivities in schooling and capital good production. The respective elasticities are η and $[1-\eta]$. Moreover, a larger labor force, a lower rate of time preference, and a higher intertemporal elasticity of substitution accelerate growth.[18]

The equilibrium dynamics of the present model are analogous to the model with two-stage input differentiation that we have investigated in the previous

[16] Thus, the steady-state share of schooling expenditure in total investment is constant over time, too. Using production functions (12.5) and (12.6) yields $\bar{u} = \bar{\kappa}/\{\bar{\kappa} + [\omega_K/\omega_H]\}$.

[17] Alternatively, we may use no-arbitrage (12.26) to obtain a Keynes/Ramsey rule where consumption's growth depends on the return on a skill. Inserting premium (12.20) and free entry (12.23), and using equation (12.27), yields steady-state growth rate (12.28), too.

[18] Notice that the steady-state saving rate follows as $\bar{s} = \omega_H\gamma\left[\bar{\kappa} + \omega_K/\omega_H\right] / \left[\eta\bar{\kappa}^{\eta}L^{\nu}\right]$.

chapter. In particular, this model exhibits convergence, too. That is, the longer the distance between the human capital/physical capital ratio, κ_t, and its steady-state value, $\bar{\kappa}$, the higher economic growth at time t. Accordingly, the closer the economy gets to the steady state, the lower becomes the growth rate.

12.3 Social Planner's Solution

The social planner's problem is to max U_t subject to technology constraints $\dot{H}_t = u_t I_t / \omega_H$ and $\dot{K}_t = [1 - u_t] I_t / \omega_K$. The social optimum steady-state growth rate is readily derived as

$$\gamma_S = \sigma \left[\frac{\nu}{\alpha^\eta \beta} \left[\frac{[1-\alpha]\beta}{\omega_H} \right]^\eta \left[\frac{1-\beta}{\omega_K} \right]^{1-\eta} L^\nu - \rho \right]$$

Growth increases with higher productivities in schooling and capital good production. As before, growth goes up for a larger labor force, a lower rate of time preference, and a higher intertemporal elasticity of substitution.

Both the laissez-faire outcome and the social optimum solution involve a steady-state equilibrium condition (CC), given by

$$r = r_S = \rho + \frac{1}{\sigma}\gamma \qquad (CC)$$

The laissez-faire equilibrium condition (MM) follows as

$$r = \left[\frac{[1-\alpha]\beta}{\omega_H} \right]^\eta \left[\frac{1-\beta}{\omega_K} \right]^{1-\eta} L^\nu \qquad (MM)$$

It social optimum counterpart (PP) may be derived as

$$r_S = \frac{\nu}{\alpha^\eta \beta} \left[\frac{[1-\alpha]\beta}{\omega_H} \right]^\eta \left[\frac{1-\beta}{\omega_K} \right]^{1-\eta} L^\nu \qquad (PP)$$

Whereas the CC line is upward-sloping, the graphs that are given by conditions (MM) and (PP) are horizontal in γ-r-space [cf. figure (12.2)]. We find that laissez-faire growth is unambiguously below the social optimum, i.e. $\gamma < \gamma_S$. The difference between the two growth rates increases with the degrees of imperfectness of competition in labor market and intermediates market. Furthermore, it increases with stronger economies of scale.[19]

[19] If the economy exhibited constant returns to scale, i.e. $\nu = 1$, and both the labor market and the intermediates market were perfectly competitive, i.e. $\alpha = \beta = 1$, this inefficiency would vanish. If the markets were perfectly competitive, individuals would invest neither in schooling nor in firm capital.

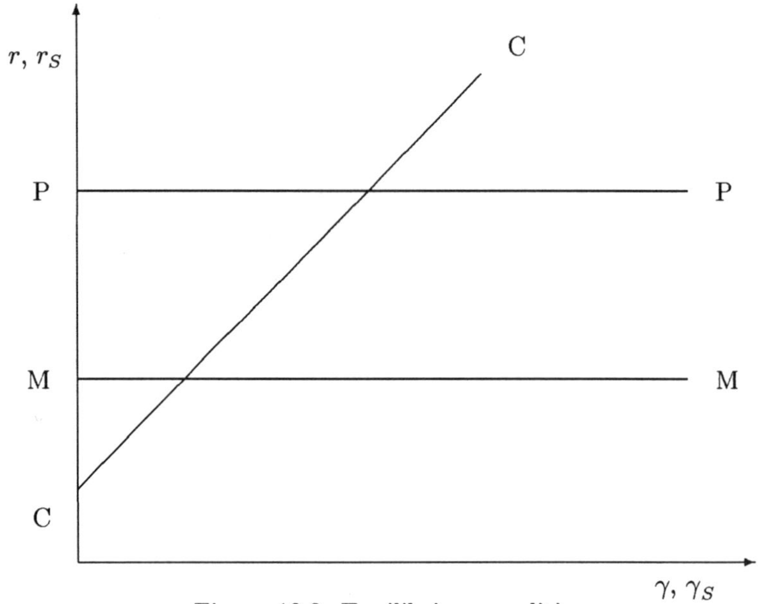

Figure 12.2: Equilibrium conditions.

Social planner's calculus implies for the steady-state social optimum human capital/physical capital ratio $\bar{\kappa}_S$ the subsequent equation

$$\frac{H_t}{K_t} = \frac{\omega_K}{\omega_H} \frac{[1-\alpha]\,\beta}{\alpha\,[1-\beta]} = \frac{\omega_K}{\omega_H} \frac{\eta}{[1-\eta]} \equiv \bar{\kappa}_S \tag{12.29}$$

The ratio increases with schooling's relative productivity. A lower substitutability between skills and a higher substitutability between intermediates raise the ratio. As its laissez-faire counterpart, the steady-state social optimum human capital/physical capital ratio is constant.

A comparison of laissez-faire ratio (12.27) and social optimum ratio (12.29) reveals a further inefficiency: with laissez-faire, the ratio of human capital stock to physical capital stock is unambiguously too low, i.e. $\kappa < \kappa_S$. Stated differently: the steady-state share of total investment that is spent on schooling is too small, i.e. $\bar{u} < \bar{u}_S$, where u_S is the steady-state social optimum schooling share of total investment. The inefficiency increases with a lower substitutability between skills.[20]

[20] If the labor market were perfectly competitive, i.e. $\alpha = 1$, this inefficiency would vanish, while no schooling would be undertaken. If the intermediates market were perfectly competitive, i.e. $\beta = 1$, the capital good sector would collapse, and the inefficiency would vanish, too.

12.4 Policy Implications

We introduce a government which faces the following flow budget constraint

$$\begin{aligned} & t_\pi \left[\pi_{Ht} H_t + \pi_{Kt} K_t\right] + t_I I_t \\ & + t_{\pi_H} \pi_{Ht} H_t + t_{I_H} u_t I_t \\ & + t_{\pi_K} \pi_{Kt} K_t + t_{I_K} \left[1 - u_t\right] I_t \\ + T_t L &= 0 \end{aligned}$$

where t_π is a general tax that affects skill premia and profits, t_I is a general investment tax, t_{π_H} is a tax on skill premia, t_{I_H} is a tax on schooling, t_{π_K} is a tax on profits, t_{I_K} is a tax on investment in shares, and T_t is a lump-sum tax. Taxes obey the condition $-1 < t_\pi, t_I, t_{\pi_H}, t_{I_H}, t_{\pi_K}, t_{I_K} < 1$.

First, we derive optimum policy measures to address the difference between the steady-state growth rates of laissez-faire and social optimum. The after-tax steady-state rate of return may be derived as

$$r_T = \frac{1 - t_\pi}{1 + t_I} \left[\frac{[1 - t_{\pi_H}]}{[1 + t_{I_H}]} \frac{[1 - \alpha]\beta}{\omega_H} \right]^\eta \left[\frac{[1 - t_{\pi_K}]}{[1 + t_{I_K}]} \frac{1 - \beta}{\omega_K} \right]^{1-\eta} L^\nu \qquad (TT)$$

Accordingly, optimum combinations of subsidies $[t_\pi, t_I]^*$ which close this gap obey the condition

$$t_\pi = 1 - [1 + t_I] \frac{\nu}{\alpha^\eta \beta} \qquad (12.30)$$

Thus, investment subsidization and profit subsidization prove to be substitutes. The stronger the economies of scale, and the higher the degrees of imperfectness of competition in labor market and intermediates market, the higher – ceteris paribus – the optimum subsidies. For $t_I = 0$, equation (12.30) implies an optimum subsidy on skill premia and profits that is given by $t_\pi^* = 1 - \{\nu / [a^\eta \beta]\}$. For $t_\pi = 0$, we obtain the optimum investment subsidy $t_I^* = \{[a^\eta \beta] / \nu\} - 1$.

Second, we investigate optimum policy measures to tackle the inefficiency of the steady-state laissez-faire allocation of savings on human capital and physical capital. In order to rule out an interference with the intertemporal allocation of final output, the economy's rate of return must not be affected by these policy measures. The optimum combination of a subsidy on skill premia and a tax on profits is given by[21]

$$[t_{\pi_H}, t_{\pi_K}]^* = \left[- \left[\alpha^{-[1-\eta]} - 1 \right], 1 - \alpha^\eta \right]$$

Alternatively, κ's bias may be corrected by a direct subsidy on schooling

[21] It is readily shown that the optimum overall profit tax is negative, i.e. $t_{\pi K}^{overall*} = - \{[\nu / \beta] - 1\}$.

and a tax on investment in shares. The respective optimum subsidy-tax-combination can be stated as[22]

$$[t_{I_H}, t_{I_K}]^* = \left[-\left[1-\alpha^{1-\eta}\right], \alpha^{-\eta}-1\right]$$

A subsidy on skill premia may be substituted by a direct subsidy on schooling, i.e. $dt_{\pi_H}/dt_{I_H} = -\alpha^{-[1-\eta]}$. Analogously, a tax on profits may be substituted by a tax on investment in shares, i.e. $dt_{\pi_K}/dt_{I_K} = -\alpha^{\eta}$.

12.5 Discussion

In this chapter, we present a growth model with individuals investing in their own skills and in firms' shares. The complementarity of schooling and capital accumulation sets off the market-saturation effect, which otherwise would lead to a petering-out of growth. Thus, while schooling triggers investment in physical capital by raising profits, the stimulus works the other way round, too: investment in physical capital triggers schooling by raising the wages of skilled labor. It becomes apparent that, in the long run, neither schooling nor capital accumulation were to sustain without the other.

For laissez-faire, we find a double suboptimality. First, saving is inefficiently low. This inefficiency increases with higher degrees of imperfectness of competition in labor market and intermediates market. Stronger economies of scale enlarge the inefficiency, too.

Second, the allocation of the inefficiently low savings is inefficient: there is too little schooling relative to investment in physical capital. This inefficiency increases with a higher degree of imperfectness of competition in the labor market. This second finding – which proposes that schooling is inefficiently low – replicates the result of growth models of the Uzawa/Lucas-type. Nevertheless, our explanation is innovative: here, the inefficiency is not the result of an outstanding nature of human capital spillovers, but a consequence of workers' relatively inferior pricing capability.

The policy implications are readily derived. First, to raise the decentralized growth rate to the social optimal level, policy measures that encourage saving are suggested. Second, governments should advance human capital formation through a direct subsidization of schooling, or through a subsidization of the wages of skilled labor.

---

[22]The optimum overall tax on investment in shares is negative, i.e. $t_{I_K}^{overall*} = -\{1-[\beta/\nu]\}$.

Concluding Remarks

In the present study, we investigate the relation between investment, R&D, and long-run growth. The study's contribution encompasses three points.

First, we explain evidence that shows a close relation between capital accumulation and economic growth within an imperfect competition framework. In our analysis, we employ two approaches. In a first approach, we model a homogeneous capital stock, assuming that capital equipment embodies technical knowledge. In a second approach, we turn the complementarity of different kinds of capital explicit. That is, in the respective models, individuals may invest separately in physical capital and R&D capital, respectively human capital.

Second, we represent the capability of physical capital investment to differentiate products. Our modeling is in line with real world experience according to which product differentiation is not restricted to be the outcome of mere R&D investment. It is apparent that, in real world, a firm may appropriate market power by physical capital investment, too. Moreover, workers may differentiate their skills by human capital investment, i.e. schooling. We present models that capture these phenomena.

Third, we investigate the external effects of physical capital investment, research, and schooling. Our finding is striking: in a world with imperfectly competitive markets, laissez-faire growth is most likely below the social optimum. To summarize our results on investment externalities, it is helpful to divide the models into two groups: models without an intertemporal investment spillover [chapters 5-6, 11-12], and models with an intertemporal investment spillover [chapters 7-10].

The result for models without an intertemporal investment spillover is unambiguous. There, laissez-faire growth is inefficiently low. By the Ramsey model with imperfect competition, we show that even without a network externality, the mere monopoly distortion effect leads to a suboptimal laissez-faire outcome [cf. chapter 5]. Considering a network externality as in the generalized AK model, the result of inefficiently low laissez-faire growth is confirmed [cf. chapter 6]. Furthermore, the result of inefficiently low laissez-faire growth is supported by models that capture a heterogeneous capital stock [chapters 11, 12]. Whereas the models with an intertemporal investment spillover represent cases of excessive growth, they also imply that it is very unlikely that excessive growth is a real world phenomenon [cf. chapters 7-10]. Thus, the result that excessive growth is probably not a real world phenomenon proves to be stable.

The policy implication of our finding of inefficiently low laissez-faire growth is straightforward: governments may raise social welfare by promoting investment. The reasoning behind this policy recommendation is shared by all presented models: since individuals disregard the positive external effects of their investment, governments ought to promote entrepreneurial activity, i.e. set incentives for an increase in capital accumulation. The models propose supply side policies that strengthen the incentive to invest: either subsidizing profits, respectively skill premia, or reducing investment costs by appropriate transfers.

Appendices

A A Suggestive Procedure to Eliminate Scale Effects

In the current appendix, we show that by the consideration of matching and shipping costs, scale effects may be readily eliminated. For this investigation, we use the basic model of the present study, i.e. chapter 5's Ramsey model with imperfect competition. Regarding the other models of this study, the elimination of scale effects may be attained in an analogous manner.

Whereas final output Y_t is, as before, produced according to the CES production function

$$Y_t = \left[\int_0^{K_t} x_{kt}^{\alpha} dk \right]^{\frac{1}{\alpha}} \tag{A.1}$$

where $0 < \alpha < 1$, we modify the technology of the intermediate goods sector to

$$x_{kt} = l_{kt} L^{-\phi} \tag{A.2}$$

where $k \in [0, K_t]$. Recall that it takes a unit of physical capital to open up an intermediates production unit, and that the output of the production unit k, i.e. x_{kt}, is determined by the size of the labor force l_{kt} that it employs. By equation (A.2), we model that at the stage at which differentiated goods are produced, scale-dependent costs are incurred. Accordingly, in equation (A.2), the output of intermediates production unit k is negatively related to the size of the economy's total labor force, L_t. The magnitude of the scale-dependent costs depends on the size of the parameter $\phi > 0$.

The scale-dependent costs may be motivated by matching and shipping costs. Employers incur *matching costs* when they recruit workers. These costs increase with the size of the economy, since in a larger economy, more highly diversified employers have to search appropriate workers out of a larger labor force. The presence of this effect is reflected in the high earnings that "head-hunters" typically obtain in highly differentiated economies. Apart from such matching costs, *shipping costs* are scale-dependent, too: the average distance between plant and customer increases with the size of the economy.

The profit rates of the intermediates suppliers at time t are given by

$$\pi_{kt} = p_{x_k t}(x_{kt})x_{kt} - w_t x_{kt} \tag{A.3}$$

where $p_{x_k t}$ denotes the price of the intermediate k, where $k \in [0, K_t]$. The suppliers maximize their flow profits by charging $p_{x_k t} = w_t/\alpha$. Thus, we obtain a symmetric solution that allows to restate production functions (A.1) and (A.2) as

$$x_t = K_t^{-1} L^{1-\phi} \tag{A.4}$$

and

$$Y_t = K_t^{\frac{1-\alpha}{\alpha}} L^{1-\phi} \tag{A.5}$$

To rule out exploding as well as endogenous growth, we assume $0 < [1-\alpha]/\alpha < 1$, i.e. $0.5 < \alpha < 1$.

The cost function C_Y that is dual to production function (A.1) may be stated as[23]

$$C_Y(\{p_{x_k t}\}_{k=0}^{K_t}, Y_t) = \left[\int_0^{K_t} p_{x_k t}^{\frac{-\alpha}{1-\alpha}} dk\right]^{-\left[\frac{1-\alpha}{\alpha}\right]} Y_t$$

By symmetry, total cost follows as $C_Y(p_{xt}, L) = p_{xt}$. Since perfect competition prevails on the market for final output, revenue equals cost. Accordingly, the price of final output, p_{Yt}, is equal to aggregate cost over aggregate output. Setting $p_{Yt} = 1$ for all t, and solving for p_{xt} yields the subsequent intermediates price

$$p_{xt} = K_t^{\frac{1-\alpha}{\alpha}} L^{1-\phi} \tag{A.7}$$

The wage rate follows as

$$w_t = \alpha K_t^{\frac{1-\alpha}{\alpha}} L^{1-\phi}$$

Using $w_t = \alpha p_{xt}$ as well as equations (A.4) and (A.7), we may restate profit rate (A.3) as

$$\pi_t = [1-\alpha] K_t^{-\left[1-\frac{1-\alpha}{\alpha}\right]} L^{1-\phi} \tag{A.9}$$

Accordingly, an increase in the economy's scale has two opposite effects on the profit rate of the representative intermediates firm. First, with a larger

[23]The cost function is the solution to the problem $\min\left\{\int_0^{K_t} p_{x_k t} x_{kt} dk + \mu\left[Y_t - \left[\int_0^{K_t} x_{kt}^{\alpha} dk\right]^{1/\alpha}\right]\right\}$.

magnitude of the market, sales increase, and, in turn, the profit rate rises. Second, with a larger size of the economy, the matching and shipping costs at the intermediates production stage increase, and, hence, the profit rate decreases. The size of the latter effect hinges on the magnitude of elasticity ϕ. For $0 < \phi < 1$, the overall effect of a larger market on the profit rate is positive, i.e. the economy exhibits scale effects. For $\phi = 1$, the two effects neutralize, and the scale effects vanish.[24]

The Keynes/Ramsey rule is given by $\dot{c}_t/c_t = \sigma\left[\pi_t/v_t - \dot{v}_t/v_t\right]$, where $\rho, \sigma > 0$. Using $v_t = 1$ and profit rate (A.9), we obtain the following equation of motion for the level of consumption

$$\frac{\dot{c}_t}{c_t} = \sigma\left[[1-\alpha]K_t^{-\left[1-\frac{1-\alpha}{\alpha}\right]}L^{1-\phi} - \rho\right] \tag{A.10}$$

where $[1-\alpha]K_t^{-\{1-[1-\alpha]/\alpha\}}L^{1-\phi} > \rho$. Together with the equation of motion for the capital stock, i.e. $\dot{K}_t = K_t^{[1-\alpha]/\alpha}L^{1-\phi} - c_t L$, and the transversality condition, we obtain a two-dimensional system of differential equations in K-c space. Existence and stability of the unique saddle path equilibrium are analogous to the Ramsey model with imperfect competition [cf. chapter 5 and appendix B].

Notice that the current model fits the empirical evidence on aggregate production technology, national income distribution, and the speed of convergence very well [cf. chapter 2]. In this model, the output elasticity to capital is given by $[1-\alpha]/\alpha$, whereas the capital share follows as $[1-\alpha]$. Hence, consistently with the data, the former exceeds the latter. The output elasticity to labor is given by $[1-\phi]$, while the labor share follows as α. Thus, the model permits the labor share to exceed labor's output elasticity. Finally, the present modification of our basic model relaxes the restrictive predictions concerning the returns to scale that the basic model draws [cf. production function (A.5)].

Moreover, we have shown that by taking matching and shipping costs into account, we may indeed eliminate the scale effects. In particular, in our modified basic model, for $\phi = 1$, neither the profit rate nor the growth rate depend on the size of the labor force [cf. equations (A.9) and (A.10)]. Our approach to eliminate the scale effects deviates from the procedures that are proposed by the existing literature. In semi-endogenous growth models, exhaustion to research is employed to eliminate the scale effects [cf. Jones (1995a), Kortum (1997), Segerstrom (1998)]. In recent endogenous growth models, a process of imitation suppresses the scale effects [cf. chapter 10, Aghion/Howitt (1998, ch. 3), Dinopoulos/Thompson (1998), Peretto (1998), Young (1998)].

---

[24] Hence, as in the recent endogenous growth models without scale effects, the non-scale property hinges on a knife-edge solution [cf. endogenous growth III, i.e. Aghion/Howitt (1998, ch. 3), Dinopoulos/Thompson (1998), Peretto (1998), Young (1998)].

B Stability of the Steady-State Equilibrium in the Ramsey Model with Imperfect Competition

The two-dimensional dynamic system of the Ramsey model with imperfect competition is given by differential equations (5.11) and (5.12). We linearize this system in the neighborhood of steady state $[\bar{K}, \bar{c}]$, with $\bar{K} = \{[\{1-\alpha\} L] / \rho\}^{1/\{1-[\{1-\alpha\}/\alpha]\}}$ and $\bar{c} = \bar{K}^{[1-\alpha]/\alpha}$. We obtain the following two differential equations:

$$\dot{c}_t = -\frac{1}{[1-\alpha] L}\left[1-\frac{1-\alpha}{\alpha}\right]\rho^2\sigma\left[K_t - \bar{K}\right] \tag{B.1}$$

and

$$\dot{K}_t = \frac{\rho}{\alpha}\left[K_t - \bar{K}\right] - L\left[c_t - \bar{c}\right] \tag{B.2}$$

We reduce this dynamic system to a single second-order differential equation in K_t. First, we differentiate equation (B.2) with respect to time. Thus,

$$\ddot{K}_t = \frac{\rho}{\alpha}\dot{K}_t - L\dot{c}_t \tag{B.3}$$

Second, we insert equation (B.1) into equation (B.3). We obtain the following second-order differential equation in K_t:

$$\ddot{K}_t - \frac{\rho}{\alpha}\dot{K}_t - \frac{1}{1-\alpha}\left[1-\frac{1-\alpha}{\alpha}\right]\rho^2\sigma K_t = -\frac{1}{1-\alpha}\left[1-\frac{1-\alpha}{\alpha}\right]\rho^2\sigma\bar{K} \tag{B.4}$$

The characteristic equation associated with equation (B.4) is given by

$$\xi^2 - \frac{\rho}{\alpha}\xi - \frac{1}{1-\alpha}\left[1-\frac{1-\alpha}{\alpha}\right]\rho^2\sigma = 0 \tag{B.5}$$

The solution to characteristic equation (B.5) encompasses two roots. First, a root given by

$$\xi_1 = \frac{\rho}{2\alpha}\left[1-\sqrt{1+4\sigma\frac{\alpha^2}{1-\alpha}\left[1-\frac{1-\alpha}{\alpha}\right]}\right]$$

i.e. $\xi_1 < 0$, and, second, a root denoted by

$$\xi_2 = \frac{\rho}{2\alpha}\left[1+\sqrt{1+4\sigma\frac{\alpha^2}{1-\alpha}\left[1-\frac{1-\alpha}{\alpha}\right]}\right]$$

i.e. $\xi_2 > 0$. Recall that we have restricted the parameter α to $\alpha > 0.5$ [cf. production function (5.3)]. Hence, one root is negative and the other positive. The presence of a positive root implies that, for arbitrary initial conditions, the system explodes. The presence of a negative root, though, ensures that for any given value of K_0, there is a unique value of $\dot{K}_0$ so that the system converges to the steady state. Accordingly, our dynamic system proves to be stable, exhibiting saddle point behavior.

Trajectories that satisfy equation (B.4) are given by

$$K_t - \bar{K} = m_1 e^{\xi_1 t} + m_2 e^{\xi_2 t} \tag{B.6}$$

where m_1 and m_2 are arbitrary constants. Since K_0 is historically given, we require for m_1 and m_2 that

$$K_0 - \bar{K} = m_1 e^0 + m_2 e^0 = m_1 + m_2$$

Moreover, since root ξ_2 is positive, for K_t to converge to $\bar{K}$, m_2 must be equal to zero. Accordingly, $m_1 = K_0 - \bar{K}$. This implies, using equation (B.6), that

$$K_t = \bar{K} + \left[K_0 - \bar{K}\right] e^{\xi_1 t}$$

Hence, the speed of convergence in our linearized two-dimensional dynamic system is given by $|\xi_1|$.

C Stability of the Steady-State Equilibrium in the Models with Two-Stage Input Differentiation

In the present study, we set forth two models with two-stage input differentiation. In chapter twelve, we present a model that considers investment in R&D capital and physical capital. In chapter thirteen, we construe a model with investment in human capital and physical capital. The two models share a common dynamic behavior. Accordingly, in the present appendix, we focus merely on the stability of chapter twelve's model. The analysis for chapter thirteen's model is analogous.

In chapter twelve's model, the economy is initially endowed with capital stocks A_0 and K_0. Suppose that the ratio $\kappa_0 \equiv A_0/K_0$ deviates from the value given by equation (11.32). In our analysis, we distinguish two cases: case I in which $\kappa_0 = A_0/K_0 < \kappa$, and case II in which $\kappa_0 = A_0/K_0 > \kappa$.

First, we investigate the stability of the system that describes case I, i.e. the case where $\kappa_0 = A_0/K_0 < \kappa$. The two-dimensional dynamic system is given by differential equations (11.34) and (11.36). We linearize this system in the neighborhood of steady state $[\bar{\kappa}_I, \bar{\chi}_I]$, with $\bar{\kappa}_I = \{[1-\alpha]\beta L^\nu/\omega_A \rho\}^{1/[1-\eta]}$ and $\bar{\chi}_I = \bar{\kappa}_I^\eta L^\nu$. We obtain the following two differential equations:

$$\dot{\chi}_t = -\omega_A \frac{1-\eta}{[1-\alpha]\beta} \rho^2 \sigma \left[\kappa_t - \bar{\kappa}_I\right] \tag{C.1}$$

and

$$\dot{\kappa}_t = \omega_A \frac{\nu}{\alpha\beta}\rho\left[\kappa_t - \bar{\kappa}_I\right] - \left[\chi_t - \bar{\chi}_I\right] \tag{C.2}$$

We reduce this dynamic system to a single second-order differential equation in κ_t. Differentiating equation (C.2) with respect to time yields

$$\ddot{\kappa}_t = \omega_A \frac{\nu}{\alpha\beta}\rho\dot{\kappa}_t - \dot{\chi}_t \tag{C.3}$$

Inserting equation (C.1) into equation (C.3) implies the following second-order differential equation in κ_t:

$$\ddot{\kappa}_t - \omega_A \frac{\nu}{\alpha\beta}\rho\dot{\kappa}_t - \omega_A \frac{1-\eta}{\left[1-\alpha\right]\beta}\rho^2\sigma\kappa_t = -\omega_A \frac{1-\eta}{\left[1-\alpha\right]\beta}\rho^2\sigma\bar{\kappa}_I \tag{C.4}$$

The characteristic equation associated with equation (C.4) is given by

$$\xi^2 - \omega_A \frac{\nu}{\alpha\beta}\rho\xi - \omega_A \frac{1-\eta}{\left[1-\alpha\right]\beta}\rho^2\sigma = 0 \tag{C.5}$$

The solution to characteristic equation (C.5) encompasses two roots. First, a root given by

$$\xi_1 = \frac{1}{2}\omega_A \frac{\nu}{\alpha\beta}\rho\left[1 - \sqrt{1 + 4\sigma\frac{\alpha\beta}{\omega_A\nu\eta}\left[1-\eta\right]}\right]$$

i.e. $\xi_1 < 0$, and, second, a root denoted by

$$\xi_2 = \frac{1}{2}\omega_A \frac{\nu}{\alpha\beta}\rho\left[1 + \sqrt{1 + 4\sigma\frac{\alpha\beta}{\omega_A\nu\eta}\left[1-\eta\right]}\right]$$

i.e. $\xi_2 > 0$. Thus, one root is negative and the other positive. Accordingly, our dynamic system proves to be stable, exhibiting saddle point behavior. The speed of convergence in our linearized two-dimensional dynamic system is given by $|\xi_1|$.

Second, we investigate the stability of the system that is associated with case II, i.e. the case where $\kappa_0 = A_0/K_0 > \kappa$. The two-dimensional dynamic system is given by differential equations (11.38) and (11.40). We linearize this system in the neighborhood of steady state $\left[\bar{\kappa}_{II}, \bar{\chi}_{II}\right]$, with $\bar{\kappa}_{II} = \left\{\omega_K\rho/\left[\left\{1-\beta\right\}L^\nu\right]\right\}^{1/\eta}$ and $\bar{\chi}_{II} = \bar{\kappa}_{II}^\eta L^\nu$. We obtain the subsequent equations of motion:

$$\dot{\chi}_t = \eta L^\nu \rho\sigma\bar{\kappa}_{II}^{-[1-\eta]}\left[\kappa_t - \bar{\kappa}_{II}\right] \tag{C.6}$$

and

$$\dot{\kappa}_t = -\omega_K \frac{\eta}{1-\beta}\rho\left[\kappa_t - \bar{\kappa}_{II}\right] + \bar{\kappa}_{II}\left[\chi_t - \bar{\chi}_{II}\right] \tag{C.7}$$

We reduce this dynamic system to a single second-order differential equation in κ_t. Differentiating equation (C.7) with respect to time implies

$$\ddot{\kappa}_t = -\omega_K \frac{\eta}{1-\beta} \rho \dot{\kappa}_t + \bar{\kappa}_{II} \dot{\chi}_t \tag{C.8}$$

Inserting equation (C.6) into equation (C.8), we obtain the following second-order differential equation in κ_t:

$$\ddot{\kappa}_t + \omega_K \frac{\eta}{1-\beta} \rho \dot{\kappa}_t - \omega_K \frac{\eta}{1-\beta} \rho^2 \sigma \kappa_t = -\omega_K \frac{\eta}{1-\beta} \rho^2 \sigma \bar{\kappa}_{II} \tag{C.9}$$

The characteristic equation that corresponds to equation (C.9) is given by

$$\xi^2 + \omega_K \frac{\eta}{1-\beta} \rho \xi - \omega_K \frac{\eta}{1-\beta} \rho^2 \sigma = 0 \tag{C.10}$$

The solution to characteristic equation (C.10) consists of two roots. First, a root given by

$$\xi_1 = -\frac{1}{2} \omega_K \frac{\eta}{1-\beta} \rho \left[1 + \sqrt{1 + 4\sigma \frac{1-\beta}{\omega_K \eta}} \right]$$

i.e. $\xi_1 < 0$, and, second, a root denoted by

$$\xi_2 = -\frac{1}{2} \omega_K \frac{\eta}{1-\beta} \rho \left[1 - \sqrt{1 + 4\sigma \frac{1-\beta}{\omega_K \eta}} \right]$$

i.e. $\xi_2 > 0$. Thus, our system shows stable saddle point behavior. The speed of convergence in our linearized two-dimensional dynamic system is given by $|\xi_1|$.

D Equilibrium Dynamics with High σ in the Models with Two-Stage Input Differentiation

In the present appendix, we focus on the equilibrium dynamics of chapter twelve's two-stage input differentiation model. We analyze the system's behavior for a relatively high elasticity of intertemporal substitution, i.e. for $\sigma \geq \omega_K / [1-\beta]$. Notice that the respective analysis for chapter thirteen's two-stage input differentiation model is analogous to the subsequent investigation.

Whereas the dynamics for case I, i.e. $\kappa_0 < \kappa$ are straightforward, it is worth to investigate the dynamics for case II, i.e. $\kappa_0 > \kappa$ more detailed. Our dynamic system features two loci that are of particular interest. First, the $\dot{\kappa}_t = 0$-locus is given by

$$\chi_t = \kappa_t^\eta L^\nu$$

Hence, the $\dot{\kappa}_t = 0$-locus is an upward-sloping concave curve. A value of χ_t above the curve corresponds to $\dot{\kappa}_t > 0$, whereas a value of χ_t below the curve implies $\dot{\kappa}_t < 0$.

Second, the $\dot{\chi}_t = 0$-locus is denoted by

$$\chi_t = \left\{ 1 - \sigma \frac{1}{\omega_K} [1 - \beta] \right\} \kappa_t^{\eta} L^{\nu} + \sigma\rho$$

Hence, with respect to the slope of the $\dot{\chi}_t = 0$-locus, we may distinguish three cases: first, $\sigma < \omega_K / [1 - \beta]$, second, $\sigma = \omega_K / [1 - \beta]$, and, third, $\sigma > \omega_K / [1 - \beta]$. In either case, a value of χ_t above this locus corresponds to $\dot{\chi}_t > 0$, whereas a value of χ_t below this curve corresponds to $\dot{\chi}_t < 0$.

First, for $\sigma < \omega_K / [1 - \beta]$, the $\dot{\chi}_t = 0$-locus is an upward-sloping concave curve in κ-χ-space. The case of a relatively low elasticity of intertemporal substitution is investigated in chapter twelve [cf. figure 11.3].

Second, for $\sigma = \omega_K / [1 - \beta]$, the $\dot{\chi}_t = 0$-locus is a horizontal line. The existence of a steady-state equilibrium follows. In this case, the stable saddle path ABC coincides with the $\dot{\chi}_t = 0$-locus. That is, along the trajectory, the ratio of R&D capital stock over physical capital stock, κ_t, decreases, while the ratio of consumption over physical capital stock, χ_t, remains constant.

Third, for $\sigma > \omega_K / [1 - \beta]$, the $\dot{\chi}_t = 0$-locus is a downward-sloping convex curve. The existence of a steady-state equilibrium follows. As the $\dot{\chi}_t = 0$-locus, the stable saddle path ABC is downwardly sloped, and shows a convex shape. The path runs above the $\dot{\chi}_t = 0$-locus. Along the trajectory, the ratio of R&D capital stock over physical capital stock, κ_t, decreases, while the ratio of consumption over physical capital stock, χ_t, increases. Moreover, in this case of a relatively high elasticity of intertemporal substitution, the speed of convergence is high.

References

Abramovitz, Moses (1956), Resource and Output Trends in the United States Since 1870, *American Economic Review* 46, pp. 5-23.

Aghion, Philippe, and Peter Howitt (1992), A Model of Growth Through Creative Destruction, *Econometrica* 60, pp. 323-351.

Aghion, Philippe, and Peter Howitt (1998), *Endogenous Growth Theory*, Cambridge/MA: MIT Press.

Aitken, Brain (1991), Measuring Trade Policy Intervention: A Cross-Country Index of Relative Price Dispersion, *Mimeo*, World Bank.

Argote, Linda, and Dennis Epple (1990), Learning Curves in Manufacturing, *Science* 247, pp. 920-924.

Arrow, Kenneth J. (1962), The Economic Implications of Learning by Doing, *Review of Economic Studies* 29, pp. 155-173.

Backus, David K., Patrick J. Kehoe, and Timothy J. Kehoe (1992), In Search of Scale Effects in Trade and Growth, *Journal of Economic Theory* 58, pp. 377-409.

Barro, Robert J. (1974), Are Government Bonds Net Wealth?, *Journal of Political Economy* 81, pp. 1095-1117.

Barro, Robert J. (1991), Economic Growth in a Cross Section of Countries, *Quarterly Journal of Economics* 106, pp. 407-443.

Barro, Robert J. (1996), Democracy and Growth, *Journal of Economic Growth* 1, pp. 1-27.

Barro, Robert J. (1997), *Determinants of Economic Growth*, Cambridge/MA: MIT Press.

Barro, Robert J., and Jong-Wha Lee (1993), International Comparisons of Educational Attainment, *Journal of Monetary Economics* 32, pp. 363-394.

Barro, Robert J., and Jong-Wha Lee (1994), Sources of Economic Growth, *Carnegie-Rochester Conference Series on Public Policy* 40, pp. 1-57.

Barro, Robert J., and Xavier X. Sala-i-Martin (1992), Convergence, *Journal of Political Economy* 100, pp. 223-251.

Barro, Robert J., and Xavier X. Sala-i-Martin (1995), *Economic Growth*, New York: McGraw-Hill.

Benhabib, Jess, and Mark M. Spiegel (1994), The Role of Human Capital in Economic Development: Evidence from Aggregate Cross-Country Data, *Journal of Monetary Economics* 34, pp. 143-173.

Bental, Benjamin, and Dan Peled (1996), The Accumulation of Wealth and the Cyclical Generation of New Technologies: A Search Theoretic Approach, *International Economic Review* 37, pp. 687-718.

Blanchard, Olivier J., and Stanley Fischer (1989), *Lectures on Macroeconomics*, Cambridge/MA: MIT Press.

Bretschger, Lucas (1997), International Trade, Knowledge Diffusion, and Growth, *International Trade Journal* 9, pp. 327-348.

Bretschger, Lucas (1999), Dynamik der realwirtschaftlichen Integration am Beispiel der EU-Osterweiterung, *Jahrbücher für Nationalökonomie und Statistik* 218, pp. 276-293.

Bretschger, Lucas (2000), Asymmetrical Distribution of Gains from Trade: Externalities and Dynamics, *Mimeo*, University of Greifswald.

Caballero, Ricardo J., and Richard K. Lyons (1990), Internal Versus External Economies in European Industry, *European Economic Review* 34, pp. 805-830.

Caballero, Ricardo J., and Richard K. Lyons (1992a), External Effects in U.S. Procyclical Productivity, *Journal of Monetary Economics* 29, pp. 209-225.

Caballero, Ricardo J., and Richard K. Lyons (1992b), The Case of External Economies, in: Alex Cukierman, Zvi Hercowitz, and Leonardo Leiderman, eds., *Political Economy, Growth and Business Cycles*, Cambridge/MA: MIT Press.

Cass, David (1965), Optimum Growth in an Aggregative Model of Capital Accumulation, *Review of Economic Studies* 32, pp. 223-240.

Chatterjee, Satyajit, and Russel W. Cooper (1993), Entry and Exit, Product Variety and the Business Cycle, *NBER Working Paper* No. 4562, Cambridge/MA.

Crafts, Nicholas (2000), Globalization and Growth in the Twentieth Century, *IMF Working Paper* No. 44/00.

Davis, Steven, and John Haltiwanger (1990), Gross Job Creation and Destruction: Microeconomic Evidence and Macroeconomic Implications, *NBER Macroeconomics Annual*, pp. 126-168.

De Long, J. Bradford (2000), The Shape of Twentieth Century Economic History, *NBER Working Paper* No. 7569.

De Long, J. Bradford, and Lawrence H. Summers (1991), Equipment Investment and Economic Growth, *Quarterly Journal of Economics* 106, pp. 445-502.

De Long, J. Bradford, and Lawrence H. Summers (1993), How Strongly Do Developing Countries Benefit from Equipment Investment?, *Journal of Monetary Economics* 32, pp. 395-415.

Denison, Edward F. (1962), *The Sources of Economic Growth in the United States and the Alternatives Before Us*, New York: Committee for Economic Development.

Denison, Edward F. (1967), *Why Growth Rates Differ: Post-War Experience in Nine Western Countries*, Washington D.C.: Brookings Institution.

Dinopoulos, Elias, and Peter Thompson (1998), Schumpeterian Growth without Scale Effects, *Journal of Economic Growth* 3, pp. 313-335.

Dixit, Avinash K., and Joseph E. Stiglitz (1977), Monopolistic Competition and Optimum Product Diversity, *American Economic Review* 67, pp. 297-308.

Dowrick, Steve, and Duc-Tho Nguyen (1989), OECD Comparative Economic Growth 1950-85: Catch-Up and Convergence, *American Economic Review* 79, pp. 1010-1030.

Duguet, Emmanuel, and Isabelle Kabla (1998), Appropriation Strategy and the Motivations to Use the Patent System: An Econometric Analysis at the Firm Level in French Manufacturing, *Annales d'Economie et de Statistique* 49/50, pp. 289-327.

Durlauf, Steven N., and Danny T. Quah (1999), The New Empirics of Economic Growth, in: John B. Taylor and Michael Woodford, eds., *Handbook of Macroeconomics*, Amsterdam: North-Holland Elsevier, pp. 231–304.

Encaoua, David, Bronwyn H. Hall, François Laisney, and Jacques Mairesse (1998), The Economics and Econometrics of Innovation, *Annales d'Economie et de Statistique* 49/50, pp. 27-51.

Ethier, Wilfried J. (1982), National and International Returns to Scale in the Modern Theory of International Trade, *American Economic Review* 72, pp. 389-405.

Evenson, Robert E. (1984), International Invention: Implications for Technology Market Analysis, in: Zvi Griliches, ed., *R&D, Patents, and Productivity*, Chicago: University of Chicago Press, pp. 89-123.

Evenson, Robert E. (1991), Patent Data by Industry: Evidence for Invention Potential Exhaustion?, in: *Technology and Productivity: The Challenge for Economic Policy*, Paris: OECD, pp. 233-248.

Fagerberg, Jan (1987), A Technology Gap Approach to Why Growth Rates Differ, *Research Policy* 16, pp. 87-99.

Fagerberg, Jan (1988), Why Growth Rates Differ, in: Giovanni Dosi et al., eds., *Technical Change and Economic Theory*, London: Pinter, pp. 432-457.

Frankel, Jeffrey A., and David Romer (1996), Trade and Growth: An Empirical Investigation, *NBER Working Paper* No. 5476, Cambridge/MA.

Frankel, Jeffrey A., David Romer, and Teresa Cyrus (1996), Trade and Growth in East Asian Countries: Cause and Effect?, *NBER Working Paper* No. 5732, Cambridge/MA.

Funke, Michael, and Ralf Ruhwedel (1999), Product Variety and Economic Growth – Empirical Evidence for the OECD Countries, *Quantitative Macroeconomics Working Paper* No. 4/99, Department of Economics, Hamburg University.

Gerschenkron, Alexander (1962), *Economic Backwardness in Historical Perspective*, Cambridge/MA: Harvard University Press.

Goldsmith, Raymond W. (1969), *Financial Structure and Development*, New Haven/CT: Yale University Press.

Gordon, Robert J. (1990), *The Measurement of Durable Goods Prices*, Chicago: University of Chicago Press.

Goto, Akira, and Kazuyuki Suzuki (1989), R&D Capital, Rate of Return on R&D Investment and Spillover of R&D in Japanese Manufacturing Industries, *Review of Economics and Statistics* 71, pp. 555-564.

Griliches, Zvi (1992), The Search for R&D Spillovers, *Scandinavian Journal of Economics* 94, pp. S29-S47.

Griliches, Zvi (1994), Productivity, R&D and the Data Constraint, *American Economic Review* 84, pp. 1-23.

Griliches, Zvi, and Frank R. Lichtenberg (1984), Interindustry Technology Flows and Productivity Growth: A Reexamination, *Review of Economics and Statistics* 66, pp. 324-329.

Grossman, Gene M., and Elhanan Helpman (1991a), *Innovation and Growth in the Global Economy*, Cambridge/MA: MIT Press.

Grossman, Gene M., and Elhanan Helpman (1991b), Quality Ladders in the Theory of Growth, *Review of Economic Studies* 58, pp. 43-61.

Hall, Robert E., and Charles I. Jones (1997), Fundamental Determinants of Output per Worker across Countries, *Mimeo*, Stanford University.

Hamilton, James D., and Josefina Monteagudo (1998), The Augmented Solow Model and the Productivity Slowdown, *Journal of Monetary Economics* 42, pp. 495-509.

Harrison, Ann (1995), Openness and Growth: A Time-Series, Cross-Country Analysis for Developing Countries, *NBER Working Paper* No. 5221, Cambridge/MA.

Helpman, Elhanan (1993), Innovation, Imitation, and Intellectual Property Rights, *Econometrica* 61, pp. 1247-1280.

Hornstein, Andreas (1993), Monopolistic Competition, Increasing Returns to Scale, and the Importance of Productivity Shocks, *Journal of Monetary Economics* 31, pp. 299-316.

Islam, Nazrul (1995), Growth Empirics: A Panel Data Approach, *Quarterly Journal of Economics* 110, pp. 1127-1170.

Jones, Charles I. (1994), Economic Growth and the Relative Price of Capital, *Journal of Monetary Economics* 34, pp. 359-382.

Jones, Charles I. (1995a), R&D-Based Models of Economic Growth, *Journal of Political Economy* 103, pp. 759-784.

Jones, Charles I. (1995b), Time Series Tests of Endogenous Growth Models, *Quarterly Journal of Economics* 110, pp. 495-525.

Jones, Charles I. (1999), With or Without Scale Effects?, *American Economic Review* 89, pp. 139-144.

Jones, Charles I., and John C. Williams (1998), Measuring the Social Return to R&D, *Quarterly Journal of Economics* 113, pp. 1119-1135.

Jones, Charles I., and John C. Williams (1999), Too Much of a Good Thing? The Economics of Investment in R&D, *NBER Working Paper* No. 7283, Cambridge/MA.

Jones, Larry E., and Rodolfo E. Manuelli (1990), A Convex Model of Equilibrium Growth: Theory and Policy Implications, *Journal of Political Economy* 98, pp. 1008-1038.

Jorgenson, Dale W. (1988), Productivity and Postwar U.S. Economic Growth, *Journal of Economic Perspectives* 2, pp. 23-41.

Jorgenson, Dale W., Frank M. Gollop, and Barbara M. Fraumeni (1987), *Productivity and U.S. Economic Growth*, Cambridge/MA: Harvard University Press.

Jovanovic, Boyan (1993), The Diversification of Production, *Brookings Papers on Economic Activity: Microeconomics*, pp. 197-247.

Judd, Kenneth L. (1999), Optimal Taxation and Spending in General Competitive Growth Models, *Journal of Public Economics* 71, pp. 1-26.

King, Robert G., and Ross Levine (1993a), Finance and Growth: Schumpeter Might Be Right, *Quarterly Journal of Economics* 108, pp. 717-737.

King, Robert G., and Ross Levine (1993b), Finance, Entrepreneurship, and Growth: Theory and Evidence, *Journal of Monetary Economics* 32, pp. 513-542.

King, Robert G., and Ross Levine (1993c), Financial Intermediation and Economic Development, in: Colin Mayer and Xavier Vives, eds., *Financial Intermediation in the Construction of Europe*, London: CEPR, pp. 156-189.

King, Robert G., and Sérgio Rebelo (1993), Transitional Dynamics and Economic Growth in the Neoclassical Model, *American Economic Review* 83, pp. 908-931.

Kiyotaki, Nobuhiro (1988), Multiple Expectational Equilibria under Monopolistic Competition, *Quarterly Journal of Economics* 103, pp. 695-713.

Koopmans, Tjalling C. (1965), On the Concept of Optimal Growth, in: *The Econometric Approach to Development Planning*, Amsterdam: North Holland.

Kormendi, Roger C., and Philip G. Meguire (1985), Macroeconomic Determinants of Growth: Cross-Country Evidence, *Journal of Monetary Economics* 16, pp. 141-163.

Kortum, Samuel S. (1993), Equilibrium R&D and the Patent-R&D Ratio: U.S. Evidence, *American Economic Review* 83, pp. 450-457.

Kortum, Samuel S. (1997), Research, Patenting, and Technological Change, *Econometrica* 65, pp. 1389-1419.

Kravis, Irving B. (1984), Comparative Studies of National Incomes and Prices, *Journal of Economic Literature* 22, pp. 1-39.

Kremer, Michael (1993), Population Growth and Technological Change: One Million B.C. to 1990, *Quarterly Journal of Economics* 108, pp. 681-716.

Krusell, Per (1998), Investment-Specific R&D and the Decline in the Relative Price of Capital, *Journal of Economic Growth* 3, pp. 131-141.

Kyriacou, George (1991), Level and Growth Effects of Human Capital, *Working Paper* 26/1991, C.V. Starr Center, New York.

Landau, Daniel (1983), Government Expenditure and Economic Growth: A Cross-Country Study, *Southern Economic Journal* 49, pp. 783-792.

Landes, David (1969), *The Unbound Prometheus*, Cambridge/MA: Cambridge University Press.

Lee, Jong-Wha (1992), *Trade, Distortion, and Growth*, Ph.D. Thesis, Harvard University.

Lee, Ronald (1988), Induced Population Growth and Induced Technological Progress: Their Interaction in the Accelerating Stage, *Mathematical Population Studies* 1, pp. 265-288.

Levine, Ross (1997), Financial Development and Economic Growth: Views and Agenda, *Journal of Economic Literature* 35, pp. 688-726.

Levine, Ross, and David Renelt (1992), A Sensitivity Analysis of Cross-Country Growth Regressions, *American Economic Review* 82, pp. 942-963.

Levine, Ross, and Sara Zervos (1998), Stock Markets, Banks, and Economic Growth, *American Economic Review* 88, pp. 537-558.

Lichtenberg, Frank R., and Donald Siegel (1991), The Impact of R&D Investment on Productivity: New Evidence Using Linked R&D-LRD Data, *Economic Inquiry* 29, pp. 203-229.

Lucas, Robert E. Jr. (1988), On the Mechanics of Economic Development, *Journal of Monetary Economics* 22, pp. 3-42.

Maddison, Angus (1987), Growth and Slowdown in Advanced Capitalist Economies: Techniques of Quantitative Assessment, *Journal of Economic Literature* 25, pp. 649-698.

Mankiw, N. Gregory, David Romer and David N. Weil (1992), A Contribution to the Empirics of Economic Growth, *Quarterly Journal of Economics* 107, pp. 407-437.

Mohnen, Pierre (1990), R&D and Productivity Growth: A Survey of the Literature, *Working Paper*, Centre de Recherche sur les Politiques Economiques, Université du Québec à Montréal.

Mokyr, Joel (1990), *The Lever of Riches*, New York: Oxford University Press.

Peretto, Pietro (1998), Technological Change and Population Growth, *Journal of Economic Growth* 3, pp. 283-311.

Pollard, Sidney (1982), *Peaceful Conquest: The Industrialization of Europe 1760-1970*, Oxford: Oxford University Press.

Pritchett, Lant (1996), Where Has All the Education Gone?, *World Bank Working Paper* No. 1581.

Ramsey, Frank P. (1928), A Mathematical Theory of Saving, *Economic Journal* 38, pp. 543-559.

Rebelo, Sérgio (1991), Long-Run Policy Analysis and Long-Run Growth, *Journal of Political Economy* 99, pp. 500-521.

Rivera-Batiz, Francisco L., and Paul M. Romer (1991), Economic Integration and Endogenous Growth, *Quarterly Journal of Economics* 106, pp. 531-555.

Robinson, Sherman (1971), Sources of Growth in Less Developed Countries: A Cross-Section Study, *Quarterly Journal of Economics* 85, pp. 391-408.

Romer, Paul M. (1986), Increasing Returns and Long-Run Growth, *Journal of Political Economy* 98, pp. 71-103.

Romer, Paul M. (1987), Growth Based on Increasing Returns Due to Specialization, *American Economic Review* 77, pp. 56-62.

Romer, Paul M. (1990), Endogenous Technological Change, *Journal of Political Economy* 98, pp. 71-102.

Rostow, Walt Whitman (1958), *The Stages of Economic Growth*, London: Macmillan.

Rostow, Walt Whitman (1959), The Stages of Economic Growth, *Economic History Review* 12, pp. 1-16.

Sala-i-Martin, Xavier X. (1997), I Just Ran Two Million Regressions, *American Economic Review* 87, pp. 178-183.

Scherer, Frederic M. (1982), Inter-Industry Technology Flows and Productivity Growth, *Review of Economics and Statistics* 64, pp. 627-634.

Schmookler, Jacob (1966), *Invention and Economic Growth*, Cambridge/MA: Harvard University Press.

Schumpeter, Joseph A. (1942), *Capitalism, Socialism and Democracy*, New York.

Segerstrom, Paul S. (1998), Endogenous Growth Without Scale Effects, *American Economic Review* 88, pp. 1290-1310.

Segerstrom, Paul S., T. C. A. Anant, and Elias Dinopoulos (1990), A Schumpeterian Model of the Product Life Cycle, *American Economic Review* 80, pp. 1077-1092.

Shell, Karl (1966), Toward a Theory of Inventive Activity and Capital Accumulation, *American Economic Review* 56, pp. 56-62.

Shell, Karl (1967), A Model of Inventive Activity and Capital Accumulation, in: Karl Shell, ed., *Essays on the Theory of Optimal Growth*, Cambridge/MA: MIT Press.

Shell, Karl (1973), Inventive Activity, Industrial Organization, and Economic Activity, in: James A. Mirrlees and Nicholas H. Stern, eds., *Models of Economic Growth*, London: Macmillan.

Sheshinski, Eytan (1967a), Optimal Accumulation with Learning by Doing, in: Karl Shell, ed., *Essays on the Theory of Optimal Economic Growth*, Cambridge/MA: MIT Press, pp. 31-52.

Sheshinski, Eytan (1967b), Tests of the Learning by Doing Hypothesis, *Review of Economics and Statistics* 49, pp. 568-578.

Sokoloff, Kenneth L. (1988), Inventive Activity in Early Industrial America: Evidence from Patent Records, 1790-1846, *Journal of Economic History* 48, pp. 813-850.

Solow, Robert M. (1956), A Contribution to the Theory of Economic Growth, *Quarterly Journal of Economics* 70, pp. 65-94.

Solow, Robert M. (1957), Technical Change and the Aggregate Production Function, *Review of Economics and Statistics* 34, pp. 312-320.

Summers, Robert, and Alan Heston (1988), A New Set of International Comparisons of Real Product and Price Levels: Estimates for 130 Countries, 1950-1985, *Review of Income and Wealth* 34, pp. 1-25.

Summers, Robert and Alan Heston (1991), The Penn World Table (Mark 5): An Expanded Set of International Comparisons, 1950-1988, *Quarterly Journal of Economics* 106, pp. 327-368.

Swan, Trevor W. (1956), Economic Growth and Capital Accumulation, *Economic Record* 32, pp. 334-364.

Temple, Jonathan (1999), The New Growth Evidence, *Journal of Economic Literature* 37, pp. 112-156.

Terleckyj, Nestor E. (1982), R&D and U.S. Industrial Productivity in the 1970s, in: D. Sahal, ed., *The Transfer and Utilization of Technical Knowledge*, Lexington: Lexington Books.

Uzawa, Hirofumi (1965), Optimum Technical Change in an Aggregative Model of Economic Growth, *International Economic Review* 6, pp. 18-31.

Varian, Hal R. (1992), *Microeconomic Analysis*, 3rd ed., New York: Norton.

Walz, Uwe (1995), A Dynamic Model of Economic Geography and the Enlargement of a Common Market, *Discussion Paper* 525/1995, Institut für Volkswirtschaftslehre und Statistik, Universität Mannheim.

Wolff, Edward N. (1996), The Productivity Slowdown: The Culprit at Last? Follow-Up on Hulten and Wolff, *American Economic Review* 86, pp. 1239-1252.

Wright, Theodore P. (1936), Factors Affecting the Cost of Airplanes, *Journal of the Aeronautical Sciences* 3, pp. 122-128.

Young, Alwyn (1998), Growth without Scale Effects, *Journal of Political Economy* 106, pp. 41-63.

Vol. 410: R. Winkelmann, Count Data Models. XI, 213 pages. 1994.

Vol. 411: S. Dauzère-Péres, J.-B. Lasserre, An Integrated Approach in Production Planning and Scheduling. XVI, 137 pages. 1994.

Vol. 412: B. Kuon, Two-Person Bargaining Experiments with Incomplete Information. IX, 293 pages. 1994.

Vol. 413: R. Fiorito (Ed.), Inventory, Business Cycles and Monetary Transmission. VI, 287 pages. 1994.

Vol. 414: Y. Crama, A. Oerlemans, F. Spieksma, Production Planning in Automated Manufacturing. X, 210 pages. 1994.

Vol. 415: P. C. Nicola, Imperfect General Equilibrium. XI, 167 pages. 1994.

Vol. 416: H. S. J. Cesar, Control and Game Models of the Greenhouse Effect. XI, 225 pages. 1994.

Vol. 417: B. Ran, D. E. Boyce, Dynamic Urban Transportation Network Models. XV, 391 pages. 1994.

Vol. 418: P. Bogetoft, Non-Cooperative Planning Theory. XI, 309 pages. 1994.

Vol. 419: T. Maruyama, W. Takahashi (Eds.), Nonlinear and Convex Analysis in Economic Theory. VIII, 306 pages. 1995.

Vol. 420: M. Peeters, Time-To-Build. Interrelated Investment and Labour Demand Modelling. With Applications to Six OECD Countries. IX, 204 pages. 1995.

Vol. 421: C. Dang, Triangulations and Simplicial Methods. IX, 196 pages. 1995.

Vol. 422: D. S. Bridges, G. B. Mehta, Representations of Preference Orderings. X, 165 pages. 1995.

Vol. 423: K. Marti, P. Kall (Eds.), Stochastic Programming. Numerical Techniques and Engineering Applications. VIII, 351 pages. 1995.

Vol. 424: G. A. Heuer, U. Leopold-Wildburger, Silverman's Game. X, 283 pages. 1995.

Vol. 425: J. Kohlas, P.-A. Monney, A Mathematical Theory of Hints. XIII, 419 pages, 1995.

Vol. 426: B. Finkenstädt, Nonlinear Dynamics in Economics. IX, 156 pages. 1995.

Vol. 427: F. W. van Tongeren, Microsimulation Modelling of the Corporate Firm. XVII, 275 pages. 1995.

Vol. 428: A. A. Powell, Ch. W. Murphy, Inside a Modern Macroeconometric Model. XVIII, 424 pages. 1995.

Vol. 429: R. Durier, C. Michelot, Recent Developments in Optimization. VIII, 356 pages. 1995.

Vol. 430: J. R. Daduna, I. Branco, J. M. Pinto Paixão (Eds.), Computer-Aided Transit Scheduling. XIV, 374 pages. 1995.

Vol. 431: A. Aulin, Causal and Stochastic Elements in Business Cycles. XI, 116 pages. 1996.

Vol. 432: M. Tamiz (Ed.), Multi-Objective Programming and Goal Programming. VI, 359 pages. 1996.

Vol. 433: J. Menon, Exchange Rates and Prices. XIV, 313 pages. 1996.

Vol. 434: M. W. J. Blok, Dynamic Models of the Firm. VII, 193 pages. 1996.

Vol. 435: L. Chen, Interest Rate Dynamics, Derivatives Pricing, and Risk Management. XII, 149 pages. 1996.

Vol. 436: M. Klemisch-Ahlert, Bargaining in Economic and Ethical Environments. IX, 155 pages. 1996.

Vol. 437: C. Jordan, Batching and Scheduling. IX, 178 pages. 1996.

Vol. 438: A. Villar, General Equilibrium with Increasing Returns. XIII, 164 pages. 1996.

Vol. 439: M. Zenner, Learning to Become Rational. VII, 201 pages. 1996.

Vol. 440: W. Ryll, Litigation and Settlement in a Game with Incomplete Information. VIII, 174 pages. 1996.

Vol. 441: H. Dawid, Adaptive Learning by Genetic Algorithms. IX, 166 pages.1996.

Vol. 442: L. Corchón, Theories of Imperfectly Competitive Markets. XIII, 163 pages. 1996.

Vol. 443: G. Lang, On Overlapping Generations Models with Productive Capital. X, 98 pages. 1996.

Vol. 444: S. Jørgensen, G. Zaccour (Eds.), Dynamic Competitive Analysis in Marketing. X, 285 pages. 1996.

Vol. 445: A. H. Christer, S. Osaki, L. C. Thomas (Eds.), Stochastic Modelling in Innovative Manufactoring. X, 361 pages. 1997.

Vol. 446: G. Dhaene, Encompassing. X, 160 pages. 1997.

Vol. 447: A. Artale, Rings in Auctions. X, 172 pages. 1997.

Vol. 448: G. Fandel, T. Gal (Eds.), Multiple Criteria Decision Making. XII, 678 pages. 1997.

Vol. 449: F. Fang, M. Sanglier (Eds.), Complexity and Self-Organization in Social and Economic Systems. IX, 317 pages, 1997.

Vol. 450: P. M. Pardalos, D. W. Hearn, W. W. Hager, (Eds.), Network Optimization. VIII, 485 pages, 1997.

Vol. 451: M. Salge, Rational Bubbles. Theoretical Basis, Economic Relevance, and Empirical Evidence with a Special Emphasis on the German Stock Market.IX, 265 pages. 1997.

Vol. 452: P. Gritzmann, R. Horst, E. Sachs, R. Tichatschke (Eds.), Recent Advances in Optimization. VIII, 379 pages. 1997.

Vol. 453: A. S. Tangian, J. Gruber (Eds.), Constructing Scalar-Valued Objective Functions. VIII, 298 pages. 1997.

Vol. 454: H.-M. Krolzig, Markov-Switching Vector Autoregressions. XIV, 358 pages. 1997.

Vol. 455: R. Caballero, F. Ruiz, R. E. Steuer (Eds.), Advances in Multiple Objective and Goal Programming. VIII, 391 pages. 1997.

Vol. 456: R. Conte, R. Hegselmann, P. Terna (Eds.), Simulating Social Phenomena. VIII, 536 pages. 1997.

Vol. 457: C. Hsu, Volume and the Nonlinear Dynamics of Stock Returns. VIII, 133 pages. 1998.

Vol. 458: K. Marti, P. Kall (Eds.), Stochastic Programming Methods and Technical Applications. X, 437 pages. 1998.

Vol. 459: H. K. Ryu, D. J. Slottje, Measuring Trends in U.S. Income Inequality. XI, 195 pages. 1998.

Vol. 460: B. Fleischmann, J. A. E. E. van Nunen, M. G. Speranza, P. Stähly, Advances in Distribution Logistic. XI, 535 pages. 1998.

Vol. 461: U. Schmidt, Axiomatic Utility Theory under Risk. XV, 201 pages. 1998.

Vol. 462: L. von Auer, Dynamic Preferences, Choice Mechanisms, and Welfare. XII, 226 pages. 1998.

Vol. 463: G. Abraham-Frois (Ed.), Non-Linear Dynamics and Endogenous Cycles. VI, 204 pages. 1998.

Vol. 464: A. Aulin, The Impact of Science on Economic Growth and its Cycles. IX, 204 pages. 1998.

Vol. 465: T. J. Stewart, R. C. van den Honert (Eds.), Trends in Multicriteria Decision Making. X, 448 pages. 1998.

Vol. 466: A. Sadrieh, The Alternating Double Auction Market. VII, 350 pages. 1998.

Vol. 467: H. Hennig-Schmidt, Bargaining in a Video Experiment. Determinants of Boundedly Rational Behavior. XII, 221 pages. 1999.

Vol. 468: A. Ziegler, A Game Theory Analysis of Options. XIV, 145 pages. 1999.

Vol. 469: M. P. Vogel, Environmental Kuznets Curves. XIII, 197 pages. 1999.

Vol. 470: M. Ammann, Pricing Derivative Credit Risk. XII, 228 pages. 1999.

Vol. 471: N. H. M. Wilson (Ed.), Computer-Aided Transit Scheduling. XI, 444 pages. 1999.

Vol. 472: J.-R. Tyran, Money Illusion and Strategic Complementarity as Causes of Monetary Non-Neutrality. X, 228 pages. 1999.

Vol. 473: S. Helber, Performance Analysis of Flow Lines with Non-Linear Flow of Material. IX, 280 pages. 1999.

Vol. 474: U. Schwalbe, The Core of Economies with Asymmetric Information. IX, 141 pages. 1999.

Vol. 475: L. Kaas, Dynamic Macroeconomics with Imperfect Competition. XI, 155 pages. 1999.

Vol. 476: R. Demel, Fiscal Policy, Public Debt and the Term Structure of Interest Rates. X, 279 pages. 1999.

Vol. 477: M. Théra, R. Tichatschke (Eds.), Ill-posed Variational Problems and Regularization Techniques. VIII, 274 pages. 1999.

Vol. 478: S. Hartmann, Project Scheduling under Limited Resources. XII, 221 pages. 1999.

Vol. 479: L. v. Thadden, Money, Inflation, and Capital Formation. IX, 192 pages. 1999.

Vol. 480: M. Grazia Speranza, P. Stähly (Eds.), New Trends in Distribution Logistics. X, 336 pages. 1999.

Vol. 481: V. H. Nguyen, J. J. Strodiot, P. Tossings (Eds.). Optimation. IX, 498 pages. 2000.

Vol. 482: W. B. Zhang, A Theory of International Trade. XI, 192 pages. 2000.

Vol. 483: M. Königstein, Equity, Efficiency and Evolutionary Stability in Bargaining Games with Joint Production. XII, 197 pages. 2000.

Vol. 484: D. D. Gatti, M. Gallegati, A. Kirman, Interaction and Market Structure. VI, 298 pages. 2000.

Vol. 485: A. Garnaev, Search Games and Other Applications of Game Theory. VIII, 145 pages. 2000.

Vol. 486: M. Neugart, Nonlinear Labor Market Dynamics. X, 175 pages. 2000.

Vol. 487: Y. Y. Haimes, R. E. Steuer (Eds.), Research and Practice in Multiple Criteria Decision Making. XVII, 553 pages. 2000.

Vol. 488: B. Schmolck, Ommitted Variable Tests and Dynamic Specification. X, 144 pages. 2000.

Vol. 489: T. Steger, Transitional Dynamics and Economic Growth in Developing Countries. VIII, 151 pages. 2000.

Vol. 490: S. Minner, Strategic Safety Stocks in Supply Chains. XI, 214 pages. 2000.

Vol. 491: M. Ehrgott, Multicriteria Optimization. VIII, 242 pages. 2000.

Vol. 492: T. Phan Huy, Constraint Propagation in Flexible Manufacturing. IX, 258 pages. 2000.

Vol. 493: J. Zhu, Modular Pricing of Options. X, 170 pages. 2000.

Vol. 494: D. Franzen, Design of Master Agreements for OTC Derivatives. VIII, 175 pages. 2001.

Vol. 495: I Konnov, Combined Relaxation Methods for Variational Inequalities. XI, 181 pages. 2001.

Vol. 496: P. Weiß, Unemployment in Open Economies. XII, 226 pages. 2001.

Vol. 497: J. Inkmann, Conditional Moment Estimation of Nonlinear Equation Systems. VIII, 214 pages. 2001.

Vol. 498: M. Reutter, A Macroeconomic Model of West German Unemployment. X, 125 pages. 2001.

Vol. 499: A. Casajus, Focal Points in Framed Games. XI, 131 pages. 2001.

Vol. 500: F. Nardini, Technical Progress and Economic Growth. XVII, 191 pages. 2001.

Vol. 501: M. Fleischmann, Quantitative Models for Reverse Logistics. XI, 181 pages. 2001.

Vol. 502: N. Hadjisavvas, J. E. Martínez-Legaz, J.-P. Penot (Eds.), Generalized Convexity and Generalized Monotonicity. IX, 410 pages. 2001.

Vol. 503: A. Kirman, J.-B. Zimmermann (Eds.), Economics with Heterogenous Interacting Agents. VII, 343 pages. 2001.

Vol. 504: P.-Y. Moix (Ed.),The Measurement of Market Risk. XI, 272 pages. 2001.

Vol. 505: S. Voß, J. R. Daduna (Eds.), Computer-Aided Scheduling of Public Transport. XI, 466 pages. 2001.

Vol. 506: B. P. Kellerhals, Financial Pricing Models in Continuous Time and Kalman Filtering. XIV, 247 pages. 2001.

Vol. 507: M. Koksalan, S. Zionts, Multiple Criteria Decision Making in the New Millenium. XII, 481 pages. 2001.

Vol. 508: K. Neumann, C. Schwindt, J. Zimmermann, Project Scheduling with Time Windows and Scarce Resources. XI, 335 pages. 2002.

Vol. 509: D. Hornung, Investment, R&D, and Long-Run Growth. XVI, 194 pages. 2002.